Eugene V. Debs Speaks

THE SOCIALIST PARTY'S 1920 CAMPAIGN BUTTON

EUGENE V. DEBS
SPEAKS

with an introduction by James P. Cannon

Pathfinder

New York   London   Montreal   Sydney

Edited by Jean Y. Tussey

ISBN 0-87348-132-1
Library of Congress Catalog Card Number 72-108720
Manufactured in the United States of America

First edition, 1970
Fifth printing, 1996

Cover design by Toni Gorton
Cover photo courtesy of Tamiment Institute Library, New York University

The publisher wishes to thank the Eugene V. Debs Foundation,
Terre Haute, Indiana, and Mr. Ned A. Bush, Sr., executive
vice-president of the foundation, for their courtesy in making available
the photographs in this book.

Pathfinder
410 West Street, New York, NY 10014, U.S.A.
Fax: (212) 727-0150
CompuServe: 73321,414 • Internet: pathfinder@igc.apc.org

Pathfinder distributors around the world:

Australia (and Asia and the Pacific):
    Pathfinder, 19 Terry St., Surry Hills, Sydney, N.S.W. 2010
    Postal address: P.O. Box K879, Haymarket, N.S.W. 2000

Canada:
    Pathfinder, 4581 rue St-Denis, Montreal, Quebec, H2J 2L4

Iceland:
    Pathfinder, Klapparstíg 26, 2d floor, 101 Reykjavík
    Postal address: P. Box 233, 121 Reykjavík

New Zealand:
    Pathfinder, La Gonda Arcade, 203 Karangahape Road, Auckland
    Postal address: P.O. Box 8730, Auckland

Sweden:
    Pathfinder, Vikingagatan 10, S-113 42, Stockholm

United Kingdom (and Europe, Africa except South Africa, and Middle East):
    Pathfinder, 47 The Cut, London, SE1 8LL

United States (and Caribbean, Latin America, and South Africa):
    Pathfinder, 410 West Street, New York, NY 10014

CONTENTS

INTRODUCTION

E. V. Debs: The Socialist Movement
of His Time — Its Meaning for Today
by James P. Cannon

The centennial of the birth of Debs coincided with the merger of the AFL and CIO in a year of standstill, which appears to present a mixed picture of progress and reaction. The organized labor movement as it stands today, with industrial unionism predominant, owes a lot to Debs, but his name was not mentioned at the merger convention. Debs was the greatest of the pioneers of industrial unionism who prepared the way—but that was yesterday. The smug bureaucrats who ran the convention are practical men who live strictly in the present, and they are convinced that progress is something you can see and count, here and now.

They counted approximately 15 million members in the affiliated organizations, and even more millions of dollars in the various treasuries, and found the situation better than ever. The official mood was never more complacent and conservative.

On the other hand, various groups and organizations calling themselves socialists, taking the numerical size of the present-day movement of political radicalism as their own criterion, found nothing to cheer about in Debs' centennial year. They compared the present membership and support of all the radical organizations with the tens of thousands of members and hundreds of thousands of votes of the Socialist Party in Debs' time, and concluded that things were never so bad. Their celebrations of the Debs Centennial were devoted mainly to nostalgic reminiscences about the "Golden Age of American Socialism" and sighs and lamentations for a return to "the way of Debs."

In my opinion, both of these estimates derive from a misunderstanding of the present reality of the labor movement and of its perspectives for the future. The changes since the time of Debs are not all progressive as the complacent trade-union bureaucrats imagine, and not all reactionary as some others assume, but a combination of both.

The organization of 15 million workers in the AFL-CIO, plus about 2 million more in the independent unions — and the acquisition of a trade-union consciousness that has come with it — represents in itself a progressive achievement of incalculable significance. And more than trade-union expansion is involved in this achievement.

There has been a transformation of the position of the working class in American capitalist society, which is implicitly revolutionary. Properly understood, the achievements on the trade-union field represent a tremendous advance of the cause of American socialism, since the socialist movement is a part of the general movement of the working class and has no independent interests or meaning of its own.

In addition to that — and no less important — the revolutionary socialist movement of the present, although numerically smaller, is ideologically richer than its predecessors. Insofar as it has assimilated the experience of the past, in this and other countries, and incorporated their lessons in its program, it is better prepared to understand its tasks. That represents progress for American socialism in the highest degree, for in the last analysis the program decides everything.

At the same time, it is obvious that the progressive growth of the industrial labor movement has not been accompanied by a corresponding development of the class consciousness of the workers. On the contrary, the recent

years have seen a decline in this respect; and this is reflected in the numerical weakness of socialist political
organization.

That is certainly a reactionary manifestation, but it is
far outweighed by the other factors in the situation. The
overall picture is one of tremendous progress of the American working class since the time of Debs. And the present
position is a springboard for another forward leap.

In their next advance the organized trade unionists will
become class-conscious and proceed to class political organization and action. That will be accomplished easier than
was the first transformation of a disorganized, atomized
class into the organized labor movement of the present
day. And most probably it will take less time.

The same conditions and forces, arising from the contradictions of the class society, which produced the one will
produce the other. We can take it for granted without fear
of going wrong, that the artificial prosperity of present-day
American capitalism will explode sooner and more devas-
tatingly than did the more stable prosperity of expanding
capitalism in the time of Debs; and that the next explosion
will produce deeper changes in the consciousness of the
workers than did the crisis of the Thirties, which brought
about the CIO.

In the light of that perspective, the work of revolutionary
socialists in the present difficult period acquires an extraordinary historical significance. With that prospect in view,
the present momentary lull in the class struggle, which
gives time for thought and reflection, can be turned to
advantage. It can be, and probably will be, one of the
richest periods in the history of American socialism — a
period of preparation for great events to come. A study
of the socialist movement of the past can be a useful part
of this preparation for the future.

That is the only sensible way to observe the Debs Centennial. It should be an occasion, not for nostalgic remi-
niscence, not for moping and sighing for the return of
times and conditions that are gone beyond recall, but for

a thoroughgoing examination and critical evaluation of the early socialist movement. It should be seen as a stage of development, not as a pattern to copy. The aim should be to study its defeats as well as its victories, in order to learn something from the whole experience.

The first rule for such an inquiry should be to dig out the truth and to tell it; to represent the Debsian movement as it really was. Debs deserves this, and he can stand it too. Even his mistakes were the mistakes of a giant and a pioneer. In an objective survey they only make his monumental virtues stand out more sharply in contrast.

The real history of America is the history of a process leading up to socialism, and an essential part of that process is the activity of those who see the goal and show it to others. From that point of view Eugene V. Debs is a man to remember. The day of his birth one hundred years ago — November 5, 1855 — was a good day for this country. Debs saw the future and worked for it as no one else has been privileged to do. On the honor roll of the socialist pioneers his name leads all the rest.

The life of Debs is a great American story; but like everything else American, it is partly foreign. He was truly indigenous, about as American as you can get, and he did far more than anyone else to "Americanize" socialism. But he was not, as he is sometimes pictured, the exponent of a peculiar homemade socialism, figured out all by himself, without benefit of "foreign" ideas and influences.

Debs was the perfect example of an American worker whose life was transformed by the ideas of others, and imported ideas at that. Many influences, national and international, his own experiences and the ideas and actions of others at home and abroad, conspired to shape his life, and then to transform it when he was already on the threshold of middle age.

The employers and their political tools did all they could to help. When President Cleveland sent federal troops to break the strike of the American Railway Union in 1894, and a federal judge put Debs in jail for violating an injunction, they made a great, if unintended, contribution to the auspicious launching of the native American socialist movement.

The inspired agitator began to "study socialism" in Woodstock Jail. That was the starting point of the great change in the life of Debs, and thereby in the prospects of socialism in this country. It was to lead a little later to the organization of the first indigenous movement of American socialism under the name of the Socialist Party.

The transformation of Debs, from a progressive unionist and Populist into a revolutionary socialist, didn't happen all at once, as if by a sudden revelation. It took him several more years after he left Woodstock Jail, carefully checking the new idea against his own experiences in the class struggle, and experimenting with various reformist and utopian conceptions along the route, to find his way to the revolutionary socialism of Marx and Engels.

But when he finally got it, he got it straight and never changed. Debs learned the basic essentials from Kautsky, the best popularizer of Marxism known in this country in the epoch before the First World War. Thereafter the Marxist theory of the class struggle was the central theme of all his agitation. He scornfully denouced the Gompers theory that the interests of capital and labor are identical. And he would have no truck with the delusive theory that capitalism will grow into socialism through a series of reforms.

Debs campaigned for the overthrow of capitalism by workers' revolution, and refused to settle for anything less. As he himself expressed it, he "determined to stick to the main issue and stay on the main track, no matter how alluring some of the byways may appear."

Debs was the main influence and most popular attraction making possible the formation of the Socialist Party of America at the "Unity Convention" in 1901, and the party became an important factor in American life mainly because of him.

There had been socialists and socialist organizations in this country for a half-century before that; but they had been derailed every time by a combination of objective circumstances and their own misunderstanding of the doctrine they espoused. The original socialists had been mainly utopians of various kinds, or German immigrants who brought their socialist ideas with them and never learned to relate them to American conditions.

Engels who, like Marx, was foreign to no country, saw no future for that kind of socialism in the United States. In his letters to friends in this country, up to the time of his death in 1895, he continuously insisted that American socialism would never amount to anything until it learned to "speak English" and find expression through the native workers.

In Debs the movement finally found a man who really spoke the language of the country, and who knew how to explain the imported idea of socialism to the American workers in relation to their own experiences.

When he came to socialism, Debs had already attained national fame as a labor leader. He brought to the new party the rich benefits of his reputation and popularity, the splendor of his oratorical gifts, and a great good will to work for the cause. Debs made the difference; Debs, plus conditions at the time which produced an audience ready to respond. With Debs as its outstanding spokesman after the turn of the century, socialism began for the first time to get a hearing in this country.

Part of what I have to say about Debs and the movement he symbolized is the testimony of a witness who was there at the time. The rest is afterthought. My own appreciation of Debs goes all the way back to the beginning of my conscious life as a socialist. I never knew Debs personally, but I heard him speak several times and he loomed large in my life, as in the lives of all other radicals of my generation.

Debs was an ever-present influence in the home where I was raised. My father was a real Debs man — all the way through. Of all the public figures of the time, Debs was his favorite. Debs' character and general disposition, his way of life — his whole radiant personality — appealed strongly to my father. Most of the pioneer socialists I came to know were like that. They were good people, and they felt warmly toward Debs as one of their own — the best representative of what they themselves were, or wanted to be. It would not be an exaggeration to say that they loved Debs as a man, as a fellow human being, as much as they admired and trusted him as a socialist leader and orator.

My father's political evolution had been along the same line as that of Debs. He had been a "labor man" since the old Knights of Labor days, then a Populist, then a Bryanite in the presidential campaign of '96, and he finally came to socialism, along with Debs, around the turn of the century.

The *Appeal to Reason*, for which Debs was then the chief editorial writer, came to our house in the little town of Rosedale, Kansas, every week. When Moyer and Haywood, then leaders of the Western Federation of Miners, were arrested in 1906 on a framed-up charge of murder, the *Appeal*, with Debs in the lead, opened up a tremendous campaign for their defense. Debs called for revolutionary action to prevent the judicial murder, with his famous declaration: "If they hang Moyer and Haywood, they will have to hang me!"

That was when I first began to take notice of the paper and of Debs. From week to week I was deeply stirred by the thunderous appeals of Debs and the dispatches of George H. Shoaf, the *Appeal's* "war correspondent" in the Western mine fields. My father and other local socialists chipped in to order extra bundles of the paper for free distribution. I was enlisted to help in that work. My first activity for the movement — in the memory of which I still take pride — was to distribute these special Moyer-Haywood editions of the *Appeal* from house to house in Rosedale.

The campaign for the defense of Moyer and Haywood was the biggest socialist action of the time. All the agitation seemed to center around that one burning issue, and it really stirred up the people. I believe it was the action itself, rather than the political arguments, that influenced me most at first. It was an action for justice, and that always appeals powerfully to the heart of youth. My commitment to the action led to further inquiry into the deeper social issues involved in the affair.

It was this great Moyer-Haywood campaign of Debs and the *Appeal to Reason* that started me on the road to socialism while I was still a boy, and I have always remembered them gratefully for that. In later years I met many people all around the country whose starting impulse had been the same as mine. Debs and the *Appeal to Reason* were the most decisive influences inspiring my generation of native radicals with the great promise of socialism.

Debs was a man of many talents, but he played his greatest role as an agitator, stirring up the people and sowing the seed of socialism far and wide. He was made for that and he gloried in it. The enduring work of Debs and the *Appeal to Reason*, with which he was long associated, was to wake people up, to shake them loose from habits of conformity and resignation, to show them a new road.

Debs denounced capitalism with a tongue of fire, but that was only one side of his agitation. He brought a message of hope for the good time coming. He bore down heavily on the prospect of a new social order based on cooperation and comradeship, and made people see it and believe in it. The socialist movement of the early days was made up, in the main, of people who got their first introduction to socialism in the most elementary form from Debs and the *Appeal to Reason*.

That's a long time ago. In the meantime history has moved at an accelerated pace, here and everywhere else. Many things have happened in the world of which America is a part — but only a part — and these world events have had their influence on American socialism. The modern revolutionary movement has drawn its inspiration and its ideas from many sources and many experiences since the time of Debs, and these later acquisitions have become an essential part of its program.

But for all that, the movement of the present and the future in the United States is the lineal descendant of the earlier movement for which Debs was the outstanding spokesman, and owes its existence to that pioneering endeavor. The centennial of the birth of Debs is a good time to remind ourselves of that and to take a deeper look at the movement of his time.

Those of the younger generation who want to study the ancestral origins of their movement, can easily find the necessary material already assembled. A group of conscientious scholars have been at work reclaiming the record as it was actually written in life and pointing it up with all the necessary documentation.

The published results of their work are already quite substantial. Almost as though in anticipation of the Debs Centennial, we have seen the publication of a number of books on the theme of Debs and American socialism within the last decade.

The Forging of American Socialism, by Howard H. Quint, gives an account of the tributary movements and organizations in the nineteenth century and ends with the launching of the Socialist Party at the Unity Convention in 1901.

The American Socialist Movement — 1897-1912, by Ira Kipnis, takes the story up to the presidential campaign of 1912, and gives an extensive report of the internal conflicts in the Socialist Party up to that time. The reformist leaders of the party come off badly in this account. The glaring contrast between them and Debs is fully documented on every point.

Following that, the Debs Centennial this year [1955] coincides with the publication of a rather concise history of *The Socialist Party of America* by David A. Shannon. Professor Shannon's research has evidently been thoroughgoing and his documentary references are valuable. In his interpretation, however, he appears to be moved by a tolerance for the reformist bosses of the party, who did an efficient job of exploiting the popularity of Debs and counteracting his revolutionary policy at the same time.

On top of these historical works, Debs speaks for himself in *Writings and Speeches of Eugene V. Debs*. This priceless volume, published in 1948, contains an "explanatory" introduction by Arthur Schlesinger, Jr., which in simple decency had better been left out.

Schlesinger, the sophisticated apologist of American imperialism, has no right to introduce Debs, the thoroughgoing and fully committed revolutionary socialist; and still less right to "explain" him because he can't begin to understand him. Schlesinger's ruminations stick out of this treasury of Debs' own speeches like a dirty thumb; but everything else in the book is clean and clear. It is the real Debs, explained in his own words.

Finally, there is the truly admirable biography of Debs by Ray Ginger, entitled *The Bending Cross*. Following after earlier biographies by David Karsner and McAlister Coleman, Ginger gives a more complete and rounded report. This is a sweet book if there ever was one; the incomparable Gene comes to life in its pages. All the lights and shadows in that marvelous life as it was actually lived are there, the shadows making the lights shine brighter.

Out of this imposing mass of documentary material — allowing for the shadings of opinion and interpretation by the authors — emerges a pretty clear picture of what the Socialist Party was and what Debs was. Debs was by far the most popular socialist in the heyday of the party, and in the public mind he stood for the party. But the history of American socialism in the first two decades of this century is a double story.

It is the story of the party itself — its official policies and actions — and the story of the unofficial and largely independent policies and actions of Debs. They were related to each other and they went on at the same time, but they were not the same thing. Debs was in and of the party, but at the same time he was bigger than the party — bigger and better.

Ray Ginger, the biographer of Debs, remarks that he was a legendary figure while he was still alive. Many stories — some of them of doubtful authenticity — were told about him, and many people professed devotion to him for different and even contradictory reasons.

Debs was a many-sided man, the like of which the movement has not seen, and this gave rise to misinterpretations by some who saw only one facet of his remarkable personality; and to misrepresentations by others who knew the whole man but chose to report only that part which seemed to serve their purpose. This business of presenting fragmentary pictures of Debs is still going on.

There is no doubt that Debs was friendly and generous, as befits a socialist, and that he lived by the socialist ideal even in the jungle of class society. For that he was praised more than he was imitated, and attempts were often made to pass him off as a harmless saint. It was the fashion to say Debs was a good man, but that's not what they put him in prison for. There was nothing saintly about his denunciation of the exploiters of the workers and the labor fakers who preached the brotherhood of workers and exploiters.

For all the complexity of his personality, Debs was as rigidly simple in his dedication to a single idea, and in suiting his actions to his words, as was John Brown, his acknowledged hero. His beliefs and his practices as a socialist agitator were related to each other with a singular consistency in everything he said and did. The record is there to prove it.

He was a famous labor organizer and strike leader — a man of action — long before he came to socialism, and he never lost his love and feel for the firing line of the class struggle after he turned to the platform. Striking workers in trouble could always depend on Gene. He responded to every call, and wherever there was action he was apt to turn up in the thick of it.

Debs was a plain man of the people, of limited formal education, in a party swarming with slick lawyers, professional writers and unctuous doctors of divinity. It was customary for such people to say — flattering themselves by implication — that Debs was a good fellow and a great orator, but not the "brains" of the party; that he was no good for theory and politics.

The truth is, as the documentary record clearly shows, that as a political thinker on the broad questions of working-class policy in his time, Debs was wiser than all the pretentious intellectuals, theoreticians and politicians in the Socialist Party put together. On practically all such questions his judgment was also better than that of any of the left-wing leaders of his time, most of whom turned to syndicalism to one degree or another.

Debs' own speeches and writings, which stand up so well even today, make the Socialist Party for which he spoke appear better than it really was. The simplicity, clarity and revolutionary vigor of Debs were part of the party's baggage — but only a part. The Socialist Party, by its nature and composition, had other qualities and the other qualities predominated.

The political law that every workers' party develops through internal struggles, splits and unifications is vividly illustrated in the stormy history of the Socialist Party — from start to finish. There is nothing obscure about this history; it is quite fully documented in the historical works previously mentioned.

The Socialist Party came into existence at the "Unity Convention" of 1901, but it had roots in the movements of the past. The new unity followed from and was made possible by a split in the old Socialist Labor Party, which was left on the sidelines in dogmatic isolation; a split in the original, short-lived "Social Democracy," in which Debs and Berger broke away from the utopian colonist elements of that organization; and an earlier split of thousands of native radicals — including Debs and J. A. Wayland, the famed publisher of the *Appeal to Reason* — from the Populist movement, which in its turn had been "united" with the Democratic Party and swallowed up by it.

These currents of different origins, plus many other local groups and individuals who had begun to call themselves socialists, were finally brought together in one camp in the Socialist Party.

Revolutionists and reformists were present at the first convention, and even after, until the definitive split in 1919. In addition, the new organization made room for a wide variety of people who believed in socialism in general and had all kinds of ideas as to what it really meant and how it was to be achieved. All hues of the political rainbow, from dogmatic ultraradicalism to Christian Socialism, showed up in the party from the start.

The mixed assemblage was held together in uneasy unity by a loose organizational structure that left all hands free from any real central control. The principle of "states' rights" was written into the constitution by a provision for the complete autonomy of the separate state organizations; each one retained the right to run its own affairs and, by implication, to advocate its own brand of socialism. Decentralization was further reinforced by the refusal to sanction a national official organ of the party. This measure was designed to strengthen the local and state publications — and incidentally, the local bosses such as Berger — in their own bailiwicks.

The party's principle of the free press included "free enterprise" in that domain. The most influential national publications of large circulation — *Appeal to Reason, Wilshire's Magazine, The Ripsaw,* and *The International Socialist Review* — were all privately owned. The individual owners interpreted socialism as they saw fit and the party members had no say, and this was accepted as the natural order of things.

To complete the picture of a socialist variety store, each

party speaker, writer, editor and organizer, and—in actual practice—each individual, promoted his own kind of socialism in his own way; and the general unification, giving rise to the feeling of greater strength, stimulated all of them to greater effort. The net result was that socialism as a general idea got a good workout, and many thousands of people heard about it for the first time, and accepted it as a desirable goal.

That in itself was a big step forward, although the internal conflict of tendencies was bound to store up problems and difficulties for the future. Such a heterogeneous party was made possible, and perhaps was historically justified as an experimental starting point, by the conditions of the of the time.

The socialist movement, such as it was, was new in this country. In its experiences, as well as in its thinking, it lagged far behind the European movement. The different groups and tendencies espousing socialism had yet to test out the possibility of working out a common policy by working together in a single organization. The new Socialist Party provided an arena for the experiment.

The trade unions embraced only a narrow stratum of the skilled and privileged workers; the problem of organizing the basic proletariat in the trustified industries—the essential starting point in the development of a real class movement—had not yet been seriously tackled. It was easier to organize general centers of radicalism, in the shape of socialist locals, than industrial unions which brought down the direct and immediate opposition of the entrenched employers in the basic industries.

In the country at large there was widespread discontent with the crude brutalities of expanding capitalism, just entering into its first violent stage of trustification and crushing everything in its path. Workers exploited without the restraints of union organization; tenant and mortgaged farmers waging an unequal struggle to survive on the land; and small businessmen squeezed to the wall by the trend to monopolization—they all felt the oppression of the "money power" and were looking about for some means of defense and protest.

The ruling capitalists, for their part, were happy with things as they were. They thought everything was fine and saw no need of ameliorating reforms. The two big political parties of capitalism had not yet developed the flexibility and capacity for reformist demagogy which they displayed in later decades; they stood pat on the status quo and showed little interest in the complaints of its victims. The collapse of the Populist Party had left a political vacuum.

The stage was set in the first decade of the present century for a general movement of social protest. And the new Socialist Party, with its appeal to all people with grievances, and its promise of a better deal all the way around in a new social order, soon became its principal rallying center.

With Debs as its presidential candidate and most popular agitator, and powerfully supported by the widely circulated *Appeal to Reason,* the new party got off to a good start and soon began to snowball into a movement of imposing proportions. Already in 1900, as the presidential candidate of the new combination of forces before the formal unification in the following year, Debs polled nearly 100,000 votes. This was about three times the vote for a presidential candidate of any previous socialist ticket.

In 1904 the Debs vote leaped to 402,283, a sensational fourfold increase; and many people, calculating the *rate* of growth, began to predict a socialist majority in the foreseeable future. In 1908 the presidential vote remained stationary at 420,713; but this electoral disappointment was more than counterbalanced by the organizational growth of the party.

In the intervening four years the party membership had doubled, going from 20,763 in 1904 to 41,751 in 1908 (official figures cited by Shannon). The party still had the wind in its sails, and the next four years saw spectacular advances all along the line.

Socialist mayors were elected all the way across the

country from Schenectady, New York, to Berkeley, California, with Milwaukee, the home of small-time municipal reform socialism — almost as famous and even milder than its beer — the shining light in between.

We had a socialist mayor in New Castle, Pennsylvania, when I was there in 1912-1913, working on *Solidarity,* eastern organ of the IWW. Ohio, a center of "red socialism," had a number of socialist mayors in the smaller industrial towns. On a tour for the IWW Akron rubber strike in 1913, I spoke in the City Hall at Saint Marys, Ohio, with Scott Wilkins, the socialist mayor of the town, as chairman of the meeting. Scott was a "red socialist," friendly to the IWW.

By 1912, according to official records cited by Kipnis, the party had "more than one thousand of its members elected to political office in 337 towns and cities. These included 56 mayors, 305 aldermen and councilmen, 22 police officials, 155 school officials and four pound-keepers."

If the transformation of society from capitalism to socialism was simply a process of electing enough socialist mayors and aldermen, as a great many leaders of the Socialist Party — especially its candidates for office — fervently believed, the great change was well underway by 1912.

In the campaign of 1912 the socialist cause was promoted by 323 papers and periodicals — 5 dailies, 262 weeklies and 10 monthlies, plus 46 publications in foreign languages, of which 8 were dailies. The *Appeal to Reason,* always the most widely read socialist paper, reached a circulation of over 600,000 in that year. The party membership, from a claimed 10,000 (probably an exaggeration) at the formation of the party 11 years earlier, had climbed to an average of 117,984 dues-payers for 1912, according to official records cited by Shannon.

In the 1912 presidential election Debs polled 897,000 votes on the Socialist ticket. This was before woman suffrage, and it was about 6 percent of the total vote that year. Proportionally, this showing would represent more than 3 million votes in the 1952 election.

Considering that Debs, as always, campaigned on a program of straight class-struggle socialism, the 1912 vote was an impressive showing of socialist sentiment in this country at that time, even though a large percentage of the total must be discounted as protest, rather than socialist, votes, garnered by the reform socialists working the other side of the street.

But things were not as rosy as this statistical record of growth and expansion might seem to indicate. The year 1912 was the Socialist Party's peak year, in terms of membership as well as votes, and it never reached that peak again. The decline, in fact, had already set in before the votes were counted. This was due, not to public disfavor at the time, but to internal troubles.

At the moment of its greatest external success the contradictions of the "all-inclusive party" were beginning to catch up with it and tear it apart. After 1912 the Socialist Party's road was downhill to catastrophe.

The Socialist Party was more radical in its first years than it later became. The left wing was strong at the founding convention and still stronger at the second convention in 1904. As we see it now, the original left wing was faulty in some of its tactical positions; but it stood foursquare for industrial unionism and took a clear and definite stand on the basic principle of the class struggle — the essential starting point of any real socialist policy. The class struggle was the dominant theme of the party's pronouncements in its first — and best — period.

A loose alliance of the left and center constituted the party majority at that time. The right-wing faction led by Berger, the Milwaukee slow-motion, step-at-a-time municipal reformer, was a definite minority. But the opportunists fought for control of the party from the very beginning. As a pressure tactic in the fight, Berger threatened, at least once a year, to split off his Wisconsin section.

Soon after the 1904 convention the centrists led by Hillquit combined with the Milwaukee reformists against the proletarian left wing. Thereafter the policy of Berger — with a few modifications provided by Hillquit to make it go down easier — became the prevailing policy of the party. With this right-wing combination in control, "political action" was construed as the pure and simple business of socialists getting elected and serving in public office, and the party organization became primarily an electoral machine.

The fight for industrial unionism — the burning issue of the labor movement championed by Debs and the left wing — was abandoned and betrayed by the opportunists in the hope of propitiating the AFL bureaucracy and roping in the votes of conservative craft unionists. The doctrine of socialism was watered down to make it more acceptable to "respectable" middle-class voters. The official Socialist Party turned more and more from the program of the class struggle to the scramble for electoral success by a program of reform.

This transformation did not take place all at once and without internal convulsions. The battle between left and right — the revolutionists and the reformists — raged without letup in all sections of the party. Many locals and state organizations were left-wing strongholds, and there is little room for doubt that the majority sentiment of the rank and file leaned toward the left.

Debs, who voiced the sentiments of the rank and file more sensitively and accurately than anyone else, always stood for the class-struggle policy, and always made the same kind of speeches no matter what the official party platform said. But Debs poured out all his energies in external agitation; the full weight of his overwhelming influence was never brought to bear in the internal struggle.

The professional opportunists, on the other hand, worked at internal party politics all the time. They wangled their way into control of the national party machinery, and used it unscrupulously in their unceasing factional maneuvers and manipulations. They fought, not only to impose their policy on an unwilling party, whose majority never trusted them, but also to drive out the revolutionary workers who consciously opposed them.

In 1910 Victor Berger, promoting the respectable reformist brand of socialism, was elected as the first socialist congressman; and a socialist city administration was swept into office in Milwaukee in the same year. These electoral victories had the double effect of strengthening the reformist influence in the party and of stimulating the hunger and thirst for office in other parts of the country by the Milwaukee method. Municipal elections, in which the opportunist wing of the party specialized, on a program of petty municipal reform, yielded many victories for socialist office-seekers, if not for socialism.

Says Kipnis: "Few of these local victories were won on the issue of capitalism versus socialism. In fact, this issue was usually kept well in the background. The great majority of Socialists elected to office between 1910 and 1912 were ministers and professional men who conducted their successful campaigns on reform questions that appeared crucial in their own communities; local option, prohibition, liquor law enforcement; corruption, inefficiency, maladministration, graft, and extravagance; bi-partisan combinations, boss and gang rule, and commission government; public improvements, aid to schools, playgrounds, and public health; municipal ownership, franchises, and equitable taxation; and, in a small minority of the elections, industrial depression and labor disputes."

The steady shift of the official policy from the class struggle to reformist gradualism, and the appeal to moderation and respectability that went with it, had its effects on the social composition of the party. Droves of office-hunting careerists, ministers of the gospel, businessmen, lawyers and other professional people were attracted to the organization which agreeably combined the promise of free and easy social progress with possible personal advantages for the ambitious. In large part they came, not to serve in the ranks but to take charge and run the show.

Lawyers, professional writers and preachers became the
party's most prominent spokesmen and candidates for
office.

At a Christian Socialist Congress in 1908 it was claimed
that more than 300 preachers belonged to the Socialist
Party. The preachers were all over the place; and in the
nature of things they exerted their influence to blunt the
edge of party policy. Kipnis pertinently remarks: "Since
the Christian Socialists based their analysis on the brotherhood of man rather than on the class struggle, they
aligned themselves with the opportunist, rather than the
revolutionary, wing of the party."

The revolutionary workers in the party ranks were re-
pelled by this middle-class invasion, as well as by the
policy that induced it. Thousands left the party by the
other door. Part of them, recoiling against the parliamen-
tary idiocy of the official policy, renounced "politics" alto-
gether and turned onto the bypath of syndicalism. Others
simply dropped out. Thousands of revolutionary-minded
workers, first-class human material out of which a great
party might have been built, were scattered and lost to
the movement in this period.

The revolutionary militants who remained in the party
found themselves fighting a losing battle as a minority,
without adequate leadership. In a drawn-out process the
"all-inclusive" Socialist Party was being transformed into a
predominantly reformist organization in which revolutionary workers were no longer welcome.

At the 1912 convention the right-wing majority mobilized
to finish the job. They pushed through an amendment to
the constitution committing the party to bourgeois law and
order, and proscribing the advocacy of any methods of
working-class action which might infringe upon it. This
amendment—the notorious "Article II, Section 6"—which
later was included almost verbatim in the "Criminal Syndicalism" laws adopted by various states to outlaw the
IWW—read as follows:

"Any member of the party who opposes political action

or advocates crime, sabotage, or other methods of violence as a weapon of the working class to aid in its emancipation shall be expelled from membership in the party. Political action shall be construed to mean participation in elections for public office and practical legislative and administrative work along the lines of the Socialist Party platform."

This trickily worded amendment was deliberately designed to split the party by forcing out the revolutionary workers. This aim was largely realized. The convention action was followed by the recall of Bill Haywood, the fighting leader of the left wing, from the National Executive Committee, and a general exodus of revolutionary workers from the party.

The reformist bosses had also calculated that their demonstration of respectability would gain more recruits and more votes for the Socialist Party, if not for socialism. But in this they were sadly disappointed. The party membership declined precipitately after that, and so did the votes. By 1916 the party membership was down to an average of 83,138, a drop of close to 35,000 from the 1912 average. And the party vote that year — with Benson, a reformist, as presidential candidate in place of Debs — fell to 588,-113, a decline of one-third from the Debs vote of 1912.

The Socialist Party never recovered from the purge of 1912, and came up to the First World War in a weakened condition. The war brought further mass desertions — this time primarily from the right-wing elements, who were finding the struggle for socialism far more difficult and dangerous than the program of reformist gradualism had made it appear. At the same time, the war, and then the Russian Revolution, also brought a new influx of foreign-born workers who swelled the membership of the language federations and provided a new base of support for a reinvigorated left wing.

This new left wing, armed with the great ideas of the Russian Revolution, fought far more effectively than its predecessor. There was no disorganized withdrawal and dispersal this time. The opportunist leaders, finding themselves in a minority, resorted to wholesale expulsions, and the split became definitive. The new left wing emerged from the internal struggle and split as the Communist Party.

The new Communist Party became the pole of attraction for all the vital elements in American radicalism in the next decade. The Socialist Party was left on the sidelines; after the split it declined steadily. The membership in 1922 was down to 11,277; and by 1928 it had declined to 7,793, of which almost half were foreign-language affiliates (all figures from official records cited by Shannon).

Debs remained a member of the shattered organization, but that couldn't save it. Nothing could save it. The Socialist Party had lost its appeal to the rebel youth, and not even the magic name of Debs could give it credit any more. The great agitator died in 1926. In the last years of his life the Socialist Party had fewer members and less influence — less everything — than it had started with a quarter of a century before.

The Socialist Party was bound to change in any case. It could begin as an all-inclusive political organization, hospitably accommodating all shades and tendencies of radical thought; but it could not permanently retain the character of its founding days. It was destined, by its nature, to move toward a more homogeneous composition and a more definite policy. But the direction of the change, and the eventual transformation of the party into a reformist electoral machine, were not predetermined. Here individuals, by their actions and omissions, played their parts, and the most decisive part of all was played by Debs.

The role of Debs in the internal struggles of the Socialist Party is one of the most interesting and instructive aspects of the entire history of the movement. By a strange anomaly, the conduct of this irreproachable revolutionist was the most important single factor enabling the reformist right wing to control the party and drive out the revolutionary workers.

He didn't want it that way, and he could have prevented

it, but he let it happen just the same. That stands out clearly in the record, and it cannot be glossed over without falsifying the record and concealing one of the most important lessons of the whole experience.

Debs was by far the most popular and influential member of the party. If he had thrown his full weight into the internal conflict there is no doubt that he could have carried the majority with him. But that he would never do. At every critical turning point he stepped aside. His abstention from the fight was just what the reformists needed to win, and they could not have won without it.

Debs never deviated from the class-struggle line in his own public agitation. He fought steadfastly for industrial unionism, and he never compromised or dodged that issue as the official party did. He had no use for vote-catching nostrums. He was opposed to middle-class intellectuals and preachers occupying positions of leadership in the party. His stand against the war was magnificent. He supported the Russian Revolution and proclaimed himself a Bolshevik.

On all these basic issues his sympathies were always consistently with the left wing, and he frequently took occasion to make his own position clear in the *International Socialist Review*, the organ of the left wing. But that's as far as he would go. Having stated his position, he withdrew from the conflict every time.

This seems paradoxical, for Debs certainly was no pacifist. In the direct class struggle of the workers against the capitalists Debs was a fighter beyond reproach. Nothing and nobody could soften him up or cool his anger in that domain. He didn't waste any of his good nature on the capitalist-minded labor fakers either.

Debs' blind spot was the narrower, but no less important, field of party politics and organization. On that field he evaded the fight. This evasion was not inspired by pacifism; it followed from his own theory of the party.

As far as I know, Debs' theory of the party was never formally stated, but it is clearly indicated in the course he consistently followed in all the internal conflicts of the party—from beginning to end. He himself always spoke for a revolutionary program. But at the same time he thought the party should have room for other kinds of socialists; he stood for an all-inclusive socialist party, and party unity was his first consideration.

Debs was against expulsions and splits from either side. He was opposed to the split in 1919 and saddened by it. Even after the split had become definitive, and the Rights and Lefts had parted company for good, he still appealed for unity.

Debs believed that all who called themselves socialists should work together in peace and harmony in one organization. For him all members of the party, regardless of their tendency, were comrades in the struggle for socialism, and he couldn't stand quarreling among comrades.

This excellent sentiment, which really ought to govern the relations between comrades who are united on the basic principles of the program, usually gets lost in the shuffle when factions fight over conflicting programs which express conflicting class interests. The reformists see to that, if the revolutionists don't. That's the way it was in the Socialist Party. Debs held aloof from the factions, but that didn't stop the factional struggles. And there was not much love lost in them either.

Debs' course in the internal conflicts of the party was also influenced by his theory of leadership, which he was inclined to equate with bureaucracy. He deliberately limited his own role to that of an agitator for socialism; the rest was up to the rank and file.

His repeated declarations—often quoted approvingly by thoughtless people—that he was not a leader and did not want to be a leader, were sincerely meant, like everything else he said. But the decisive role that leadership plays in every organization and every collective action cannot be wished away. Debs' renunciation of leadership created a vacuum that other leaders—far less worthy—came to fill. And the program they brought with them was not the program of Debs.

Debs had an almost mystic faith in the rank and file, and repeatedly expressed his confidence that, with good will all around, the rank and file, with its sound revolutionary instincts, would set everything straight. Things didn't work out that way, and they never do. The rank and file, in the internal conflicts of the party, as in the trade unions, and in the broader class struggle, can assert its will only when it is organized; and organization never happens by itself. It requires leadership.

Debs' refusal to take an active part in the factional struggle, and to play his rightful part as the leader of an organized left wing, played into the hands of the reformist politicians. There his beautiful friendliness and generosity played him false, for the party was also an arena of the struggle for socialism. Debs spoke of "the love of comrades" — and he really meant it — but the opportunist sharpers didn't believe a word of it. They never do. They waged a vicious, organized fight against the revolutionary workers of the party all the time. And they were the gainers from Debs' abstention.

Debs' mistaken theory of the party was one of the most costly mistakes a revolutionist ever made in the entire history of the American movement.

The strength of capitalism is not in itself and its own institutions; it survives only because it has bases of support in the organizations of the workers. As we see it now, in the light of what we have learned from the Russian Revolution and its aftermath, nine-tenths of the struggle for socialism is the struggle against bourgeois influence in the workers' organizations, including the party.

The reformist leaders were the carriers of bourgeois influence in the Socialist Party, and at bottom the conflict of factions was an expression of the class struggle. Debs obviously didn't see it that way. His aloofness from the conflict enabled the opportunists to dominate the party machine and to undo much of his great work as an agitator for the cause.

Debs' mistaken theory of the party was one of the most important reasons why the Socialist Party, which he did more than anyone else to build up, ended so disgracefully and left so little behind.

Here we can make an instructive comparison between the course of Debs — to whom we owe so much — and that of Lenin — to whom we owe even more.

As we see them in their words and works, which were always in harmony, they were much alike in character — honest and loyal in all circumstances; unselfish; big men, free from all pettiness. For both of them the general welfare of the human race stood higher than any concerns of self. Each of them, in his own way, has given us an example of a beautiful, heroic life devoted to a single idea which was also an ideal. There was a difference in one of their conceptions of method to realize the ideal.

Both men started out from the assumption that the transformation of society requires a workers' revolution. But Lenin went a step farther. He saw the workers' revolution as a concrete actuality of this epoch; and he concerned himself particularly with the question of how it was to be prepared and organized.

Lenin believed that for victory the workers required a party fit to lead a revolution; and to him that meant a party with a revolutionary program and leadership — a party of revolutionists. He concentrated the main energies of his life on the construction of just such a party, and on the struggle to keep it free from bourgeois ideas and influences.

Lenin recognized that this involved internal discussion and conflict, and he never shirked it. The Menshevik philistines — the Russian counterparts of the American Bergers and Hillquits — hated him for that, especially for his single-minded concentration on the struggle for a revolutionary program, and for his effectiveness in that struggle, but that did not deter him. Lenin believed in his bones that the internal problems of the party were the problems of the revolution, and he was on top of them all the time.

After 1904 Debs consistently refused to attend party conventions, where policy was decided, and always declined nomination for the National Committee, where policy was interpreted and put into practice. Lenin's attitude was directly opposite. He saw the Party Congress as the highest expression of party life, and he was always on hand there, ready to fight for his program. He regarded the Central Committee as the executive leadership of the movement, and he took his place at the head of it.

Lenin wrote a whole book about the conflict at the Second Congress of the party in 1903, where the first basic division between the Bolsheviks and the Mensheviks took place. He was in his element there, in that internal struggle which was to prove so fateful for the Russian Revolution and the future of all mankind.

Contrasting his own feeling about it to that of another delegate dismayed by the conflict, Lenin wrote:

"I cannot help recalling in this connection a conversation I happened to have at the Congress with one of the 'Centre' delegates. 'How oppressive the atmosphere is at our Congress!' he complained. 'This bitter fighting, this agitation one against the other, this biting controversy, this uncomradely attitude . . .'

"'What a splendid thing our Congress is!' I replied. 'A free and open struggle. Opinions have been stated. The shades have been brought out. The groups have taken shape. Hands have been raised. A decision has been taken. A stage has been passed. Forward! That's the stuff for me! That's life! That's not like the endless, tedious, word-chopping of intellectuals which terminates not because the question has been settled, but because they are too tired to talk any more . . .'

"The comrade of the 'Centre' stared at me in perplexity and shrugged his shoulders. We were talking in different languages." (*One Step Forward, Two Steps Back*, p. 225 footnote.)

In her book, *Memories of Lenin*, Krupskaya, his widow, quoted those words of Lenin with the remark: "That quotation sums up Ilyich to a 't'."

The practical wiseacres in Lenin's time looked disdainfully at the ideological conflicts of the Russian emigres, and regarded Lenin as a sectarian fanatic who loved factional squabbling for its own sake. But Lenin was not fighting over trifles. He saw the struggle against opportunism in the Russian Social Democratic Party as an essential part of the struggle for the revolution. That's why he plunged into it.

It is important to remember that the Bolshevik Party, constructed in the course of that struggle, became the organizer and leader of the greatest revolution in history.

Debs and Lenin, united on the broad program of revolutionary socialism, were divided on the narrower question of the character and role of the party. This turned out to be the most important question of our epoch for socialists in this country, as in every other country.

The Russian Revolution of 1917 clarified the question. Lenin's party of revolutionists stood up and demonstrated its historical rightness at the same time that the all-inclusive party of Debs was demonstrating its inadequacy.

This is the most important lesson to be derived from the experiences in the two countries, so far apart from each other yet so interdependent and alike in their eventual destiny.

The validity of the comparison is not impaired by reference to the well-known fact that Russia came to a revolutionary situation before America, which hasn't come to it yet. Lenin's greatest contribution to the success of the Russian Revolution was the work of *preparation* for it. That began with the construction of a revolutionary party in a time of reaction, *before* the revolution; and the Bolshevik Party, in turn, began with *Lenin's theory of the party*.

The Socialist Party of Debs' time has to be judged, not for its failure to lead a revolution, but for its failure to work with that end in view and to select its membership accordingly. Socialism signifies and requires the revolutionary transformation of society; anything less than that is mere bourgeois reform. A socialist party deserves the name only to the extent that it acts as the conscious agency in preparing the workers for the necessary social revolution. That can only be a party of revolutionists; an all-inclusive party of diverse elements with conflicting programs will not do.

The achievements of American socialism in the early years of the present century are not to be discounted, but it would be well to understand just what these achievements were. The movement, of which the party was the central organizing force, gave many thousands of people their first introduction to the general perspective of socialism; and it provided the arena where the main cadres of the revolutionary movement of the future were first assembled. These were the net results that remained after everything else became only a memory, and they stand to the historic credit of the early Socialist Party — above all to Debs.

But these irrevocable achievements were rather the by-products of an experimental form of socialist organization which, by its nature, could only be transitory. By including petty-bourgeois reformists and proletarian revolutionists in one political organization, the Socialist Party, presumed to be an instrument of the class struggle of the workers against the capitalists, was simply introducing a form of the class struggle into its own ranks. The result was unceasing internal conflict from the first day the party was constituted. The eventual breakup of the party, and the decision of the revolutionary elements to launch a party of their own, was the necessary outcome of the whole experiment.

In the Russian movement Lenin saw all that beforehand, and the revolution was the gainer for it. After the Russian Revolution, the left wing of the American Socialist Party, and some of the syndicalists too, recognized the superiority of Lenin's method. Those who took the program of socialism seriously had no choice but to follow the path of Lenin.

The Bolshevik Party of Lenin rightly became the model for the revolutionary workers in all countries, including this country.

The launching of the Communist Party in 1919 represented, not simply a break with the old Socialist Party, but even more important, a break with the whole conception of a common party of revolutionists and opportunists. That signified a new beginning for American socialism, far more important historically than everything that had happened before, including the organization of the Socialist Party in 1901. There can be no return to the outlived and discredited experiment of the past.

The reconstituted movement has encountered its own difficulties and made its own mistakes since that new beginning in 1919. But these are of a different order from the difficulties and mistakes of the earlier time and have to be considered separately. In any case, the poor ideological equipment of the old movement cannot help in their solution.

The struggle against the crimes and betrayals of Stalinism, the prerequisite for the construction of an honest revolutionary party, requires weapons from a different arsenal. Here also the Russians are our teachers. The programmatic weapons for this fight against Stalinist treachery were given to us by Trotsky, the coequal and successor of Lenin.

There can be no return to the past of the American movement. In connection with the Debs Centennial some charlatans, who measure the worth of a socialist movement by its numerical strength at the moment, have discovered new virtues in the old Socialist Party, which polled so many votes in the time of Debs, and have recommended a new experiment on the same lines. Besides its worthlessness as advice to the socialist vanguard of the present day, that prescription does an injustice to the memory of Debs.

He deserves to be honored for his great positive contributions to the cause of socialism, not for his mistakes. The lifework of Debs, as the foremost agitator for socialism we have ever had, as the man of principle who always stood at his post in the class struggle in times of danger and difficulty, will always remain a treasured heritage of the revolutionary workers.

It is best — and it is enough — to honor him for that. The triumph of the cause he served so magnificently will require a different political instrument — a different kind of party — than the one he supported. The model for that is the party of Lenin.

BIOGRAPHICAL NOTE

Born November 5, 1855, in Terre Haute, Indiana, Eugene Victor Debs dropped out of high school at the age of fourteen to go to work in a railroad paint shop. From 1871 to 1874 he worked as a fireman on the railroad, then as a billing clerk for a wholesale grocer for the next five years.

He joined the Brotherhood of Locomotive Firemen at an organizing meeting in 1875 and served as the first secretary of the Terre Haute local. He remained active in the union movement as an officer, organizer, editor and strike leader — officially and unofficially — for some thirty years. In 1905 he helped organize the Industrial Workers of the World.

His political activity started with two 2-year terms as city clerk (1879-1883) and one term in the Indiana State Legislature, to which he was elected in 1884 on the Democratic ticket.

In 1897 Debs helped organize the Social Democracy of America, in 1898 the Social Democratic Party of America and in 1901 the Socialist Party.

He was a candidate for President of the United States five times: on the Social Democratic ticket in 1900, and on the Socialist Party ticket in 1904, 1908, 1912 and 1920, receiving almost a million votes — the highest socialist vote in American history—in his last campaign, when he was in prison.

He served six months in jail in 1895 for violating a court injunction against his leadership of a railroad strike involving more than a hundred thousand workers.

In 1919, charged with violating the Espionage Act for having made an antiwar speech, he went to prison and served two years and eight months of a ten-year sentence.

Upon his release from prison he continued to serve the labor and socialist movement, speaking and writing, as long as he was physically able, until his death on October 20, 1926.

DEBS AT 14 (FIRST ROW, LEFT) ON THE PAINT GANG OF THE TERRE HAUTE, INDIANAPOLIS, & RICHMOND RR

1

HOW I BECAME A SOCIALIST

This article first appeared in the April 1902 issue of The Comrade, *a popular socialist monthly magazine then published in New York City.*

The anarchists Debs refers to in this article were the four labor leaders hanged November 11, 1887, by the State of Illinois. The charge against them was that their ideas had led to the bombing and death of police in the May 4, 1886, Haymarket Square demonstration in Chicago against police brutality to strikers.

As I have some doubt about the readers of *The Comrade* having any curiosity as to "how I became a socialist" it may be in order to say that the subject is the editor's, not my own; and that what is here offered is at his bidding — my only concern being that he shall not have cause to wish that I had remained what I was instead of becoming a socialist.

On the evening of February 27, 1875, the local lodge of the Brotherhood of Locomotive Firemen was organized at Terre Haute, Indiana, by Joshua A. Leach, then grand master, and I was admitted as a charter member and at once chosen secretary. "Old Josh Leach," as he was affectionately called, a typical locomotive fireman of his day, was the founder of the brotherhood, and I was instantly

attracted by his rugged honesty, simple manner and home-
ly speech. How well I remember feeling his large, rough
hand on my shoulder, the kindly eye of an elder brother
searching my own as he gently said: "My boy, you're a
little young, but I believe you're in earnest and will make
your mark in the brotherhood." Of course, I assured him
that I would do my best. What he really thought at the
time flattered my boyish vanity not a little when I heard
of it. He was attending a meeting at St. Louis some months
later, and in the course of his remarks said: "I put a tow-
headed boy in the brotherhood at Terre Haute not long
ago, and some day he will be at the head of it."

Twenty-seven years, to a day, have played their pranks
with "Old Josh" and the rest of us. When last we met, not
long ago, and I pressed his good right hand, I observed
that he was crowned with the frost that never melts; and
as I think of him now:

> Remembrance wakes, with all her busy train,
> Swells at my breast and turns the past to pain.

My first step was thus taken in organized labor and a
new influence fired my ambition and changed the whole
current of my career. I was filled with enthusiasm and
my blood fairly leaped in my veins. Day and night I
worked for the brotherhood. To see its watchfires glow
and observe the increase of its sturdy members were the
sunshine and shower of my life. To attend the "meeting"
was my supreme joy, and for ten years I was not once
absent when the faithful assembled.

At the convention held in Buffalo in 1878 I was chosen
associate editor of the magazine, and in 1880 I became
grand secretary and treasurer. With all the fire of youth
I entered upon the crusade which seemed to fairly glitter
with possibilities. For eighteen hours at a stretch I was
glued to my desk reeling off the answers to my many
correspondents. Day and night were one. Sleep was time
wasted and often, when all oblivious of her presence in

the still small hours my mother's hand turned off the light, I went to bed under protest. Oh, what days! And what quenchless zeal and consuming vanity! All the firemen everywhere — and they were all the world — were straining:

> To catch the beat
> On my tramping feet

My grip was always packed; and I was darting in all directions. To tramp through a railroad yard in the rain, snow or sleet half the night, or till daybreak, to be ordered out of the roundhouse for being an "agitator," or put off a train, sometimes passenger, more often freight, while attempting to deadhead over the division, were all in the program, and served to whet the appetite to conquer. One night in midwinter at Elmira, New York, a conductor on the Erie kindly dropped me off in a snowbank, and as I clambered to the top I ran into the arms of a policeman, who heard my story and on the spot became my friend.

I rode on the engines over mountain and plain, slept in the cabooses and bunks, and was fed from their pails by the swarthy stokers who still nestle close to my heart, and will until it is cold and still.

Through all these years I was nourished at Fountain Proletaire. I drank deeply of its waters and every particle of my tissue became saturated with the spirit of the working class. I had fired an engine and been stung by the exposure and hardship of the rail. I was with the boys in their weary watches, at the broken engine's side and often helped to bear their bruised and bleeding bodies back to wife and child again. How could I but feel the burden of their wrongs? How could the seed of agitation fail to take deep root in my heart?

And so I was spurred on in the work of organizing, not the firemen merely, but the brakemen, switchmen, telegraphers, shopmen, trackhands, all of them in fact, and as I had now become known as an organizer, the calls came from all sides and there are but few trades I have not helped to organize and less still in whose strikes I have not at some time had a hand.

In 1894 the American Railway Union was organized and a braver body of men never fought the battle of the working class.

Up to this time I had heard but little of socialism, knew practically nothing about the movement, and what little I did know was not calculated to impress me in its favor. I was bent on thorough and complete organization of the railroad men and ultimately the whole working class, and all my time and energy were given to that end. My supreme conviction was that if they were only organized in every branch of the service and all acted together in concert they could redress their wrongs and regulate the conditions of their employment. The stockholders of the corporation acted as one, why not the men? It was such a plain proposition — simply to follow the example set before their eyes by their masters — surely they could not fail to see it, act as one, and solve the problem.

It is useless to say that I had yet to learn the workings of the capitalist system, the resources of its masters and the weakness of its slaves. Indeed, no shadow of a "system" fell athwart my pathway; no thought of ending wage misery marred my plans. I was too deeply absorbed in perfecting wage servitude and making it a "thing of beauty and a joy forever."

It all seems very strange to me now, taking a backward look, that my vision was so focalized on a single objective point that I utterly failed to see what now appears as clear as the noonday sun — so clear that I marvel that any workingman, however dull, uncomprehending, can resist it.

But perhaps it was better so. I was to be baptized in socialism in the roar of conflict and I thank the gods for reserving to this fitful occasion the fiat, "Let there be light!"—the light that streams in steady radiance upon the broad way to the socialist republic.

The skirmish lines of the A. R. U. were well advanced. A series of small battles was fought and won without the loss of a man. A number of concessions was made by the corporations rather than risk an encounter. Then came the fight on the Great Northern, short, sharp, and decisive. The victory was complete—the only railroad strike of magnitude ever won by an organization in America.

Next followed the final shock—the Pullman strike—and the American Railway Union again won, clear and complete. The combined corporations were paralyzed and helpless. At this juncture there was delivered, from wholly unexpected quarters, a swift succession of blows that blinded me for an instant and then opened wide my eyes—and in the gleam of every bayonet and the flash of every rifle *the class struggle was revealed.* This was my first practical lesson in socialism, though wholly unaware that it was called by that name.

An army of detectives, thugs and murderers was equipped with badge and beer and bludgeon and turned loose; old hulks of cars were fired; the alarm bells tolled; the people were terrified; the most startling rumors were set afloat; the press volleyed and thundered, and over all the wires sped the news that Chicago's white throat was in the clutch of a red mob; injunctions flew thick and fast, arrests followed, and our office and headquarters, the heart of the strike, was sacked, torn out and nailed up by the "lawful" authorities of the federal government; and when in company with my loyal comrades I found myself in Cook County Jail at Chicago, with the whole press screaming conspiracy, treason and murder, and by some fateful coincidence I was given the cell occupied just previous to his execution by the assassin of Mayor Carter Harrison, Sr., overlooking the spot, a few feet distant, where the anarchists were hanged a few years before, I had another exceedingly practical and impressive lesson in socialism.

Acting upon the advice of friends we sought to employ John Harlan, son of the Supreme Justice, to assist in our defense — a defense memorable to me chiefly because of the skill and fidelity of our lawyers, among whom were the brilliant Clarence Darrow and the venerable Judge Lyman Trumbull, author of the thirteenth amendment to the Constitution, abolishing slavery in the United States.

Mr. Harlan wanted to think of the matter overnight; and the next morning gravely informed us that he could not afford to be identified with the case, "for," said he, "you will be tried upon the same theory as were the anarchists, with probably the same result." That day, I remember, the jailer, by way of consolation, I suppose, showed us the bloodstained rope used at the last execution and explained in minutest detail, as he exhibited the gruesome relic, just how the monstrous crime of lawful murder is committed.

But the tempest gradually subsided and with it the bloodthirstiness of the press and "public sentiment." We were not sentenced to the gallows, nor even to the penitentiary — though put on trial for conspiracy — for reasons that will make another story.

The Chicago jail sentences were followed by six months at Woodstock and it was here that socialism gradually laid hold of me in its own irresistible fashion. Books and pamphlets and letters from socialists came by every mail and I began to read and think and dissect the anatomy of the system in which workingmen, however organized, could be shattered and battered and splintered at a single stroke. The writings of Bellamy and Blatchford early appealed to me. The *Cooperative Commonwealth* of Gronlund also impressed me, but the writings of Kautsky were so clear and conclusive that I readily grasped not merely his argument, but also caught the spirit of his socialist utterance — and I thank him and all who helped me out of darkness into light.

It was at this time, when the first glimmerings of social-

ism were beginning to penetrate, that Victor L. Berger—
and I have loved him ever since—came to Woodstock, as
if a providential instrument, and delivered the first impas-
sioned message of socialism I had ever heard—the very
first to set the "wires humming in my system." As a souvenir of that visit there is in my library a volume of *Capital*, by Karl Marx, inscribed with the compliments of
Victor L. Berger, which I cherish as a token of priceless
value.

The American Railway Union was defeated but not conquered—overwhelmed but not destroyed. It lives and pul-
sates in the socialist movement, and its defeat but blazed
the way to economic freedom and hastened the dawn of
human brotherhood.

2

THE ROLE OF THE COURTS

*The lessons of his experience with the federal courts in
the Pullman strike were expressed by Debs in a speech delivered November 23, 1895, on his return to Terre Haute
the day after his release from Woodstock jail.*

In our cases at Chicago an injunction was issued at a
time when the American Railway Union had its great
struggle for human rights and they were triumphant in
restraining myself and colleagues from doing what we
never intended to do and never did do; and then we were
put in jail for not doing it.

When that injunction was served on me, to show that
I acted in good faith, I went to two of the best constitutional lawyers in the city of Chicago and said, "What
rights, if any, have I under this injunction? I am a law-
abiding citizen; I want to do what is right. I want you to
examine this injunction and then advise me what to do."

They examined the injunction. They said, "Proceed just
as you have been doing. You are not committing any
violence; you are not advising violence, but you are trying
to do everything in your power to restrain men from the
commission of crime or violating the law." I followed their
advice and got six months for it. [*Laughter and applause.*]

What does Judge Lyman Trumbull say upon that subject? Judge Trumbull is one of the most eminent jurists

the country has produced. He served sixteen years in the United States Senate; he was chairman of the Senate Committee on Judiciary; he was on the Supreme Bench of the state of Illinois; he has held all of the high offices but he is a poor man. There is not a scar nor a blemish upon his escutcheon. No one ever impugned his integrity. What does he say about this subject?

To use his exact language he says: "The decision carried to its logical conclusion means that any federal judge can imprison any citizen at his own will. If this be true, it is judicial despotism, pure and simple, whatever you may choose to call it."

When the trials were in progress at Chicago Mr. George M. Pullman was summoned to give some testimony. Mr. Pullman attached his car to the New York train and went East, and in some way the papers got hold of the matter and made some publication about it and the judge said that Mr. Pullman would be dealt with drastically. In a few days Mr. Pullman returned and he went into chambers, made a few personal explanations and that is the last we heard about it. Had it been myself, I would have to go to jail. That is the difference.

Only a little while ago Judge Henford cited Henry C. Payne, of the Northern Pacific, to appear before him to answer certain charges, and he went to Europe and is there yet. Will he go to jail on his return? Of course not. The reason suggests itself. If it were a railroad striker he would be in Woodstock instead of Berlin.

Governor Altgeld, in many respects the greatest governor in the United States, says: "The precedent has now been established and any federal judge can now enjoin any citizen from doing anything and then put him in jail."

Now what is an injunction? It has all of the force and vital effect of a law, but it is not a law in and by the representatives of the people; it is not a law signed by a President or by a governor. It is simply the wish and will of the judge. A judge issues an injunction; serves it upon his intended victim. The next day he is arrested. He is brought into the presence of the same judge. Sentence is pronounced upon him by the same judge, who constitutes the judge and court and jury and he goes to jail and he has no right of appeal. Under this injunctional process the plain provisions of the Constitution have been disregarded. The right of trial by jury has been abrogated, and this at the behest of the money power of the country.

What is the effect upon the workingmen and especially railway employees to bind them to their task? The government goes into partnership with a corporation. The workingmen are intimidated; if there is a reduction of wages they submit; if unjust conditions are imposed they are silent. And what is the tendency? To demoralize, to degrade workingmen until they have reached the very deadline of degradation.

And how does it happen and why does it happen that corporations are never restrained? Are they absolutely law-abiding? Are they always right? Do they never transgress the law or is it because the federal judges are their creatures? Certain it is that the united voice of labor in this country would be insufficient to name a federal judge. If all the common people united and asked for the appointment of a federal judge their voice would not be heeded any more than if it were the chirp of a cricket. Money talks. Yes, money talks. And I have no hesitancy in declaring that money has even invaded, or the influence, that power conferred by money, has invaded the Supreme Court and left that august tribunal reeking with more stench than Coleridge discovered in Cologne and left all the people wondering how it was ever to be deodorized.

There is something wrong in this country; the judicial nets are so adjusted as to catch the minnows and let the whales slip through and the federal judge is as far removed from the common people as if he inhabited another planet. As Boyle O'Reilly would say:

His pulse, if you felt it, throbbed apart
From the throbbing pulse of the people's heart.

3

THE AMERICAN UNIVERSITY AND THE LABOR PROBLEM

As the leader of the national railroad strike that the newspapers had called the "Debs Rebellion," Eugene V. Debs, president of the American Railway Union, emerged from jail a national hero to the working men and women, the liberals and the radical youth of that day.

College students then, as now, were trying to relate to the society around them. In response to a request from the editor of the Western Reserve University publication in Cleveland, Ohio, Debs wrote this article, which appeared in the February 1896 issue of The Adelbert.

Strictly speaking, the American university is doing little, if anything, toward solving the "great labor problem" and the reason why, if sought, is found in the fact that neither the American nor the European universities were founded for any purpose directly or remotely connected with the solution of any labor problem, great or small. Such is the history of European universities and in the founding of American universities history may be said to have repeated itself.

In replying to the interrogatories addressed to me by the editor-in-chief of *The Adelbert*, "Is the American University doing its share in solving the great Labor Problem? If not, where is it lacking and what suggestions would you make for its improvement in that direction?" hypercriticism of the American university is not required and yet, facts should be courageously stated regardless of consequences.

As a general proposition, universities are aristocratic institutions. This is preeminently true of European universities and to make matters still worse they were from the date of inception hedged about with ecclesiastic prerogatives and bigotries which, *nolens volens*, created a class of superior beings as separate and distinct from labor as if the lines defining their limits had been rivers of fire.

That American universities, as in the case of Harvard and Yale, should have inherited the defects of European institutions, is of easy and satisfactory explanation. The French, English, and German universities were creations of kings and popes and within their sacred precincts no labor problem was ever considered except to find the most effective methods of enslaving the masses, and how effectively this work has gone forward in Europe for the past six hundred years the merest novice in investigation may find abundant proof; indeed, exclusiveness is the distinguishing characteristic of the ancient and modern university and no amount of learned sophistication can obscure the fact. It was true of the Lyceum when Aristotle taught, when Grecian philosophy was in its meridian glory, and the academy of Plato was not invaded except by the favored few, and it is as true now as then, that a university education is reserved for those who have money to purchase it, and the fact that universities confer degrees is in itself a power employed for constituting a species of nobility which, however well deserved in certain cases, considered from an educational point of view as rewards of merit, serves nevertheless, and has always served the purpose of creating an aristocracy of D. D.'s, LL. D.'s, etc., often as obnoxiously exclusive as a titled nobility created by kings.

The graduates of universities with their diplomas and degrees, boasting of their *alma maters*, as a rule regard themselves, as compared with the "common people," of superior mold, and this fact is scarcely less conspicuous in America than in Europe. The rule is stated: there are numerous exceptions, but observation verifies the proposition and that such defects and infirmities are largely the result of inheritance, few will be found to question the averment.

Referring directly to the interrogatory "Is the American University doing its share in solving the great Labor Problem?" after grouping all the facts the reply must be in the negative; but just what is meant by the "great labor problem" is susceptible of so many and such varied conclusions that the difficulties evoked are well calculated to involve discussion in ceaseless entanglements. Labor in the United States is confronted with numerous problems and which one should be designated as "the great labor problem" must be of necessity left to the judgment of those who are interested in such questions.

There are those who are constantly championing the hypothesis that there exists something in the nature of an irrepressible conflict between labor and capital and that to harmonize the belligerents constitutes the solution of the "great labor problem" and the error, for such it is, so permeates discussion that confusion becomes worse confounded as the debate proceeds and necessarily so, because the premise is a myth, the truth being that capital and labor instead of occupying a hostile attitude towards each other, enjoy the most peaceful relationship. This must of necessity be the condition, since the truth is axiomatic that labor, and only labor, creates capital. But when it is stated that a conflict exists between laborers and capitalists, a problem is presented worthy of the attention of the American university. It so happens, however, that the university, to use a figure of speech, is itself a capitalist and has never had anything in common with labor and, therefore, is not doing its "share," whatever that may be, in solving any labor problem.

In this there is nothing peculiar to the American university, the facts standing out as prominently in the history of all universities.

What, in this connection, could be more interesting than to know what labor problem has been solved by any of the great universities of Europe? To be more particular and pertinent, because of language inheritance, what labor problems have the great historical and wealthy universities of England solved? For more than six hundred years the Cambridge and Oxford Universities have flourished, and if either of them have solved any great labor problem for the benefit of the toilers of England, the facts should be stated. A correspondent of a Chicago paper, writing recently from London, after recapitulating numerous and aggravating afflictions of labor in England says, "The result is that England has upon her hands an enormous pauperized population and the government is seriously embarrassed by continued demands for relief." What is true of England is equally true of the United States, for notwithstanding we have Harvard and Yale and perhaps a hundred more American universities, we also have "an enormous pauperized population" and if these universities have solved any labor problem, the present is happily opportune to herald the fact.

If the American university has failed in doing its share in solving the "great labor problem," no laborious research is required to find a plausible reason for its shortcomings, and recent humiliating incidents transpiring in the operation of the Chicago University, become sufficiently explanatory to satisfy the most exacting. The dismissal of Prof. Bemis proclaims the fact that the American university is not equipped to solve labor problems, but is arrogantly hostile to labor and further proof of its opposition to labor, if demanded, is found in President Harper's explanation of the dismissal of Prof. Bemis in which he is reported to have said substantially that to "express friendship for workingmen is well enough *but we get our money from the other side.*"

The American university is not seeking to solve labor

problems because the performance of such work would require the arraignment of the capitalistic class from which it "gets its money," and the capitalistic class solves all labor problems by creating environments which pauperize labor, and reduce it to vassalage.

Suggestions for the improvement of the American university made by anyone identified with labor, though responding to a request to offer hints in that direction, would be regarded by university presidents, professors, and graduates, as impertinences, plebeian rudeness, born of ignorance and audacity, and yet it so happens that every advance step taken to solve labor problems, bearing the stamp of common sense and justice, has been made by men within the ranks of labor and not by men wearing university titles and equipped with the advantages their *alma maters* could confer.

But such statements are not put forth to indicate intentional culpability on the part of the American university. It was not founded nor endowed for solving labor problems and its curriculum never includes studies specially designed to aid in the performance of such tasks, and any improvement in that direction would involve such radical changes as would disturb their foundations.

The American university, if it would do any share in solving the "great labor problem," would be required to attack the corrupting power of money wielded by corporations, trusts and syndicates, as also the American aristocracy, whether built upon coal oil or codfish, watered stocks, banks, bullion or boodle. This, as in the case of the Chicago institution, it would not do because it is from such sources that it gets its money. It would be required to employ professors to lecture upon the degrading influences of starvation wages, which darken ten thousand American homes. It would be confronted with the exiling power of labor-saving machinery, which is filling the land with armies of enforced idlers which thoughtful men regard as dangerous and threatening the perpetuity of our republican institutions. It would have to array itself against a corrupt judiciary and hold it up as a target for the maledictions of liberty-loving Americans.

If it is held that the American university is solving labor problems by diffusing throughout the land the blessings of a "higher education," including football and other athletic tournaments, as also displays of pyrotechnic oratory, it may be said that ancient Greece and Rome indulged in such classic pastimes and after a few hundred years reached a condition of desuetude, without solving any labor problem whatever.

Gladstone, the "grand old man," the justly renowned English statesman and scholar, and graduate of Oxford, whose knowledge of Greek is so profound that he could, if required, rival Demosthenes as a Grecian orator, may have during his brilliant career solved some labor problem for which his name will be held in grateful remembrance by English workingmen, but if such is the case the fact is yet to be chronicled. And Daniel Webster, a graduate of Dartmouth University, the great expounder of the Constitution, found out by university processes of reasoning that "Government is founded on property" a heresy advocated by the American university.

If the American university would have any "share" in solving labor problems, a change in its policy will be required. It will have to renounce all allegiances which separate it from the great body of the people and permit its colleges, if need be, to become the tombs of its errors, whether inherited or adopted, that it may in its teachings represent the American democracy rather than the American aristocracy.

4

THE OUTLOOK FOR SOCIALISM
IN THE UNITED STATES

The American Railway Union convention which opened in Chicago June 15, 1897, voted to dissolve, then reorganized on June 21 as the Social Democracy of America, with Debs as chairman.

At its convention a year later it split over the issue of colonization (setting up a model cooperative community) versus political action as the road to socialism in the United States. On this principled difference the minority left and founded the Social Democratic Party as "a class-conscious, revolutionary social organization."

Debs was elected to the executive board. He played a leading role in building the new party, touring the country lecturing on socialism, selling subscriptions to the Social Democratic Herald, *recruiting and helping negotiate mergers with independent socialist groups.*

The national convention of the Social Democratic Party which met in Indianapolis, Indiana, in March 1900 nominated Debs, then forty-one years old, as its candidate for President of the United States.

His views on the outlook for socialism as he launched his first presidential campaign were published in the September 1900 International Socialist Review.

The sun of the passing century is setting upon scenes of extraordinary activity in almost every part of our capitalistic old planet. Wars and rumors of wars are of universal prevalence. In the Philippines our soldiers are civilizing and Christianizing the natives in the latest and most approved styles of the art, and at prices ($13 per month) which commend the blessing to the prayerful consideration of the lowly and oppressed everywhere.

In South Africa the British legions are overwhelming the Boers with volleys of benedictions inspired by the same beautiful philanthropy in the name of the meek and lowly Nazarene; while in China the heathen hordes, fanned into frenzy by the sordid spirit of modern commercial conquest, are presenting to the world a carnival of crime almost equaling the "refined" exhibitions of the world's "civilized" nations.

And through all the flame and furor of the fray can be heard the savage snarlings of the Christian "dogs of war" as they fiercely glare about them, and with jealous fury threaten to fly at one another's throats to settle the question of supremacy and the spoil and plunder of conquest.

The picture, lurid as a chamber of horrors, becomes complete in its gruesome ghastliness when robed ministers of Christ solemnly declare that it is all for the glory of God and the advancement of Christian civilization.

This, then, is the closing scene of the century as the curtain slowly descends upon the bloodstained stage — the central figure, the pious Wilhelm, Germany's sceptered savage, issuing his imperial "spare none" decree in the *sang-froid* of an Apache chief — a fitting climax to the rapacious regime of the capitalist system.

Cheerless indeed would be the contemplation of such sanguinary scenes were the light of socialism not breaking upon mankind. The skies of the East are even now aglow with the dawn; its coming is heralded by the dispelling of shadows, of darkness and gloom. From the first tremulous scintillation that gilds the horizon to the sublime march to meridian splendor the light increases till in mighty flood it pours upon the world.

From out of the midnight of superstition, ignorance and slavery the disenthralling, emancipating sun is rising. I am not gifted with prophetic vision, and yet I see the shadows vanishing. I behold near and far prostrate men lifting their bowed forms from the dust. I see thrones in the grasp of decay; despots relaxing their hold upon scepters, and shackles falling, not only from the limbs, but from the souls of men.

It is therefore with pleasure that I respond to the invitation of the editor of the *International Socialist Review* to present my views upon the "Outlook for Socialism in the United States." Socialists generally will agree that the past year has been marked with a propaganda of unprecedented activity and that the sentiment of the American people in respect to socialism has undergone a most remarkable change. It would be difficult to imagine a more ignorant, bitter and unreasoning prejudice than that of the American people against socialism during the early years of its introduction by the propagandists from the other side.

I never think of these despised and persecuted "foreign invaders" without a feeling of profound obligation, akin to reverence, for their noble work in laying the foundations deep and strong, under the most trying conditions, of the American movement. The ignorant mass, wholly incapable of grasping their splendid teachings or appreciating their lofty motives, reviled against them. The press inoculated the public sentiment with intolerance and malice which not infrequently found expression through the policeman's club when a few of the pioneers gathered to engraft the class-conscious doctrine upon their inhospitable "freeborn" American fellow citizens.

Socialism was cunningly associated with "anarchy and bloodshed," and denounced as a "foul foreign importation" to pollute the fair, free soil of America, and every outrage to which the early agitators were subjected won the plaudits of the people. But they persevered in their task; they could not be silenced or suppressed. Slowly they increased in number and gradually the movement began to take root and spread over the country. The industrial conditions consequent upon the development of capitalist production were now making themselves felt and socialism became a fixed and increasing factor in the economic and political affairs of the nation.

The same difficulties which other countries had experienced in the process of party organization have attended the development of the movement here, but these differences, which relate mainly to tactics and methods of propaganda, are bound to disappear as the friction of the jarring factions smoothens out the rough edges and adjusts them to a concrete body — a powerful section in the great international army of militant socialism.

In the general elections of 1898 upwards of 91,000 votes were cast for the Socialist candidates in the United States, an increase in this off year of almost two hundred percent over the general elections of two years previous, the presidential year of 1896. Since the congressional elections of 1898, and more particularly since the municipal and state elections following, which resulted in such signal victories in Massachusetts, two members of the legislature and a mayor, the first in America, being elected by decided majorities — since then socialism has made rapid strides in all directions and the old politicians no longer reckon it as a negative quantity in making their forecasts and calculating their pluralities and majorities.

The subject has passed entirely beyond the domain of sneer and ridicule and now commands serious treatment. Of course, socialism is violently denounced by the capitalist press and by all the brood of subsidized contributors to magazine literature, but this only confirms the view that the advance of socialism is very properly recognized by the capitalist class as the one cloud upon the horizon which portends an end to the system in which they have waxed fat, insolent and despotic through the exploitation of their countless wage-working slaves.

In school and college and church, in clubs and public halls everywhere, socialism is the central theme of discussion, and its advocates, inspired by its noble principles, are to be found here, there and in all places ready to give or accept challenge to battle. In the cities the corner meetings are popular and effective. But rarely is such a gathering now molested by the "authorities," and then only where they have just been inaugurated. They are too numerously attended by serious, intelligent and self-reliant men and women to invite interference.

Agitation is followed by organization, and the increase of branches, sections and clubs goes forward with extraordinary activity in every part of the land.

In New England the agitation has resulted in quite a general organization among the states, with Massachusetts in the lead; and the indications are that, with the vigorous prosecution of the campaign already inaugurated, a tremendous increase in the vote will be polled in the approaching national elections. New York and Pennsylvania will show surprising Socialist returns, while Ohio, Michigan, Indiana, Illinois, Missouri and Kentucky will all round up with a large vote. Wisconsin has already a great vote to her credit and will increase it largely this year. In the west and northwest, Kansas, Iowa and Minnesota will forge to the front, and so also will Nebraska, the Dakotas, Montana, Oregon, Washington, Idaho and Colorado. California is expected to show an immense increase, and the returns from there will not disappoint the most sanguine. In the southwest, Texas is making a stirring campaign, and several papers, heretofore Populist, will support our candidates and swell the Socialist vote, which will be an eye-opener when announced.

On the whole, the situation could scarcely be more favorable and the final returns will more than justify our sanguine expectations.

It must not be overlooked, however, when calculations are made, that this is a presidential year and that the general results will not be so favorable as if the elections were in an off year. Both the Republican and Democratic parties will, as usual, strain every nerve to whip the "voting kings" into line and every conceivable influence will be exerted to that end. These vast machines operate with marvelous precision and the wheels are already in motion. Corruption funds, national, state, and municipal, will flow out like lava tides; promises will be as plentiful as autumn leaves; from ten thousand platforms the Columbian orator will agitate the atmosphere, while brass bands, torchlight processions, glittering uniforms and free whisky, dispensed by the ward-heeler, will lend their combined influence to steer the "patriots" to the capitalist chute that empties into the ballot box.

The campaign this year will be unusually spectacular. The Republican Party "points with pride" to the "prosperity" of the country, the beneficent results of the "gold standard" and the "war record" of the administration. The Democratic Party declares that "imperialism" is the "paramount" issue, and that the country is certain to go to the "demnition bow-wows" if Democratic officeholders are not elected instead of the Republicans. The Democratic slogan is "The Republic vs. the Empire," accompanied in a very minor key by 16 to 1 and "direct legislation where practical."

Both these capitalist parties are fiercely opposed to trusts, though what they propose to do with them is not of sufficient importance to require even a hint in their platforms.

Needless is it for me to say to the thinking workingman that he has no choice between these two capitalist parties, that they are both pledged to the same system and that whether the one or the other succeeds, he will still remain the wage-working slave he is today.

What but meaningless phrases are "imperialism," "expansion," "free silver," "gold standard," etc., to the wage worker? The large capitalists represented by Mr. McKinley and the small capitalists represented by Mr. Bryan are interested in these "issues," but they do not concern the working class.

What the workingmen of the country are profoundly interested in is the private ownership of the means of production and distribution, the enslaving and degrading wage system in which they toil for a pittance at the pleasure of their masters and are bludgeoned, jailed or shot when they protest — this is the central, controlling, vital issue of the hour, and neither of the old party platforms has a word or even a hint about it.

As a rule, large capitalists are Republicans and small capitalists are Democrats, but workingmen must remember that they are all capitalists, and that the many small ones, like the fewer large ones, are all politically supporting their class interests, and this is always and everywhere the capitalist class.

Whether the means of production — that is to say, the land, mines, factories, machinery, etc. — are owned by a few large Republican capitalists, who organize a trust, or whether they be owned by a lot of small Democratic capitalists, who are opposed to the trust, is all the same to the working class. Let the capitalists, large and small, fight this out among themselves.

The working class must get rid of the whole brood of masters and exploiters, and put themselves in possession and control of the means of production, that they may have steady employment without consulting a capitalist employer, large or small, and that they may get the wealth their labor produces, all of it, and enjoy with their families the fruits of their industry in comfortable and happy homes, abundant and wholesome food, proper clothing and all other things necessary to "life, liberty and the pursuit of happiness." It is therefore a question not of "reform," the mask of fraud, but of revolution. The capitalist system must be overthrown, class rule abolished and wage slavery supplanted by cooperative industry.

We hear it frequently urged that the Democratic Party is the "poor man's party," "the friend of labor." There is but one way to relieve poverty and to free labor, and that is by making common property of the tools of labor.

Is the Democratic Party, which we are assured has "strong socialistic tendencies," in favor of collective ownership of the means of production? Is it opposed to the wage system, from which flows in a ceaseless stream the poverty, misery and wretchedness of the children of toil? If the

Democratic Party is the "friend of labor" any more than the Republican Party, why is its platform dumb in the presence of Coeur d'Alene? It knows the truth about these shocking outrages — crimes upon workingmen, their wives and children, which would blacken the pages of Siberia — why does it not speak out?

What has the Democratic Party to say about the "property and educational qualifications" in North Carolina and Louisiana, and the proposed general disfranchisement of the Negro race in the Southern states?

The differences between the Republican and Democratic parties involve no issue, no principle in which the working class has any interest, and whether the spoils be distributed by Hanna and Platt, or by Croker and Tammany Hall is all the same to it.

Between these parties socialists have no choice, no preference. They are one in their opposition to socialism, that is to say, the emancipation of the working class from wage slavery, and every workingman who has intelligence enough to understand the interest of his class and the nature of the struggle in which it is involved will once and for all time sever his relations with them both; and recognizing the class struggle which is being waged between producing workers and nonproducing capitalists, cast his lot with the class-conscious, revolutionary Socialist Party, which is pledged to abolish the capitalist system, class rule and wage slavery — a party which does not compromise or fuse, but, preserving inviolate the principles which quickened it into life and now give it vitality and force, moves forward with dauntless determination to the goal of economic freedom.

The political trend is steadily toward socialism. The old parties are held together only by the cohesive power of spoils, and in spite of this they are steadily disintegrating. Again and again they have been tried with the same results, and thousands upon thousands, awake to their duplicity, are deserting them and turning toward socialism as the only refuge and security. Republicans, Democrats, Populists, Prohibitionists, Single Taxers are having they eyes opened to the true nature of the struggle and they are beginning to

> Come as the winds come, when
>   Forests are rended;
> Come as the waves come, when
>   Navies are stranded.

For a time the Populist Party had a mission, but it is practically ended. The Democratic Party has "fused" it out of existence. The "middle-of-the-road" element will be sorely disappointed when the votes are counted, and they will probably never figure in another national campaign. Not many of them will go back to the old parties. Many of them have already come to socialism, and the rest are sure to follow.

There is no longer any room for a Populist Party, and progressive Populists realize it, and hence the "strongholds" of Populism are becoming the "hotbeds" of Socialism.

It is simply a question of capitalism or socialism, of despotism or democracy, and they who are not wholly with us are wholly against us.

Another source of strength to socialism, steadily increasing, is the trades-union movement. The spread of socialist doctrine among the labor organizations of the country during the past year exceeds the most extravagant estimates. No one has had better opportunities than the writer to note the transition to socialism among trades unionists, and the approaching election will abundantly verify it.

Promising, indeed, is the outlook for socialism in the United States. The very contemplation of the prospect is a wellspring of inspiration.

Oh, that all the working class could and would use their eyes and see; their ears and hear; their brains and think. How soon this earth could be transformed and by the alchemy of social order made to blossom with beauty and joy.

No sane man can be satisfied with the present system. If a poor man is happy, said Victor Hugo, "he is the pickpocket of happiness. Only the rich and noble are happy by right. The rich man is he who, being young, has the rights of old age; being old, the lucky chances of youth; vicious, the respect of good people; a coward, the command of the stouthearted; doing nothing, the fruits of labor."

With pride and joy we watch each advancing step of our comrades in socialism in all other lands. Our hearts are with them in their varying fortunes as the battle proceeds, and we applaud each telling blow delivered and cheer each victory achieved.

The wire has just brought the tidings of Liebknecht's death. The hearts of American Socialists will be touched and shocked by the calamity. The brave old warrior succumbed at last, but not until he heard the tramp of international socialism, for which he labored with all his loving, loyal heart; not until he saw the thrones of Europe, one by one, begin to totter, not until he had achieved a glorious immortality.

5

WHAT'S THE MATTER WITH CHICAGO?

In the presidential election of 1900 Debs received 96,878 votes. His year-in, year-out, and year-round campaigning for socialism continued, tying in with whatever were the popular issues of the day.

This article from the Chicago Socialist *of October 25, 1902, is of particular interest as an example of how a revolutionary socialist related to the chronic problem of urban decay in capitalist society.*

For some days William E. Curtis, the far-famed correspondent of the Chicago *Record-Herald*, has been pressing the above inquiry upon representative people of all classes with a view to throwing all possible light upon that vexed subject.

The inquiry is in such general terms and takes such wide scope that anything like a comprehensive answer would fill a book without exhausting the subject, while a review of the "interviews" would embrace the whole gamut of absurdity and folly and produce a library of comedy and tragedy.

Not one of the replies I have seen has sufficient merit to be printed in a paper read by grown folks, and those that purport to come from leaders of labor and representatives of the working class take the prize in what would appear to be a competitive contest for progressive asininity.

The leader, so-called, who puts it upon record in a capitalist paper and gives the libel the widest circulation, that Chicago is alright, so far as the workers are concerned, that they have plenty and are prosperous and happy, is as fit to lead the working class as is a wolf to guide a flock of spring lambs.

It is from the wage worker's point of view that I shall attempt an answer to the question propounded by Mr. Curtis, and in dealing with the subject I shall be as candid as may be expected from a Socialist agitator.

The question is opportune at this season, when the "frost is on the pumpkin," and the ballot is soon to decide to what extent the people really know "what is the matter with Chicago."

First of all, Chicago is the product of modern capitalism, and, like all other great commercial centers, is unfit for human habitation. The Illinois Central Railroad Company selected the site upon which the city is built and this consisted of a vast miasmatic swamp far better suited to mosquito culture than for human beings. From the day the site was chosen by (and of course in the interest of all) said railway company, everything that entered into the building of the town and the development of the city was determined purely from profit considerations and without the remotest concern for the health and comfort of the human beings who were to live there, especially those who had to do all the labor and produce all the wealth.

As a rule hogs are only raised where they have good health and grow fat. Any old place will do to raise human beings.

At this very hour typhoid fever and diphtheria are epidemic in Chicago and the doctors agree that these ravages are due to the microbes and germs generated in the catch-basins and sewers which fester and exhale their foul and fetid breath upon the vast swarms of human beings caught and fettered there.

Thousands upon thousands of Chicago's population have been poisoned to death by the impure water and foul atmosphere of this undrainable swamp (notwithstanding the doctored mortuary tables by which it is proven to prospective investors that it is the healthiest city on earth) and thousands more will commit suicide in the same way, but to compensate for it all Chicago has the prize location for money-making, immense advantage for profit-mongering — and what are human beings compared to money?

During recent years Chicago has expended millions to lift herself out of her native swamp, but the sewage floats back to report the dismal failure of the attempt, and every germ-laden breeze confirms the report.

That is one thing that is the matter with Chicago. It never was intended that human beings should live there. A thousand sites infinitely preferable for a city could have been found in close proximity, but they lacked the "commercial" advantages which are of such commanding importance in the capitalist system.

And now they wonder "what is the matter with Chicago!" Look at some of her filthy streets in the heart of the city, chronically torn up, the sunlight obscured, the air polluted, the water contaminated, every fountain and stream designed to bless the race poisoned at its source — and you need not wonder what ails Chicago, nor will you escape the conclusion that the case is chronic and that the present city will never recover from the fatal malady.

What is true of Chicago physically is emphasized in her social, moral and spiritual aspects, and this applies to every commercial metropolis in the civilized world.

From any rational point of view they are all dismal failures.

There is no reason under the sun, aside from the profit considerations of the capitalist system, why two million humans should be stacked up in layers and heaps until they jar the clouds, while millions of acres of virgin soil are totally uninhabited.

The very contemplation of the spectacle gives rise to serious doubt as to the sanity of the race.

Such a vast population in such a limited area cannot feed itself, has not room to move and cannot keep clean.

The deadly virus of capitalism is surging through all the veins of this young mistress of trade and the eruptions are found all over the body social and politic, and that's "what's the matter with Chicago."

Hundreds of the *Record-Herald's* quacks are prescribing their nostrums for the blotches and pustules which have broken out upon the surface, but few have sense enough to know and candor enough to admit that the virus must be expelled from the system — and these few are Socialists who are so notoriously visionary and impractical that their opinions are not worthy of space in a great paper printed to conserve the truth and promote the welfare of society.

This model metropolis of the West has broken all the records for political corruption. Her old rival on the Mississippi, catching the inspiration doubtless, has been making some effort to crown herself with similar laurels, but for smooth political jobbery and fancy manipulation of the wires, Chicago is still far in the lead. In the Windy City ward politics has long been recognized as a fine art and the collection is unrivaled anywhere.

From the millions of dollars filched from the millions of humans by the corporate owners of the common utilities, the reeking corruption funds flow like lava tides, and to attempt to purify the turbid stream by the "reform measures" proposed from time to time by the Republican-Democratic Party in its internal conflict for the spoils of office, is as utter a piece of folly as to try with beeswax to seal up Mount Pelee.

Chicago has plutocrats and paupers in the ratio of more than sixteen to one — boulevards for the exhibition of the rich and alleys for the convenience of the poor.

Chicago has also a grand army of the most skilled pickpockets, artistic confidence operators, accomplished footpads and adept cracksmen on earth. So well is this understood that on every breeze we hear the refrain:

> When Reuben comes to town,
> He's sure to be done brown —

And this lugubrious truth is treated as the richest of jokes, with utter unconsciousness of the moral degeneracy it reflects, the crime it glorifies and the indictment of capitalist society it returns in answer to the *Record-Herald's* query: "What's the matter with Chicago?"

Besides the array of "talent" above mentioned, fostered by competitive society everywhere, the marshy metropolis by the lake may boast of a vast and flourishing gambling industry, an illimitable and progressive "levee" district, sweatshops, slums, dives, bloated men, bedraggled women, ghastly caricatures of their former selves, babies cradled in rags and filth, aged children, than which nothing could be more melancholy — all these and a thousand more, the fruit of our present social anarchy, afflict Chicago; and, worst of all, our wise social philosophers, schooled in the economics of capitalist universities, preach the comforting doctrine that all these are necessary evils and at best can but be restricted within certain bounds; and this hideous libel is made a cloak that theft may continue to masquerade as philanthropy.

It is at this point that Chicago particularly prides herself upon her "charities," hospitals and eleemosynary endowments, all breathing the sweet spirit of Christian philanthropy — utterly ignorant of the fact, designedly or otherwise, that these very institutions are manifestations of social disease and are monumental of the iniquity of the system that must rear such whited sepulchers to conceal its crimes.

I do not oppose the insane asylum — but I abhor and condemn the cutthroat system that robs man of his reason, drives him to insanity and makes the lunatic asylum an indispensable adjunct to every civilized community.

With the ten thousand "charities" that are proposed to poultice the sores and bruises of society, I have little patience.

Worst of all is the charity ball. Chicago indulges in these festering festivals on a grand scale.

Think of cavorting around in a dress suit because some poor wretch is hungry; and of indulging in a royal carousal to comfort some despairing woman on the brink of suicide; and finally, that in "fashionable society" the definition of this mixture of inanity and moral perversion is "charity."

Fleece your fellows! That is "business," and you are a captain of industry. Having "relieved" your victims of their pelts, dance and make merry to "relieve" their agony. This is "charity" and you are a philanthropist.

In summing up the moral assets of a great (?) city, the churches should not be overlooked. Chicago is a city of fine churches. All the denominations are copiously represented, and sermons in all languages and of all varieties are turned out in job lots and at retail to suit the market.

The churches are always numerous where vice is rampant. They seem to spring from the same soil and thrive in the same climate.

And yet the churches are supposed to wage relentless warfare upon evil. To just what extent they have checked its spread in the Windy City may be inferred from the probing of the press into the body social to ascertain "what is the matter with Chicago."

The preachers are not wholly to blame, after all, for their moral and spiritual impotency. They are wage workers, the same as coal miners, and are just as dependent upon the capitalist class. How can they be expected to antagonize the interests of their employers and hold their jobs? The unskilled preachers, the common laborers in the arid spots of the vineyard, are often wretchedly paid, and yet they remain unorganized and have never struck for better wages.

"What's the matter with Chicago?" Capitalism!

What's the cure? Socialism!

Regeneration will only come with depopulation — when socialism has relieved the congestion and released the people and they spread out over the country and live close to the grass.

The *Record-Herald* has furnished the people of Chicago and Illinois with a campaign issue.

If you want to know more about "what is the matter with Chicago," read the Socialist papers and magazines; read the platform of the Socialist Party; and if you do, you will cut loose from the Republican-Democratic Party, the double-headed political monstrosity of the capitalist class, and you will cast your vote for the Socialist Party and your lot with the international Socialist movement, whose mission it is to uproot and overthrow the whole system of capitalist exploitation, and put an end to the poverty and misery it entails — and that's "what's the matter with Chicago."

DEBS, ORGANIZER OF THE AMERICAN RAILWAY UNION

6

THE WESTERN LABOR MOVEMENT

When Debs, the union militant, sat in the McHenry County Jail in Woodstock, Illinois, removed from activity for six months after the Pullman strike, he had time to think.

"Why is it," he asked himself, "that labor does not conquer anything? Why does it not assert its mighty power? Why does it not rule in Congress, in legislatures and in courts? I answer because it is factionized, because it will not unify, because, for some inscrutable reason, it prefers division, weakness and slavery, rather than unity, strength and victory.

"Will it always be thus unmindful of its power and prerogatives? I do not think so. . . ." (Quoted from "Labor Omnia Vincit," written in jail for the Labor Day souvenir book of the Central Labor Union, Boston, Massachusetts, September 1895.)

The rest of his life Debs worked to unify the working class economically and politically so that it could use its power to emancipate itself.

With that goal he advocated, supported and defended all developments toward industrial unionism as opposed to craft unionism; class-conscious socialist-oriented unionism as opposed to procapitalist reform unionism.

His article in the November 1902 International Socialist Review *was a reply to an attack by party leaders in the*

Socialist national office in St. Louis on members support-
ing the more militant section of the union movement in
the Western Federation of Miners and the American Labor
Union.

There seems to be considerable misapprehension, especially among Socialists, in regard to the trades-union movement of the Western states, whose delegates, recently assembled in national convention, adopted the platform of
the Socialist Party and pledged the support of their organizations to the international Socialist movement. This
radical departure from the effete and reactionary nonpolit-
ical policy of the American Federation of Labor, so long
and so earnestly striven for by the Western leaders, and
so entirely compatible with the socialist conception of class-
conscious and progressive trades unionism, should have
been met with the prompt and hearty approbation of every
unionist and every Socialist in the land. That such was
not the case, the lukewarm comment and the half-approv-
ing, half-condemning tone of the Socialist Party press, with
but one or two exceptions, bear convincing testimony,
while the uncalled for, unwise and wholly unaccountable
official pronunciamento of the St. Louis "Quorum," pur-
porting to speak for the National Committee, capped the
climax of unfairness and injustice to the Western movement.
   Stripped of unnecessary verbiage and free from subterfuge, the Socialist Party has been placed in the attitude of
turning its back upon the young, virile, class-conscious
union movement of the West, and fawning at the feet of
the "pure and simple" movement of the East, and this
anomalous thing has been done by men who are supposed
to stand sponsor to the party and whose utterance is
credited with being *ex cathedra* upon party affairs.
   They may congratulate themselves that upon this point
at least they are in perfect accord with the capitalist press,
and also with the "labor lieutenants," the henchmen and
heelers, whose duty it is to warn the union against social-

ism and guard its members against working-class political action.

The writer takes issue with these comrades upon this vital proposition; and first of all insists that they (including the members of the Quorum) speak for themselves alone, as they undoubtedly have the right to do, and that their declaration in reference to the American Labor Union is in no sense a party expression, nor is it in any matter binding upon the party, nor is the party to be held responsible for the same.

As a matter of fact, the rank and file of the Socialist Party, at least so far as I have been able to observe, rejoice in the action of the Denver convention, hail it as a happy augury for the future and welcome with open arms the Western comrades to fellowship in the party.

"Why didn't they stay in the Federation of Labor and carry on their agitation there? Why split the labor movement?" This is made the burden of the opposition to the Western unionists who refused to be assimilated by Mark Hanna's "Civic Federation"—the pretext for the scant, halfhearted recognition of their stalwart working-class organization and their ringing declaration in favor of socialism and in support of the Socialist Party.

And this objection may be dismissed with a single sentence. Why did not those who urge it remain in the Socialist Labor Party and carry on their agitation there? Why split the socialist movement?

It is not true that the Western unionists set up a rival organization from geographical or sectional considerations, or to antagonize the Federation; and they who aver the contrary know little or nothing about the Western movement, nor about the causes that brought it into existence. A brief review of these may throw some light upon the subject.

In 1896 the annual convention of the Federation of Labor was held in Cincinnati. The Western Federation of Miners, at that time an affiliated organization, was represented by President Edward Boyce and Patrick Clifford, of Colorado. The strike of the Leadville miners, more than 3,000 in number, one of the bloodiest and costliest labor battles ever fought, was then in progress and had been for several months. The drain and strain on the resources of the Western Federation had been enormous. They needed help and they needed it sorely. They had always poured out their treasure liberally when help was needed by other organizations, East as well as West and now that they had reached their limit, they naturally expected prompt and substantial aid from affiliated organizations. Boyce and Clifford appealed to the delegates. To use their own language they were "turned down," receiving but vague promises which, little as they meant, were never fulfilled. At the close of the convention they left for home, disappointed and disgusted. They stopped off at Terre Haute to urge me to go to Leadville to lend a helping hand to the striking miners, which I proceeded to do as soon as I could get ready for the journey. It was here that they told me the convention was a sore surprise to them, that three or four men had votes enough to practically control the whole affair and that the dilatory and reactionary proceedings had destroyed their confidence in the Federation.

Afterward I was told by the officers in charge of the strike that no aid of the least value, or even encouragement, had been rendered by the Federation of Labor and that the financial contributions were scarcely sufficient to cover the expense of the canvass for same.

It was not long after this that the Western miners withdrew from the Federation and a couple of years later, conceiving the necessity of organizing all classes of labor in the Western states, which as yet had received but scant attention, the American Labor Union was organized, the Western Federation of Miners being the first organization in affiliation with the new central body.

But notwithstanding the withdrawal of the Western Miners from the American Federation they continued loyally to support the Eastern boycotts levied by the Federation, and it is a fact not to be gainsaid that while some of those boycotts were so feebly supported in the East, where they had been levied, as to be practically impotent, the union men of the West recognized them as scrupulously as if imposed by their own organization, and in Montana and other states drove the boycotted Eastern products out of the Western markets.

So far as I am able to inform myself, there is no instance on record where the American Federation of Labor, or any organization affiliated with it, ever sanctioned or supported a boycott levied by the Western unions.

On the contrary, cases can be cited where the Eastern organizations bluntly refused to recognize boycotts declared by the Western organization.

Not only this, but the Western unions have always contributed promptly and liberally to the financial support of all labor unions, East and West, North and South, affiliated and otherwise, Butte leading with thousands of dollars in support of all kinds of strikes, in all sections of the country, the liberality and loyalty of the Western Federation of Miners in such cases being proverbial — and yet I have never heard of an instance where the Western unions received a dollar from any Eastern organization since the withdrawal of the Miners' Federation.

At this very time, while the miners of the East are making a desperate struggle against starvation, the miners of the Far West, affiliated with the tabooed American Labor Union, are contributing from their hard earnings to the support of the Pennsylvania strikers, though they never expect to receive a penny from the East; and President Moyer of the Western Federation of Miners is sending messages to President Mitchell of the United Mine Workers. Still more — notwithstanding the bituminous miners of the middle states, members of the same organization as the anthracite strikers, decided not to strike in support of their anthracite brethren, President Moyer and Secretary Haywood of the Western Federation wired President Mitchell that in their judgment all the miners in the country should

stand by the Pennsylvania strikers and that the coal miners
of the Western Union were ready to a man to lay down
their tools until the anthracite strike was won.

This is the militant, progressive, liberal spirit of Western
unionism — now reenforced with a class-conscious political
program — that could not brook the ultraconservative policy of the Eastern movement, and seceded from it with
motives as loyal to labor as ever prompted men to action.

The opponents of the Western Labor Union may search
the annals of organized labor in vain, all the circumstances considered, for as noble an example of fidelity to
the principles of union labor, as that of President Moyer
and Secretary Haywood of the Western Federation, speaking for the coal miners of the Western states, having no
grievance of their own and belonging to another organization, to which the East, if not hostile, was at least not
friendly, voluntarily agreeing to lay down their tools, and
give up their jobs to help their fellowmen more than two
thousands miles distant whom they had never seen and
never expected to see.

Had the situation been reversed and the miners of Montana had gone on strike, would the Eastern unions have
sent any money out there, or would the Eastern miners
have volunteered to strike in sympathy with their Western
brethren?

The conventions of the Western Labor Unions, the Western Federation of Miners and the Hotel and Restaurant
Employees' Union, held simultaneously at Denver in May
last, attracted wide attention chiefly because of their declaration in favor of socialism and their adoption of an independent political program. Prior to this these organizations
were rarely mentioned, in fact almost unknown in the Eastern and Middle states, and no reference to them was ever
made by the capitalist press outside their own immediate
jurisdiction. But the very moment they declared in favor
of socialism, the capitalist press, the "pure and simple"
union element and, strange to say, some Socialists, "cry
havoc, and let slip the dogs of war." As for the Socialists

who joined in the outcry, or "damned with faint praise," they were perhaps persuaded, after a survey of the East and then the West, that it was wiser policy to curry favor with numbers than to stand by principles.

The impression prevails in some quarters that the American Labor Union was first instituted at the convention in Denver last May. This is erroneous, as the organization has been in existence several years, and at the late convention simply changed its name from the Western Labor Union to the American Labor Union to more properly describe its expanding jurisdiction.

Fault has been found because of the rival disposition shown by the convention to the American Federation and the purpose to invade other sections and organize rival unions, thereby dividing the movement and precipitating a factional labor war.

The delegates to the Denver convention considered this phase of the question in all its bearings; they did not propose to antagonize the American Federation, nor to invade its jurisdiction, nor set up rival unions; they simply proposed to protect their own movement in the Western states and they did not propose to allow attacks to be made upon it without resenting them; and when they finally took action, even in the matter of changing their name, it was in self-defense, for from every quarter, even some of their own disgruntled element who sought to defeat the proposed adoption of socialism, came the threat that if the Western Union did not return to the American Federation, the latter would send a corps of organizers into the Western states to institute rival unions and "wipe the Western movement off the earth."

The "pure and simple" element in Denver and vicinity, affiliated with the American Federation, and not a few of the local politicians, who saw their doom in the socialist tendency of the convention, were loud and persistent in the threat of "annihilation" if the delegates refused to vote for affiliation with the American Federation. While there I heard it frequently upon the street and elsewhere and in fact Secretary Morrison, who, with Thomas I. Kidd, of the Executive Council, represented the American Federation at the convention with the purpose of inducing the Western Labor Union to dissolve, and its affiliated organizations to join the American Federation, gave it out that if the delegates declined their overtures, the American Federation would proceed to organize in all the Western states, as it acknowledged no boundary line to its jurisdiction in the United States.

The charge, therefore, of "invasion" and "rival unions" against the Western movement, falls to the ground. It can be proven beyond doubt that the Western movement acted upon the defensive in this matter and that only when the threat to "wipe them out of existence" in their own territory was made, did they conclude to extend their jurisdiction to such sections as desired to embrace their organization.

If it is held that the American Federation had prior jurisdiction, it may be answered that George the Third and Great Britain had prior jurisdiction over the colonies, and that the jurisdiction of the Knights of Labor antedated that of the American Federation, and the National Labor Union that of the Knights of Labor, and so on back without end.

Whatever difference may have prompted the separation several years ago — and whether it was wise or otherwise, I shall not now consider, having no share in the praise or blame, as the action was taken by the Western miners upon their own motion and they are entirely willing to accept the responsibility — it is certain that there is today a radical fundamental difference between the Eastern and Western wings of the American labor movement and that in their present state and with their present conflicting policies and tendencies, they cannot be united and even if they could be, factional and sectional strife would be at once engendered and disruption would be inevitable.

The Western movement could only have consented to go *back and backward* to the American Federation by stultifying itself and betraying and humiliating its thousands of progressive members who are far enough advanced to recognize the futility of labor organization without class-conscious political action and who will never retrace their steps to the fens and bogs of "pure and simple" unionism.

The Western men want unity and they want harmony, but they will not go backward, they will not sacrifice progress to reaction to secure it.

They have declared their class consciousness and they cannot and will not snuff out that beacon light to emancipation.

They have committed their organization to the Socialist Party and they cannot unite with an organization that is hostile to independent political action by the working class.

There is one way and one only to unite the American trades-union movement. The American Federation of Labor must go forward to the American Labor Union; the American Labor Union will never go back to the American Federation of Labor. Numbers count for nothing; principle and progress for everything.

When the American Federation of Labor sheds its outgrown "pure and simple" policy, when it declares against the capitalist system and for union, class-conscious action at the ballot box, as the supreme test of union principles, as the American Labor Union has done; when it relegates "leaders" to the rear who secure fat offices for themselves in reward for keeping the rank and file in political ignorance and industrial slavery, when it shall cease to rely upon cringing lobbying committees, begging, like Lazarus at the gate of Dives, for a bone from a capitalist legislature and Congress it helped to elect, and marshals its members in class array against their exploiters on election day to vote their own class into power, then unity will come and the Western men will hail with joy that day. And it is coming. It is simply bound to come.

In the meantime there need be no quarrel between the East and West and there will be none unless the threatened attempt to "snuff out" the West should materialize, in which case the "snuffers" will be entitled to the credit of having inspired a refreshing exhibition of the staying qualities of the class-conscious trades-union movement of the Western states.

The speaking tour of the national officers and executive council of the American Federation, in the Mountain states, following the Denver convention, and widely heralded by the capitalist press as an "uprising of the conservative element of organized labor to squelch the Western radicals" can claim anything but a victory if that was the program of President Gompers and his colleagues. Some of their meetings, with all the advertising they received, scarcely amounted to a corporal's guard, and where they had hundreds, the meetings held under the auspices of the Western Union had thousands in attendance without the aid of capitalist newspapers and in spite of the opposition of capitalist politicians.

As to whether the Western movement is growing or declining since the Denver convention, it is sufficient to say that the reports show that during the month of September the organizations affiliated with the American Labor Union added more than four thousand new names to their rolls of membership.

Passing through Denver recently I noticed by the papers of that city in scare-head articles, that the organizer of the American Federation, who had just been interviewed upon the subject, declared in emphatic terms that he had been instructed from headquarters at Washington to organize rival unions at every available point and where there was even one applicant, to admit him, totally regardless of the American Labor Union. If this is to be the policy of the Eastern Federation it will have to be that of the Western Union and as a result we shall have an era of unprecedented activity in the work of organizing the trades-union movement of the country.

One thing is noticeable in this connection and that is that the American Federation has evinced a greater interest in the Western states, spent more money and worked harder to organize them in the comparatively short time since the Western Union is in the field than in all previous years.

The rise of class-conscious trades unionism in the West was not the result of mere chance or personal design, but obedient to the rising tide of the revolutionary spirit of the proletariat of the rugged and sparsely settled Mountain states, a composite population composed of pioneers, the most adventurous, brave and freedom-loving men from all states of the American continent, and it is impossible that they, with their keen instinct and revolutionary tendency, could be long content to creep along in the creaking chariot of conservatism, even though it still bear traces of the union label.

The class-conscious union movement of the West is historic in origin and development and every Socialist should recognize its mission and encourage its growth. It is here that the tide of social revolution will reach its flood and thence roll into other sections, giving impetus where needed and hastening the glorious day of triumph.

I am the friend, not the enemy of the American Federation of Labor. I would conserve, not destroy it. I am opposed, not to the organization or its members, many of whom are personal friends, but to those who are restraining its evolution and preventing it from fulfilling its true mission.

I would not convert it into a political organization, but simply bring it up to date and have it, as it must become if it is to survive, a class-conscious industrial union, its members recognizing the Socialist ballot as the weapon of their class and using it accordingly, thus escaping the incongruities and self-contradictions of the present "pure and simple" union, whose members strike against and boycott the effects of the capitalist system while voting industriously to perpetuate the system.

It is true that there are elements of progress at work within the organization. Let them continue their efforts. Such men as Max S. Hayes, J. W. Slayton, J. Mahlon Barnes and many others who have done and are doing excellent work on the inside have all help and no hindrance to expect from the Western movement.

Certainly Max Hayes, elected delegate to the approaching convention of the American Federation of Labor by a popular vote of his organization, the International Typographical Union, upon the issue that he was a Socialist, and now muzzled by an order of a delegate convention instructing him to vote against Socialist measures, will not object to a little help from the outside.

In time the two progressive forces will meet and the work of redemption will have been accomplished.

Until then, as in the past, I shall support every boycott and every strike of the American Federation of Labor, and every organization affiliated with it, to the best of my ability, and when they lose in any of these struggles, no disheartening word from my lips shall darken their counsels or add to the bitterness of their defeat.

I have been plain and unreserved in my criticism as I have a right to be. For many years I have been an unofficial organizer for the Federation of Labor, and for all the trades unions connected with it, and in my travels, especially the past seven years, in which I have been almost continuously traversing the country, I have organized and been the means of organizing hundreds of unions of all kinds. In the Southern states I held the first great labor meetings when there was little or no trace of organization, in many places not even a single member, and I at once set to work organizing each point with the result that when I covered the same territory shortly after there were unions everywhere and the movement spread rapidly over that section of the country. In view of these facts I think I can consistently assert the right of candid criticism.

The attitude of the Socialist Party toward the trades-union movement broadly endorsing and commending it, but stopping there, and allowing it to manage its own internal affairs is, without doubt, the correct one, as any intermeddling must result in harm with no possible hope of good. The party, as such, must continue to occupy this friendly yet noninterfering position, but the members may, of course, and in my judgment should join the trades unions East and West and North and South, and put forth their best efforts to bring the American labor movement to its rightful position in the struggle for emancipation.

7

ON RACE PREJUDICE

As an all-inclusive party, that is, one in which there was general agreement on the goal of replacing capitalism with socialism but not on the kind of program or organization necessary for the task, the Socialist Party of Debs was beset with many contradictions. The conflict over craft versus industrial unionism was one. Another was the "Negro question."

The validity of the independent struggle for black liberation had not yet become the issue in the socialist and labor movement that it is today, but the relation of race discrimination to the class struggle had. On this Debs was uncompromising, as the two articles he wrote for the International Socialist Review *indicate. The first was published in the November 1903 issue, the second in January 1904.*

The Negro in the Class Struggle

It so happens that I write upon the Negro question, in compliance with the request of the editor of the *International Socialist Review*, in the state of Louisiana, where the race prejudice is as strong and the feeling against the "nigger" as bitter and relentless as when Lincoln's proclamation of emancipation lashed the waning Confederacy into fury and incited the final and desperate attempts to burst the bonds that held the Southern states in the federal union. Indeed, so thoroughly is the South permeated with the malign spirit of race hatred that even Socialists are to be found, and by no means rarely, who either share directly in the race hostility against the Negro, or avoid the issue, or apologize for the social obliteration of the color line in the class struggle.

The white man in the South declares that "the nigger is all right in his place"; that is, as menial, servant and slave. If he dare hold up his head, feel the thrill of manhood in his veins and nurse the hope that some day may bring deliverance; if in his brain the thought of freedom dawns and in his heart the aspiration to rise above the animal plane and propensities of his sires, he must be made to realize that notwithstanding the white man is civilized(?) the black man is a "nigger" still and must so remain as long as planets wheel in space.

But while the white man is considerate enough to tolerate the Negro "in his place," the remotest suggestion at social recognition arouses all the pent-up wrath of his Anglo-Saxon civilization; and my observation is that the less real ground there is for such indignant assertion of self-superiority, the more passionately it is proclaimed.

At Yoakum, Texas, a few days ago, leaving the depot with two grips in my hands, I passed four or five bearers of the white man's burden perched on a railing and decorating their environment with tobacco juice. One of them, addressing me, said: "There's a nigger that'll carry your grips." A second one added: "That's what he's here for," and the third chimed in with "That's right, by God." Here was a savory bouquet of white superiority. One glance was sufficient to satisfy me that they represented all there is of justification for the implacable hatred of the Negro race. They were ignorant, lazy, unclean, totally void of ambition, themselves the foul product of the capitalist system and held in lowest contempt by the master class, yet esteeming themselves immeasurably above the cleanest, most intelligent and self-respecting Negro, having by reflex absorbed the "nigger" hatred of their masters.

As a matter of fact the industrial supremacy of the South before the war would not have been possible without the Negro, and the South of today would totally collapse without his labor. Cotton culture has been and is the great staple and it will not be denied that the fineness and superiority of the fiber that makes the export of the Southern states the greatest in the world is due in large measure to the genius of the Negroes charged with its cultivation.

The whole world is under obligation to the Negro, and that the white heel is still upon the black neck is simply proof that the world is not yet civilized.

The history of the Negro in the United States is a history of crime without a parallel.

Why should the white man hate him? Because he stole him from his native land and for two centuries and a half robbed him of the fruit of his labor, kept him in beastly ignorance and subjected him to the brutal domination of the lash? Because he tore the black child from the breast of its mother and ravished the black man's daughter before her father's eyes?

There are thousands of Negroes who bear testimony in their whitening skins that men who so furiously resent the suggestion of "social equality" are far less sensitive in respect to the sexual equality of the races.

But of all the senseless agitation in capitalist society, that in respect to "social equality" takes the palm. The very instant it is mentioned the old aristocratic plantation owner's shrill cry about the "buck nigger" marrying the "fair young daughter" of his master is heard from the tomb and echoed and re-echoed across the spaces and repeated by the "white trash" in proud vindication of their social superiority.

Social equality, forsooth! Is the black man pressing his claims for social recognition upon his white burden bearer? Is there any reason why he should? Is the white man's social recognition of his own white brother such as to excite the Negro's ambition to covet the noble prize? Has the Negro any greater desire, or is there any reason why he should have, for social intercourse with the white man than the white man has for social relations with the Negro? This phase of the Negro question is pure fraud and serves to mask the real issue, which is not *social equality*, but *economic freedom*.

There never was any social inferiority that was not the shrivelled fruit of economic inequality.

The Negro, given economic freedom, will not ask the white man any social favors; and the burning question of "social equality" will disappear like mist before the sunrise.

I have said and say again that, properly speaking, there is no Negro question outside of the labor question — the working-class struggle. Our position as socialists and as a party is perfectly plain. We have simply to say: "The class struggle is colorless." The capitalists, white, black and other shades, are on one side and the workers, white, black and all other colors, on the other side.

When Marx said: "Workingmen of all countries unite," he gave concrete expression to the socialist philosophy of the class struggle; unlike the framers of the Declaration of Independence who announced that "all men are created equal" and then basely repudiated their own doctrine, Marx issued the call to all the workers of the globe, regardless of race, sex, creed or any other condition whatsoever.

As a social party we receive the Negro and all other races upon absolutely equal terms. We are the party of the working class, the whole working class, and we will not suffer ourselves to be divided by any specious appeal to race prejudice; and if we should be coaxed or driven from the straight road we will be lost in the wilderness and ought to perish there, for we shall no longer be a Socialist Party.

Let the capitalist press and capitalist "public opinion" indulge themselves in alternate flattery and abuse of the Negro; we as Socialists will receive him in our party, treat him in our counsels and stand by him all around the same as if his skin were white instead of black; and this we do, not from any considerations of sentiment, but because it accords with the philosophy of socialism, the genius of the class struggle, and is eternally right and bound to triumph in the end.

With the "nigger" question, the "race war" from the capitalist viewpoint we have nothing to do. In capitalism the Negro question is a grave one and will grow more threatening as the contradictions and complications of capitalist society multiply, but this need not worry us. Let them settle the Negro question in their way, if they can. We have nothing to do with it, for that is their fight. We have simply to open the eyes of as many Negroes as we can and bring them into the socialist movement to do battle for emancipation from wage slavery, and when the working class have triumphed in the class struggle and stand forth economic as well as political free men, the race problem will forever disappear.

Socialists should with pride proclaim their sympathy with and fealty to the black race, and if any there be who hesitate to avow themselves in the face of ignorant and unreasoning prejudice, they lack the true spirit of the slavery-destroying revolutionary movement.

The voice of socialism must be as inspiring music to the ears of those in bondage, especially the weak black brethren, doubly enslaved, who are bowed to the earth and groan in despair beneath the burden of the centuries.

For myself, my heart goes to the Negro and I make no apology to any white man for it. In fact, when I see the poor, brutalized, outraged black victim, I feel a burning sense of guilt for his intellectual poverty and moral debasement that makes me blush for the unspeakable crimes committed by my own race.

In closing, permit me to express the hope that the next convention may repeal the resolutions on the Negro question. The Negro does not need them and they serve to increase rather than diminish the necessity for explanation.

We have nothing special to offer the Negro, and we cannot make separate appeals to all the races.

The Socialist Party is the party of the working class, regardless of color — the whole working class of the whole world.

The Negro and His Nemesis

Since the appearance of my article on "The Negro in the Class Struggle" in the November *Review* I have received the following anonymous letter:

Elgin, Ill., November 25, 1903
Mr. Debs:

Sir, I am a constant reader of the *International Socialist Review*. I have analyzed your last article on the Negro question with apprehension and fear. You say that the South is permeated with the race prejudice of the Negro more than the North. I say it is not so. When it comes right down to a test, the North is more fierce in the race prejudice of the Negro than the South ever has been or ever will be. I tell you, you will jeopardize the best interests of the Socialist Party if you insist on political equality of the Negro. For that will not only mean political equality but also social equality eventually. I do not believe you realize what that means. You get social and political equality for the Negro, then let him come and ask the hand of your daughter in marriage, "For that seems to be the height of his ambition," and we will see whether you still have a hankering for social and political equality for the Negro. For I tell you, the Negro will not be satisfied with equality with reservation. It is impossible for the Anglo-Saxon and the African to live on equal terms. You try it, and he will pull you down to his level. Mr. Lincoln, himself, said, that "There is a physical difference between the white and the black races, which I believe will forever forbid them living together on terms of social and political equality." If the Socialist leaders *stoop* to this method to gain votes, then their policy and doctrine is as rotten and degraded as that of the Republican and Democratic parties, and I tell you, if the resolutions are adopted to give the African equality with the Anglo-Saxon you will lose more votes than you now think. I for my part shall do all I can to make you lose as many as possible and there will be others. For don't you know that just a little sour dough will spoil the whole batch of bread. You will do the Negro a greater favor by leaving him where he is. You elevate and educate him, and you will make his position impossible in the U. S. A. Mr. Debs, if you have any doubts on this subject, I beg you for humanity's sake to read Mr. Thomas Dixon's "The Leopard's Spots" and I hope that all others who have voiced your sentiments heretofore will do the same.

I assure you, I shall watch the *International Socialist Review* with the most intense hope of a reply after you have read Mr. Thomas Dixon's message to humanity. Respectfully yours,

So far a staunch member of the Socialist Party.

The writer, who subscribes himself "A staunch member of the Socialist Party" is the only member of that kind I have ever heard of who fears to sign his name to, and accept responsibility for what he writes. The really "staunch" Socialist attacks in the open — he does not shoot from ambush.

The anonymous writer, as a rule, ought to be ignored, since he is unwilling to face those he accuses, while he may be a sneak or coward, traitor or spy, in the role of a "staunch Socialist," whose base design it is to divide and disrupt the movement. For reasons which will appear later, this communication is made an exception and will be treated as if from a known party member in good standing.

It would be interesting to know of what branch our critic

is a member and how long he has been, and how he happened to become a "staunch member of the Socialist Party." That he is entirely ignorant of the philosophy of socialism may not be to his discredit, but that a "staunch member" has not even read the platform of his party not only admits of no excuse, but takes the "staunchness" all out of him, punctures and discredits his foolish and fanatical criticism and leaves him naked and exposed to ridicule and contempt.

The Elgin writer has all the eminent and well-recognized qualifications necessary to oppose Negro equality. His criticism and the spirit that prompts it harmonize delightfully with his assumed superiority.

That he may understand that he claims to be a "staunch member" of a party he knows nothing about I here incorporate the "Negro Resolutions" adopted by our last national convention, which constitute a vital part of the national platform of the Socialist Party and clearly defined its attitude toward the Negro:

Negro Resolution

Whereas, The Negroes of the United States, because of their long training in slavery and but recent emancipation therefrom, occupy a peculiar position in the working class and in society at large;

Whereas, The capitalist class seeks to preserve this peculiar condition, and to foster and increase color prejudice and race hatred between the white worker and the black, so as to make their social and economic interests to appear to be separate and antagonistic, in order that the workers of both races may thereby be more easily and completely exploited;

Whereas, Both the old political parties and educational and religious institutions alike betray the Negro in his present helpless struggle against disfranchisement and violence, in order to receive the economic favors of the capitalist class. Be it, therefore,

Resolved, That we, the Socialists of America, in national convention assembled, do hereby assure our Negro fellow worker of our sympathy with him in his subjection to lawlessness and oppression, and also assure him of the fellowship of the workers who suffer from the lawlessness and exploitation of capital in every nation or tribe of the world. Be it further

Resolved, That we declare to the Negro worker the identity of his interests and struggles with the interests and struggles of the workers of all lands, without regard to race or color or sectional lines; that the causes which have made him the victim of social and political inequality are the effects of the long exploitation of his labor power; that all social and race prejudices spring from the ancient economic causes which still endure, to the misery of the whole human family, that the only line of division which exists in fact is that between the producers and the owners of the world — between capitalism and labor. And be it further

Resolved, That we, the American Socialist Party, invite the Negro to membership and fellowship with us in the world movement for economic emancipation by which equal liberty and opportunity shall be secured to every man and fraternity become the order of the world.

But even without this specific declaration, the position of the party is so clear that no member and no other person of ordinary intelligence can fail to comprehend it.

The Socialist Party is the congealed, tangible expression of the socialist movement, and the socialist movement is based upon the modern class struggle in which all workers of all countries, regardless of race, nationality, creed or sex, are called upon to unite against the capitalist class, their common exploiter and oppressor. In this great class struggle the economic equality of all workers is a foregone conclusion, and he who does not recognize and subscribe to it as one of the basic principles of the socialist philosophy is not a socialist, and if a party member must have been admitted through misunderstanding or false pretense.

He should be speedily set adrift, that he may return to the capitalist parties with the social and economic strata from the "white trash" and "buck nigger" *down* to the syphilitic snob and harlot heiress who barters virtue for title in the matrimonial market.

I did not say that the race prejudice in the South was more intense than in the North. No such comparison was made and my critic's denial is therefore unnecessary upon this point. Whether the prejudice of the South differs from that of the North is quite another question and entirely aside from the one at issue, nor is it of sufficient interest to consider at this time.

The Elgin writer says that we shall "jeopardize the best interests of the Socialist Party" if we insist upon the political equality of the Negro. I say that the Socialist Party would be false to its historic mission, violate the fundamental principles of socialism, deny its philosophy and repudiate its own teachings if, on account of race considerations, it sought to exclude any human being from political equality and economic freedom. Then, indeed, would it not only "jeopardize" its best interests, but forfeit its very life, for it would soon be scorned and deserted as a thing unclean, leaving but a stench in the nostrils of honest men.

Political equality is to be denied the Negro, according to this writer, because it would lead to social equality, and this would be terrible — especially for those "white" men who are already married to Negro women and those "white" women who have long since picked the "buck nigger" in preference to the "white trash" whose social superiority they were unable to distinguish or appreciate.

Of course the Negro will "not be satisfied with equality with reservation." Why should he be? Would you?

Suppose you change places with the Negro just a year, then let us hear from you — "with reservation."

What now follows it is difficult to consider with patience: "You get social and political equality for the Negro, then let him come and ask the hand of your daughter in marriage."

In the first place *you* don't get equality for the Negro — *you* haven't got it yourself. In the present social scale there is no difference between you and the Negro — you are on the same level in the labor market, and the capitalist whose agent buys your labor power doesn't know and doesn't care if you are white or black for he deals with you simply as *labor power*, and is uninterested save as to the quality and quantity you can supply. He cares no more about the color of your hide than does Armour about that of the steers he buys in the cattle market.

In the next place the Negro will fight for his own political and economic equality. He will take his place in the Socialist Party with the workers of all colors and all countries, and all of them will unite in the fight to destroy the capitalist system that now makes common slaves of them all.

Foolish and vain indeed is the workingman who makes the color of his skin the steppingstone to his imaginary superiority. The trouble is with his head, and if he can get that right he will find that what ails him is not superiority but inferiority, and that he, as well as the Negro he despises, is the victim of wage slavery, which robs him of what he produces and keeps both him and the Negro tied down to the dead level of ignorance and degradation.

As for "the Negro asking the hand of your daughter in marriage," that is so silly and senseless that the writer is probably after all justified in withholding his name. How about the daughter asking the hand of the Negro in marriage? Don't you know that this is happening every day? Then, according to your logic, the inferiority and degeneracy of the white race is established and the Negro ought to rise in solemn protest against political equality, lest the white man ask the hand of his daughter in marriage.

"It is impossible," continues our critic, "for the Anglo-Saxon and the African to live upon equal terms. You try it and he will pull you down to his level." Our critic must have tried something that had a downward pull, for surely that is his present tendency.

The fact is that it is impossible for the Anglo-Saxon and the African to live on *unequal* terms. A hundred years of American history culminating in the Civil War proves that. Does our correspondent want a repetition of the barbarous experiment?

How does the Anglo-Saxon get along with the Anglo-Saxon — leaving the Negro entirely out of the question? Do they bill and coo and love and caress each other? Is the Anglo-Saxon capitalist so devoted to his Anglo-Saxon wage slave that he shares his burden and makes him the equal partner of his wealth and joy? Are they not as widely separated as the earth and sky, and do they not fight each other to the death? Does not the white capitalist look down with contempt upon the white wage slave? And don't you know that the plutocrat would feel himself pretty nearly, if not quite as outrageously insulted to have his Anglo-Saxon wage slave ask the hand of his daughter in marriage as if that slave were black instead of white?

Why are you not afraid that some Anglo-Saxon engine-wiper on the New York Central will ask the hand of Vanderbilt's daughter in marriage?

What social distinction is there between a white and a black deckhand on a Mississippi steamboat? Is it visible even with the aid of a microscope? They are both slaves, work side by side, sometimes a bunch of black slaves under a white "boss" and at other times a herd of white slaves under a black "boss." Not infrequently you have to take a second look to tell them apart — but all are slaves and all are humans and all are robbed by their "superior" white brother who attends church, is an alleged follower of Jesus Christ and has a horror of "social equality." To him "a slave is a slave for a' that" — when he bargains for labor power he is not generally concerned about the color of the package, but if he is, it is to give the black preference because it can be bought at a lower price in the labor market, in which equality always prevails — the equality of intellectual and social debasement. To paraphrase Wordsworth:

> A wage slave by the river's brim
> A simple wage slave is to him
> And he is nothing more.

The man who seeks to arouse race prejudice among workingmen is not their friend. He who advises the white wage worker to look down upon the black wage worker is the enemy of both.

The capitalist has some excuse for despising the slave — he lives out of his labor, out of his life, and cannot escape his sense of guilt, and so he looks with contempt upon his victim.

You can forgive the man who robs you, but you can't forgive the man you rob — in his haggard features you read your indictment and this makes his face so repulsive that you must keep it under your heels where you cannot see it.

One need not experiment with "sour dough" nor waste any time on "sour" literature turned into "Leopard Spots" to arrive at sound conclusions upon these points, and the true Socialist delights not only in taking his position and speaking out, but in inviting and accepting without complaint all the consequences of his convictions, be they what they may.

Abraham Lincoln was a noble man, but he was not an abolitionist, and what he said in reference to the Negro was with due regard to his circumscribed environs, and, for the time, was doubtless the quintessence of wisdom, but he was not an oracle who spoke for all coming ages, and we are not bound by what he thought prudent to say in a totally different situation half a century ago.

The Socialist platform has not a word in reference to "social equality." It declares in favor of political and economic equality, and only he who denies this to any other human being is unfit for it.

Socialism will give all men economic freedom, equal opportunity to work, and the full product of their labor. Their "social" relations they will be free to regulate to suit themselves. Like religion, this will be an individual matter and our Elgin Negro-hater can consider himself just as "superior" as he chooses, confine his social attentions exclusively to white folks, and enjoy his leisure time in hunting down the black specter who is bent on asking his daughter's hand in marriage.

What warrant has he to say that the height of the Negro's ambition is to marry a white woman? No more than a Negro has to say that the height of a white woman's ambition is to marry a Negro. The number of such cases is about equally divided and it is so infinitesimally small that any one who can see danger to society in it ought to have his visual organs treated for progressive exaggeration.

The normal Negro has ambition to rise. This is to his credit and ought to be encouraged. He is not asking, nor does he need, the white man's social favors. He can regulate his personal associations with entire satisfaction to himself, without Anglo-Saxon concessions.

Socialism will strike the economic fetters from his body and he himself will do the rest.

Suppose another race as much "superior" to the white as the white is to the black should drop from the skies. Would our Illinois correspondent at once fall upon his knees and acknowledge his everlasting inferiority, or would he seek to overcome it and rise to the higher plane of his superiors?

The Negro, like the white man, is subject to the laws of physical, mental and moral development. But in his case these laws have been suspended. Socialism simply proposes that the Negro shall have full opportunity to develop his mind and soul, and this will in time emancipate the race from animalism, so repulsive to those especially whose fortunes are built up out of it.

The African is here and to stay. How came he to our

shores? Ask your grandfathers, Mr. Anonymous, and if they will tell the truth you will or should blush for their crimes.

The black man was stolen from his native land, from his wife and child, brought to these shores and made a slave. He was chained and whipped and robbed by his "white superior," while the son of his "superior" raped the black child before his eyes. For centuries he was kept in ignorance and debased and debauched by the white man's law.

The rape fiend? Horrible!

Whence came he! Not by chance. He can be accounted for. Trace him to his source and you will find an Anglo-Saxon at the other end. There are no rape maniacs in Africa. They are the spawn of civilized lust.

Anglo-Saxon civilization is reaping and will continue to reap what it has sown.

For myself, I want no advantage over my fellowman and if he is weaker than I, all the more is it my duty to help him.

Nor shall my door or my heart be ever closed against any human being on account of the color of his skin.

8

THE SOCIALIST PARTY'S APPEAL
(1904)

*Following the 1900 election campaign, the Social Demo-
cratic Party concluded its unity negotiations with a group
that had left the older Socialist Labor Party of Daniel
DeLeon. A convention in 1901 named the new organization the Socialist Party.*

*The second national convention of the Socialist Party
opened May 1, 1904. It made "acceptance of the class
struggle," a requirement of membership and nominated
Debs as its standard bearer in the presidential election.*

The November 1904 issue of The Comrade *reprinted
this article by Debs published earlier in the New York*
Independent. *The spirit and enthusiasm it exudes permeated the party which, for the first time, collected a campaign fund with donations of half a day's pay from each
member and placed twenty-two organizers in the field.*

*Debs personally spoke to meetings totalling 250,000
people across the country. He received 402,283 votes,
more than four times his 1900 vote.*

For the first time the Socialists enter a national campaign
with a national party — a party that is united, aggressive
and enthusiastic from sea to sea.

The industrial conditions and tendencies are well calculated to set the working class thinking and to open their eyes to the trend of events.

In the presence of the abundance their labor has created they are idle and helpless, their wives fret and worry and their children, instead of a joy, become a burden to them.

The more industrious they are, the more they produce, the worse they are off, for the sooner does overproduction close down the mill and torture with hunger pangs the too industrious workingmen.

Something wrong! Something wrong!

That is the beginning in the mind of the intelligent worker and it never lets go until he is a socialist, and once he sees the light and becomes conscious of the latent economic power of his class he is a socialist through good and evil report to the last day of his life.

The campaign of the Socialist Party is and will be wholly educational. To arouse the consciousness of the workers to their economic interests as a class, to develop their capacity for clear thinking, to achieve their solidarity industrially and politically is to invest the working class with the inherent power it possesses to abolish the wage system and free itself from every form of servitude, and this is the mighty mission of the socialist movement.

Not a dollar for whiskey, or cigars, or carriages! Not a dollar for a vote if a single dollar could buy every office in the land!

Can the Republican Party or the Democratic Party truthfully say as much?

The campaign fund, such as it is, is wholly to print and circulate literature, defray the traveling expenses of speakers and other educational purposes, and this fund is raised, not by "frying the fat" out of law-defying corporations, nor by extorting boodle from the corrupters of legislation and the beneficiaries of debauched public morals, but by each member contributing the equivalent of a half day's work from his wages.

We can challenge the record of political integrity and

party cleanness without fear of accusation. We shall not compromise, nor shall we be deflected in the least by any consideration from the straight road to the cooperative commonwealth.

The Socialist Party is the only party that does not want a vote that is not intelligently cast. The popularity of a candidate is against him rather than for him in the Socialist Party. No vote is wanted on account of the personality of a candidate. It is the value of the socialist principle that is taught and emphasized, and if this is not understood and approved the vote is not wanted.

Mere disgust with other parties is not accepted by socialists as sufficient reason to encourage the voting of the Socialist ticket. Such votes are unreliable, deceptive, and misleading. The men who cast them are apt to desert at the very time they are most needed. Any vote that is subject to the influence of personal considerations is so vacillating that it is of no use in the constructive work of a revolutionary political movement.

Better a thousand trained, tried and true men, united on the solid basis of principle, than ten times that number thrown together on the shifting sands of personality.

In the Republican and Democratic national conventions principle is subordinated to personality. *"Who are the candidates?"* is the all-absorbing question. The people, like helpless children, are forever looking for some great man to watch over and protect them.

In the Socialist convention principles are paramount: the candidates are the last and least consideration. The supreme question is: "What are the principles?" and all the ability and interest of the delegates are absorbed in producing a scientific platform.

Socialists are not on the alert for some mythical Moses to lead them into a fabled promised land, nor do they expect any so-called "great man" to sacrifice himself upon the altar of the country for their salvation. They have made up their minds to be their own leaders and to save themselves. They know that persons have deceived them and will again, so they put their trust in principles, knowing that these will not betray them.

Between the Republican Party and the Democratic Party there is no difference so far as the workingman is concerned. He works for wages, and, as a rule, it costs him all he gets to live. If he organizes and forces up wages his exploiters raise prices. He has not the least interest in the tariff, or finance, or expansion, or imperialism. These issues concern the large capitalists represented by the Republican Party and the small capitalists represented by the Democratic Party, but they appeal to no intelligent wage worker, and the fact that workingmen divide upon these capitalistic issues accounts for their being driven out of Colorado and Idaho, and for their being the victims of wage slavery everywhere.

The Socialist Party addresses itself to the working class, seeking to develop the intelligence of that class, while it appeals to the ballot for the realization of its cooperative commonwealth.

Others than workers are welcome on condition that they recognize the class struggle and join the party on the basis of a working-class party.

Why should workingmen support the Socialist Party?

Because it is the only party that is unequivocally committed to their economic interests, to the abolition of the wage system and the freedom of the worker from exploitation and every other species of servitude.

The Socialist Party does not expect the support of the capitalist class, for it is opposed to their economic interests, and it would be foolish to expect them to abolish themselves.

Let no one charge that socialists have arrayed class against class in this struggle. That has been done long since in the evolution of capitalist society. One class now owns the tools while another class use them. One class is small and rich and the other large and poor. One wants more profit and the other more wages. One consists of capitalists and the other of workers. These two classes are at war. Every day of truce is at the expense of labor. There can be no peace and good will between these two essentially antagonistic economic classes. Nor can this class conflict be covered up or smoothed over. In Colorado, at this very moment, it is raging in full fury, and thousands of workingmen all over the United States are reading their own impending doom as wage workers in the murderous volleys of capitalist misrule that belch from the rifles of the mine owners' militia as they assault a union hall and shoot down in their tracks their fellow workingmen for no other crime than that they belong to a union that is engaged in a strike to enforce an eight-hour law voted as a constitutional amendment by a majority of more than 46,000 of the people, and then denied the people by a corrupt legislature bought bodily and brazenly by the mine owners to betray the people they were sworn to serve.

The workers are not all blind to the causes underlying this great struggle. They are beginning to see and to think, and this fall many thousands of them will begin to act.

They know that under Republican rule and Democratic rule conditions for them have remained unchanged. They know that under the administration of both the "panic" comes, that enforced idleness is certain, that strikes, boycotts, lockouts, injunctions, riots and bloodshed are inevitable, and that many of their number are doomed to drift into poverty and crime and finally end their lives as beggars, suicides, in prison cells or on the scaffold.

They know, too, that under both Democratic and Republican rule the President is on the side of the capitalists, that the governors are all on the side of the capitalists, that Congress and all the state legislatures respond to the demands of the capitalists, that the courts are uniformly with the capitalists, while soldiers and injunctions and bullpens are for the exclusive benefit of the workingmen.

The class struggle accounts for it all, and the intelligent worker takes his place on the right side of this struggle and works with all his might to bring his benighted brethren to the same side.

The Socialist Party is the party of the workers, who are on the right side of this world-wide struggle, and although a minority today, it contains all the elements of self-development and will expand to majority proportions to inaugurate the impending change as certain as the forces of industrial evolution are undermining the present system and making that change inevitable.

The Socialist Party is the party of the present and of the immediate future. It believes that the competitive system has outlived its usefulness, that it has become an obstruction in the path of progress, that, like feudalism, from which it sprang, it must pass away to make room for its cooperative successor.

The Socialist Party stands for the abolition of the wage system, for the economic freedom as well as the political equality of the working class, knowing that without the former the latter is impossible.

The Socialist Party stands for the collective ownership of the means of wealth production and distribution and the operation of industry in the interest of all.

The Socialist Party stands for industry of the people, by the people, and for the people, that wealth may be produced for the use of all instead of for the profit of a few, and as the basis of a real republic, in which every citizen shall have the inalienable right to work and to enjoy all the fruit of his labor.

The Socialist Party stands for a social order in which every human being in the full enjoyment of economic freedom, shall have full opportunity, in the best possible environment, to develop the best there is in him for his own good as well as the good of society at large.

When the Socialist Party succeeds to power, as it will as certain as the tides ebb and flow, it will inaugurate these changes and usher in the Socialist Republic.

Upon these issues the Socialist Party makes its appeal to the American people.

9

SPEECH AT THE
FOUNDING CONVENTION OF
THE INDUSTRIAL WORKERS
OF THE WORLD

"When the Founding Convention of the IWW—the Industrial Workers of the World—assembled in Chicago in June, 1905, the general strike movement initiating the first Russian revolution was already under way, and its reverberations were heard in the convention hall. The two events coincided to give the world a preview of its future. The leaders at Chicago hailed the Russian revolution as their own. The two simultaneous actions, arising independently with half a world between them, signalized the opening of a revolutionary century. They were the anticipations of things to come." —James P. Cannon, in the Summer 1955 issue of Fourth International, *a Marxist quarterly.*

The two hundred delegates at the founding convention were called to order by the chairman, William D. Haywood:

". . . This is the Continental Congress of the working class. We are here to confederate the workers of this country into a working-class movement that shall have for its purpose the emancipation of the working class from the slave bondage of capitalism. . . ."

On June 29, the third day of the convention, Debs addressed the delegates. The Socialist Trade & Labor Alliance, which Debs refers to, had been organized by Daniel DeLeon's Socialist Labor Party ten years earlier.

111

Fellow Delegates and Comrades: As the preliminaries in organizing the convention have been disposed of, we will get down to the real work before this body. We are here to perform a task so great that it appeals to our best thought, our united energies, and will enlist our most loyal support; a task in the presence of which weak men might falter and despair, but from which it is impossible to shrink without betraying the working class. [*Applause.*]

I am much impressed by this proletarian gathering. I realize that I stand in the presence of those who in the past have fought, are fighting, and will continue to fight the battles of the working class economically and politically [*applause*], until the capitalist system is overthrown and the working class are emancipated from all of the degrading thralldom of the ages. [*Applause.*] In this great struggle the working class are often defeated, but never vanquished. Even the defeats, if we are wise enough to profit by them, but hasten the day of the final victory.

In taking a survey of the industrial field of today, we are at once impressed with the total inadequacy of working-class organization, with the lack of solidarity, with the widespread demoralization we see, and we are bound to conclude that the old form of pure and simple unionism has long since outgrown its usefulness [*applause*]; that it is now not only in the way of progress, but that it has become positively reactionary, a thing that is but an auxiliary of the capitalist class. [*Applause.*]

They charge us with being assembled here for the purpose of disrupting the union movement. It is already disrupted, and if it were not disrupted we would not behold the spectacle here in this very city of a white policeman guarding a black scab, and a black policeman guarding a white scab [*applause*], while the trade unions stand by with their hands in their pockets wondering what is the matter with union labor in America. We are here today for the purpose of uniting the working class, for the purpose of eliminating that form of unionism which is responsible for the conditions as they exist today.

The trades-union movement is today under the control of the capitalist class. It is preaching capitalist economics. It is serving capitalist purposes. Proof of it, positive and overwhelming, appears on every hand. All of the important strikes during the past two or three years have been lost. The great strike of the textile workers at Fall River, that proved so disastrous to those who engaged in it; the strike of the subway employees in the city of New York, where under the present form of organization the local leaders repudiated the national leaders, the national leaders repudiated the local leaders and were in alliance with the capitalist class to crush their own followers; the strike of the stockyard's employees here in Chicago; the strike of the teamsters now in progress — all, all of them bear testimony to the fact that the pure and simple form of unionism has fulfilled its mission, whatever that may have been, and that the time has come for it to go. [*Great applause.*]

The American Federation of Labor has numbers, but the capitalist class do not fear the American Federation of Labor; quite the contrary. The capitalist papers here in this very city at this very time are championing the cause of pure and simple unionism. Since this convention met there has been nothing in these papers but a series of misrepresentations. [*Applause.*] If we had met instead in the interest of the American Federation of Labor these papers, these capitalist papers, would have had their columns filled with articles commending the work that is being done here. There is certainly something wrong with that form of unionism which has its chief support in the press that represents capitalism; something wrong in that form of unionism whose leaders are the lieutenants of capitalism; something wrong with that form of unionism that forms an alliance with such a capitalist combination as the Civic Federation, whose sole purpose it is to chloroform the working class while the capitalist class go through their pockets. [*Applause.*] There are those who believe that this form of unionism can be changed from within. They are very greatly mistaken. We might as well have remained in the Republican and Democratic parties and have expected to effect certain changes from within, instead of withdrawing from those parties and organizing a party that represented the exploited working class. [*Applause.*] There is but one way to effect this great change, and that is for the workingman to sever his relations with the American Federation and join the union that proposes upon the economic field to represent his class [*applause*], and we are here today for the purpose of organizing that union. I believe that we are capable of profiting by the experiences of the past. I believe it is possible for the delegates here assembled to form a great, sound, economic organization of the working class based upon the class struggle, that shall be broad enough to embrace every honest worker, yet narrow enough to exclude every fakir. [*Applause.*]

Now, let me say to those delegates who are here representing the Socialist Trade & Labor Alliance, that I have not in the past agreed with their tactics. I concede that their theory is right, that their principles are sound; I admit and cheerfully admit the honesty of their membership. [*Applause.*] But there must certainly be something wrong with their tactics or their methods of propaganda if in these years they have not developed a larger membership than they have to their credit.

Let me say in this connection, I am not of those who scorn you because of your small numbers. I have been taught by experience that numbers do not represent strength. [*Applause.*] I will concede that the capitalist class do not fear the American Federation of Labor because of their numbers. Let me add that the capitalist class do not fear your Socialist Trade & Labor Alliance. The one are too numerous and the other are not sufficiently numerous. The American Federation of Labor is not sound in its economics. The Socialist Trade & Labor Alliance is sound in its economics, but in my judgment it does not appeal to the American working class in the right spirit. [*Applause.*] Upon my lips there has never been a sneer for the Socialist Trade & Labor Alliance on account of the smallness of its numbers. I have been quite capable of applauding the pluck, of admiring the courage of the members of the Socialist Trade & Labor Alliance, for though few in numbers, they stay by their colors. [*Applause.*]

I wish, if I can, to point out what I conceive to be the error in their method of propaganda. Speaking of the members as I have met them, it seems to me that they are too prone to look upon a man as a fakir who happens to disagree with them. [*Applause.*] Now, I think there is no delegate in this convention who is more set against the real fakir than I am. But I believe it is possible for a workingman who has been the victim of fakirism to become so alert, to so strain his vision looking for the fakir that he sees the fakir where the fakir is not. [*Applause.*] I would have you understand that I am opposed to the fakir, and I am also opposed to the fanatic. [*Applause.*] And fanaticism is as fatal to the development of the working class movement as is fakirism. [*Applause.*] Admitting that the principle is sound, that the theory of your organization is right — and I concede both — what good avails it, what real purpose is accomplished if you cannot develop strength sufficient to carry out the declared purpose of your organization?

Now, I believe that there is a middle ground that can be occupied without the slightest concession of principle. I believe it is possible for such an organization as the Western Federation of Miners to be brought into harmonious relation with the Socialist Trade & Labor Alliance. I believe it is possible that that element of the organizations represented here have the conviction, born of experience, observation and study, that the time has come to organize a new union, and I believe it is possible for these elements to mingle, to combine here, and to at least begin the work of forming a great economic or revolutionary organization of the working class so sorely needed in the struggle for their emancipation. [*Applause.*] The supreme need of the hour, as the speaker who preceded me so clearly expressed it in his carefully and clearly thought address — the supreme need of the hour is a sound, revolutionary working-class organization. [*Applause.*] And while I am not foolish enough to imagine that we can complete this great work in a single convention of a few days' duration, I do believe it is possible for us to initiate this work, to begin it in a way for the greatest promise, with the assurance that its work will be completed in a way that will appeal with increasing force to the working class of the country.

I am satisfied that the great body of the working class in this country are prepared for just such an organization. [*Applause.*] I know, their leaders know, that if this convention is successful their doom is sealed. [*Applause.*] They can already see the handwriting upon the wall, and so they are seeking by all of the power at their command to discredit this convention, and in alliance with the cohorts of capitalism they are doing what they can to defeat this convention. It may fail in its mission, for they may continue to misrepresent, deceive and betray the working class and keep them in the clutches of their capitalist masters and exploiters. [*Applause.*]

They are hoping that we will fail to get together. They are hoping, as they have already expressed it, that this convention will consist of a prolonged wrangle; that such is our feeling and relations toward each other that it will be impossible for us to agree upon any vital proposition; that we will fight each other upon every point, and that when we have concluded our labors we will leave things in a worse condition than they were before.

If we are true to ourselves we will undeceive those gentlemen. We will give them to understand that we are animated by motives too lofty for them in their baseness and sordidness to comprehend. [*Applause.*] We will give them to understand that the motive here is not to use unionism as a means of serving the capitalist class, but that the motive of the men and women assembled here is to serve the working class by so organizing that class as to make their organization the promise of the coming triumph upon the economic field and the political field and the ultimate emancipation of the working class. [*Applause.*]

Let me say that I agree with Comrade DeLeon upon one very vital point at least. [*Applause.*] We have not been the best of friends in the past [*laughter*], but the whirligig of time brings about some wonderful changes. I find myself breaking away from some men I have been in very close touch with, and getting in close touch with some men from whom I have been very widely separated. [*Applause.*] But no matter. I have long since made up my mind to pursue the straight line as I see it. A man is not worthy, in my judgment, to enlist in the services of the working class unless he has the moral stamina, if need be, to break asunder all personal relations to serve that class as he understands his duty to that class. [*Applause.*]

I have not the slightest feeling against those who in the past have seen fit to call me a fakir. [*Laughter.*] I can afford to wait. I have waited, and I now stand ready to take by the hand every man, every woman that comes here, totally regardless of past affiliations, whose purpose it is to organize the working class upon the economic field, to launch that economic organization that shall be the expression of the economic conditions as they exist today; that organization for which the working class are prepared; that organization which we shall at least begin before we have ended our labors, unless we shall prove false to the object for which we have assembled here.

Now, I am not going to take the time to undertake to outline the form of this organization. Nor should I undertake to tax your patience by attempting to elaborate the plan of organization. But let me suggest, in a few words, that to accomplish its purpose this organization must not only be based upon the class struggle, but must express the economic condition of this time. We must have one organization that embraces the workers in every department of industrial activity. It must express the class struggle. It must recognize the class lines. It must of course be class-conscious. It must be totally uncompromising. [*Applause.*]

It must be an organization of the rank and file. [*Applause.*]
It must be so organized and so guided as to appeal to
the intelligence of the workers of the country everywhere.
And if we succeed, as I believe we will, in forming such
an organization, its success is a foregone conclusion.

I have already said the working class are ready for it.
There are multiplied thousands in readiness to join it,
waiting only to see if the organization is rightly grounded
and properly formed; and this done there will be no trouble about its development, and its development will take
proper form and expand to its true proportions. If this
work is properly begun, it will mean in time, and not a
long time at that, a single union upon the economic field.
It will mean more than that; it will mean a single party
upon the political field [*great applause*]; the one the economic expression, the other the political expression of the
working class; the two halves that represent the organic
whole of the labor movement.

Now, let me say in closing, comrades — and I have tried
to condense, not wishing to tax your patience or to take
the time of others, for I believe that in such conventions
as this it is more important that we shall perform than
that we shall make speeches — let me say in closing that
you and I and all of us who are here to enlist in the service of the working class need to have faith in each other
[*applause*], not the faith born of ignorance and stupidity,
but the enlightened faith of self-interest. We are in precisely
the same position; we depend absolutely upon each other.
We must get close together and stand shoulder to shoulder.
[*Applause.*] We know that without solidarity nothing is
possible, that with it nothing is impossible.

And so we must dispel the petty prejudices that are born
of the differences of the past, and I am of those who believe that, if we get together in the true working-class spirit,
most of these differences will disappear, and if those of
us who have differed in the past are willing to accord to
each other that degree of conciliation that we ourselves feel
that we are entitled to, that we will forget these differences,

we will approach all of the problems that confront us with our intelligence combined, acting together in concert, all animated by the same high resolve to form that great union, so necessary to the working class, without which their condition remains as it is, and with which, when made practical and vitalized and renewed, the working class is permeated with the conquering spirit of the class struggle, and as if by magic the entire movement is vitalized, and side by side and shoulder to shoulder in a class-conscious phalanx we move forward to certain and complete victory. [*Applause.*]

DEBS SPEAKING IN CHICAGO, 1910

DEBS AT FOUNTAIN CITY, TENNESSEE, 1905

10

INDUSTRIAL UNIONISM

Debs followed up his speech at the IWW convention by going out and campaigning for the organization, despite the opposition of Socialist Party leaders who favored the American Federation of Labor.

To them, the IWW was splitting the labor movement by providing an alternative to the existing unions. To Debs, the IWW, which organized all wage workers in an industry regardless of race, color, nationality, sex, age, or craft, was uniting the working class which the "American Separation of Labor" was helping the capitalists keep divided.

On December 10, 1905, Debs shared the platform with Daniel DeLeon of the Socialist Labor Party at Grand Central Palace, New York City, speaking for the IWW.

There is an inspiration in your greeting and my heart opens wide to receive it. I have come a thousand miles to join with you in fanning the flames of the proletarian revolution. [*Applause.*]

Your presence here makes this a vitalizing atmosphere for a labor agitator. I can feel my stature increasing, and this means that you are growing, for all my strength is drawn from you, and without you I am nothing.

In capitalist society you are the lower class; the capitalists are the upper class — because they are on your backs; if they were not on your backs, they could not be above you. [*Applause and laughter.*]

Standing in your presence, I can see in your gleaming eyes and in your glowing faces the vanguard; I can hear the tramp, I can feel the thrill of the social revolution. The working class are waking up. [*A voice, "You bet."*] They are beginning to understand that their economic interests are identical, that they must unite and act together economically and politically, and in every other way; that only by united action can they overthrow the capitalist system and emancipate themselves from wage slavery. [*Applause.*]

I have said that in the capitalist society the working class are the lower class; they have always been the lower class. In the ancient world for thousands of years they were abject slaves; in the Middle Ages, serfs; in modern times, wage workers; to become free men in socialism, the next inevitable phase of advancing civilization. [*Applause.*] The working class have struggled through all the various phases of their development, and they are today engaged in the last stage of the animal struggle for existence; and when the present revolution has run its course, the working class will stand forth the sovereigns of this earth.

In capitalist society the working man is not, in fact, a man at all; as a wage worker, he is simply merchandise; he is bought in the open market the same as hair, hides, salt, or any other form of merchandise. The very terminology of the capitalist system proves that he is not a man in any sense of that term.

When the capitalist needs you as a workingman to operate his machine, he does not advertise, he does not call for men, but for "hands"' and when you see a placard posted, "Fifty hands wanted," you stop on the instant; you know that that means *you*, and you take a beeline for the bureau of employment to offer yourself in evidence of the fact that you are a "hand." When the capitalist advertises for hands, that is what he wants.

He would be insulted if you were to call him a "hand." He has his capitalist politician tell you, when your vote is wanted, that you ought to be very proud of your hands because they are horny; and if that is true, he ought to be ashamed of his. [*Laughter and applause.*]

What is your status in society today? You are a human being, a wage worker. Here you stand just as you were created, and you have two hands that represent your labor power; but you do not work, and why not? For the simple reason that you have no tools with which to work; you cannot compete against the machinery of the capitalist with your bare hands; you cannot work unless you have access to it, and you can only secure access to it by selling your labor power, that is to say, your energy, your vitality, your life itself, to the capitalist who owns the tool with which you work, and without which you are idle and suffer all of the ills that idleness entails.

In the evolution of capitalism, society has been divided mainly into two economic classes; a relatively small class of capitalists who own tools in the form of great machines they did not make and cannot use, and a great body of many millions of workers who did make these tools and who do use them, and whose very lives depend upon them, yet who do not own them; and these millions of wage workers, producers of wealth, are forced into the labor market, in competition with each other, disposing of their labor power to the capitalist class, in consideration of just enough of what they produce to keep them in working order. They are exploited of the greater share of what their labor produces, so that while, upon the one hand, they can produce in great abundance, upon the other they can consume but that share of the product that their meager wages will buy; and every now and then it follows that they have produced more than can be consumed in the present system, and then they are displaced by the very products of their own labor; the mills and shops and mines and quarries in which they are employed close down, the tools are locked up and they are locked out, and they find themselves idle and helpless in the shadow of the very abundance their labor has created.

There is no hope for them in this system. They are

beginning to realize this fact, and so they are beginning to organize; they are no longer relying upon someone else, but they are making up their minds to depend upon themselves and to organize for their own emancipation.

Too long have the workers of the world waited for some Moses to lead them out of bondage. He has not come; he never will come. I would not lead you out if I could; for if you could be led out, you could be led back again. [*Applause.*] I would have you make up your minds that there is nothing that you cannot do for yourselves.

You do not need the capitalist. He could not exist an instant without you. You would just begin to live without him. [*Laughter and prolonged applause.*] You do everything and he has everything; and some of you imagine that if it were not for him you would have no work. As a matter of fact, he does not employ you at all; you employ him to take from you what you produce, and he faithfully sticks to his task. If you can stand it, he can; and if you don't change this relation, I am sure he won't. You make the autmobile, he rides in it. If it were not for you, he would walk; and if it were not for him, you would ride.

The capitalist politician tells you on occasion that you are the salt of the earth; and if you are, you had better begin to salt down the capitalist class.

The revolutionary movement of the working class will date from the year 1905, from the organization of the Industrial Workers of the World. [*Prolonged applause.*] Economic solidarity is today the supreme need of the working class. The old form of unionism has long since fulfilled its mission and outlived its usefulness, and the hour has struck for a change.

The old unionism is organized upon the basis of the identity of interests of the capitalist and working classes. It spends its time and energy trying to conciliate these two essentially antagonistic classes; and so this unionism has at its head a harmonizing board called the Civic Federation. This federation consists of three parts; a part representing the capitalist class; a part supposed to represent the working class, and still another part that is said to represent the "public." The capitalists are represented by that great union labor champion, August Belmont. [*Laughter and hisses.*] The working class by Samuel Gompers, the president of the American Federation of Labor [*hisses and cries, "sic him"*], and the public, by Grover Cleveland. [*Laughter.*]

Can you imagine a fox and goose peace congress? Just fancy such a meeting, the goose lifting its wings in benediction, and the fox whispering, "Let us prey."

The Civic Federation has been organized for the one purpose of prolonging the age-long sleep of the working class. Their supreme purpose is to keep you from waking up. [*A voice: "They can't do it."*]

The Industrial Workers has been organized for an opposite purpose, and its representatives come in your presence to tell you that there can be no peace between you, the working class, and the capitalist class who exploit you of what you produce; that as workers you have economic interests apart from and opposed to their interests, and that you must organize by and for yourselves; and that if you are intelligent enough to understand these interests you will sever your relations with the old unions in which you are divided and subdivided, and join the Industrial Workers, in which all are organized and united upon the basis of the class struggle. [*Applause.*]

The Industrial Workers is organized, not to conciliate, but to fight the capitalist class. We have no object in concealing any part of our mission; we would have it perfectly understood. We deny that there is anything in common between workingmen and capitalists. We insist that workingmen must organize to get rid of capitalists and make themselves the masters of the tools with which they work, freely employ themselves, secure to themselves all they produce, and enjoy to the full the fruit of their labors. [*Applause.*]

The old union movement is not only organized upon the

basis of the identity of interests of the exploited and exploiting classes, but it divides instead of uniting the workers, and there are thousands of unions, more or less in conflict, used against one another; and so long as these countless unions occupy the field, there will be no substantial unity of the working class. [*Applause.*]

And here let me say that the most zealous supporter of the old union is the capitalist himself. August Belmont, president of the Civic Federation, takes special pride in declaring himself a "union man" [*laughter*]; but he does not mean by that that he is an Industrial Worker; that is not the kind of a union he means. He means the impotent old union that Mr. Gompers and Mr. Mitchell lead, the kind that keeps the working class divided so that the capitalist system may be perpetuated indefinitely.

For thirty years I have been connected with the organized labor movement. I have long since been made to realize that the pure and simple union can do nothing for the working class; I have had some experience and know whereof I speak. The craft union seeks to establish its own petty supremacy. Craft division is fatal to class unity. To organize along craft lines means to divide the working class and make it the prey of the capitalist class. The working class can only be unionized efficiently along class lines; and so the Industrial Workers has been organized, not to isolate the crafts but to unite the whole working class. [*Applause.*]

The working class has had considerable experience during the past few years. In almost every conflict between labor and capital, labor has been defeated. Take the leading strikes in their order, and you will find that, without a single exception, the organized workers have been defeated, and thousands upon thousands of them have lost their jobs, and many of them have become "scabs." Is there not something wrong with a unionism in which the workers are always worsted? Let me review hurriedly some of this history of the past few years.

I have seen the conductors on the Chicago, Burlington & Quincy Railroad, organized in a craft union, take the place of the striking union locomotive engineers on the same system.

I have seen the employees of the Missouri, Kansas & Texas Railway, organized in their several craft unions, stand by the corporation as a unit, totally wiping out the union telegraphers, thirteen hundred of them losing their jobs.

I have seen these same craft unions, just a little while ago, on the Northern Pacific and Great Northern systems — I have seen them unite with the corporation to crush out the telegraphers' union, and defeat the strikers, their own co-unionists and fellow employees.

Just a few weeks ago, in the city of Chicago, the switchmen on the Grand Trunk went out on strike. All their fellow unionists remained at work and faithfully served the corporation until the switchmen were defeated, and now those union switchmen are scattered about looking for jobs.

The machinists were recently on strike in Chicago. They went out in a body under the direction of their craft union. Their fellow unionists all remained at work until the machinists were completely defeated, and now their organization in that city is on the verge of collapse.

There has been a ceaseless repetition of this form of scabbing of one craft union upon another until the workingman, if his eyes are open, is bound to see that this kind of unionism is a curse and not a benefit to the working class.

The American Federation of Labor does not learn by experience. They recently held their annual convention, and they passed the same old stereotyped resolutions; they are going to petition Congress to restrict the power of the courts; that is to say, they are going to once more petition a capitalist Congress to restrict the power of capitalist courts. That is as if a flock of sheep were to petition a pack of wolves to extract their own fangs. They have passed these resolutions over and over again. They have been totally fruitless and will continue to be.

What good came to the working class from this convention? Put your finger upon a single thing they did that will be of any real benefit to the workers of the country!

You have had some experience here in New York. You have plenty of unionism here, such as it is, yet there is not a city in the country in which the workers are less organized than they are here. It was in March last that you had here an exhibition of pure and simple unionism. You saw about six thousand craft union men go out on strike, and you saw their fellow unionists remain at work loyally until all the strikers were defeated and sacrificed. Here you have an object lesson that is well calculated to set you thinking and this is all I can hope to do by coming here, set you thinking, and for yourselves; for when you begin to think, you will soon begin to act for yourselves. You will then sever your relations with capitalist unions and capitalist parties [*applause*], and you will begin the real work of organizing your class, and that is what we of the Industrial Workers have engaged to do. We have a new mission. That mission is not merely the amelioration of the condition of the working class, but the complete emancipation of that class from slavery. [*Applause.*]

The Industrial Workers is going to do all for the working class that can be done in the capitalist system, but while it is engaged in doing that, its revolutionary eye will be fixed upon the goal; and there will be a great difference between a strike of revolutionary workers and a strike of ignorant trade unionists who but vaguely understand what they want and do not know how to get that. [*Applause.*]

The Industrial Workers is less than six months old, and already has a round hundred thousand of dues-paying members. [*Applause.*] This splendid achievement has no parallel in the annals of organized labor. From every

direction come the applications for charters and for organizers, and when the delegates of this revolutionary economic organization meet in the city of Chicago, next year,
it will be the greatest convention that ever met in the United
States in the interest of the working class. [*Applause.*]

This organization has a world-wide mission; it makes
its appeal directly to the working class. It asks no favors
from capitalists.

No organization of workingmen has ever been so fla-
grantly misrepresented by the capitalist press as has been
the Industrial Workers of the World; every delegate to the
Chicago convention will bear testimony to this fact; and
this is as it should be; the capitalist press is the mouth-
piece of the capitalist class, and the very fact that the capitalist press is the organ, virtually, of the American Federation of Labor, is in itself sufficient to open the eyes of the
working class.

If the American Federation of Labor were not in alliance with the capitalist class, the capitalist press would
not pour its fulsome eulogy upon it.

This press has not one friendly word for the Industrial
Workers, not one, and we do not expect it to have. These
papers of the plutocrats know us and we know them [*applause*]; between us there is no misunderstanding.

The workers of the country (the intelligent ones at least)
readily see the difference between revolutionary and reactionary unionism, and that is why they are deserting the
old and joining the new; that is why the Industrial Workers is building up so rapidly; that is why there is such a
widespread demand for organizers and for literature and
for all other means of building up this class-conscious
economic organization. [*Applause.*]

As I have said, the Industrial Workers begin by declaring that there is nothing in common between capitalists
and wage workers.

The capitalists own the tools they do not use, and the
workers use the tools they do not own.

The capitalists, who own the tools that the working class

use, appropriate to themselves what the working class produce, and this accounts for the fact that a few capitalists become fabulously rich while the toiling millions remain in poverty, ignorance and dependence.

Let me make this point perfectly clear for the benefit of those who have not thought it out for themselves. Andrew Carnegie is a type of the capitalist class. He owns the tools with which steel is produced. These tools are used by many thousands of workingmen. Andrew Carnegie, who owns these tools, has absolutely nothing to do with the production of steel. He may be in Scotland, or where he will, the production of steel goes forward just the same. His mills at Pittsburgh, Duquesne and Homestead, where these tools are located, are thronged with thousands of toolless wage workers, who work day and night, in winter's cold and summer's heat, who endure all the privations and make all the sacrifices of health and limb and life, producing thousands upon thousands of tons of steel, yet not having an interest, even the slightest, in the product. Carnegie, who owns the tools, appropriates the product, and the workers, in exchange for their labor power, receive a wage that serves to keep them in producing order; and the more industrious they are, and the more they produce, the worse they are off; for the sooner they have produced more than Carnegie can get rid of in the markets, the tool houses are shut down and the workers are locked out in the cold.

This is a beautiful arrangement — for Mr. Carnegie; he does not want a change, and so he is in favor of the Civic Federation, and a leading member of it; and he is doing what he can to induce you to think that this ideal relation ought to be maintained forever.

Now, what is true of steel production is true of every other department of industrial activity; you belong to the millions who have no tools, who cannot work without selling your labor power, and when you sell that, you have to deliver it in person; you cannot send it to the mill, you have got to carry it there; you are inseparable from your labor power.

You have got to go to the mill at seven in the morning and work until six in the evening, producing, not for yourself, but for the capitalist who owns the tools you made and use, and without which you are almost as helpless as if you had no arms.

This fundamental fact in modern industry you must recognize, and you must organize upon the basis of this fact; you must appeal to your class to join the union that is the true expression of your economic interests, and this union must be large enough to embrace you all, and such is the Industrial Workers of the World.

Every man and every woman who works for wages is eligible to membership.

Organized into various departments, when you join you become a member of the department that represents your craft, or occupation, whatever it may be; and when you have a grievance, your department has supervision of it; and if you fail to adjust it in that department, you are not limited to your craft alone for support, but, if necessary, all the workers in all other departments will unite solidly in your defense to the very last. [*Applause.*]

Take a plant in modern industry. The workers, under the old form of unionism, are parceled out to a score or more of unions. Craft division incites craft jealousy and so they are more or less in conflict with each other, and the employer constructively takes advantage of this fact, and that is why he favors pure and simple unionism.

It were better for the workers who wear craft fetters if they were not organized at all, for then they could and would spontaneously go out on strike together; but they cannot do this in craft unionism, for certain crafts bind themselves up in craft agreements, and after they have done this, they are at the mercy of the capitalist; and when their fellow unionists call upon them for aid, they make the very convenient excuse that they cannot help them, that they must preserve the sanctity of the contract they have made with the employer. This so-called contract is regarded as of vastly more importance than the jobs, aye, the very lives of the workingmen themselves.

We do not intend that certain departments shall so attach themselves to the capitalist employers. We purpose that the workers shall all be organized, and if there is any agreement, it will embrace them all; and if there is any violation of the agreement, in the case of a single employee, it at once becomes the concern of all. [*Applause.*] That is unionism, industrial unionism, in which all of the workers, totally regardless of occupation, are united compactly within the one organization, so that at all times they can act together in the interests of all. It is upon this basis that the Industrial Workers of the World is organized. It is in this spirit and with this object in view that it makes its appeal to the working class.

Then, again, the revolutionary economic organization has a new and important function which has never once been thought of in the old union, for the simple reason that the old union intends that the wage system shall endure forever.

The Industrial Workers declares that the workers must make themselves the masters of the tools with which they work; and so a very important function of this new union is to teach the workers, or, rather, have them teach themselves the necessity of fitting themselves to take charge of the industries in which they are employed when they are wrested, as they will be, from their capitalist masters. [*Applause.*]

So when you join the Industrial Workers you feel the thrill of a new aspiration; you are no longer a blind, dumb wage slave. You begin to understand your true and vital relation to your fellow workers. In the Industrial Workers you are correlated to all other workers in the plant, and thus you develop the embryonic structure of the cooperative commonwealth. [*Applause.*]

The old unionism would have you contented. We Industrial Workers are doing what we can to increase your discontent. We would have you rise in revolt against wage slavery. The workingman who is contented today is truly a pitiable object. [*Applause.*]

Victor Hugo once said: "Think of a smile in chains,"— that is a workingman who, under the influence of the Civic Federation, is satisfied with his lot; he is glad he has a master, some one to serve; for, in his ignorance, he imagines that he is dependent upon the master.

The Industrial Workers is appealing to the working class to develop their latent powers and above all, their capacity for clear thinking.

You are a workingman and you have a brain and if you do not use it in your own interests, you are guilty of treason to your manhood. [*Applause.*]

It is for the very reason that you do not use your brain in your interests that you are compelled to deform your body in the interests of your master.

I have already said that the capitalist is on your back; he furnishes the mouth, you the hands; he consumes, you produce. That is why he runs largely to stomach and you to hands. [*Laughter.*]

I would not be a capitalist: I would be a man; you cannot be both at the same time. [*Applause.*]

The capitalist exists by exploitation, lives out of the labor, that is to say the life, of the workingman; consumes him, and his code of morals and standard of ethics justify it and this proves that capitalism is cannibalism. [*Applause.*]

A man, honest, just, high-minded, would scorn to live out of the sweat and sorrow of his fellowman—by preying upon his weaker brother.

We purpose to destroy the capitalist and save the man. [*Applause.*] We want a system in which the worker shall get what he produces and the capitalist shall produce what he gets. [*Applause.*] That is a square deal.

The prevailing lack of unity implies the lack of class consciousness. The workers do not yet understand that they are engaged in a class struggle, that they must unite their class and get on the right side of that struggle economically, politically and in every other way [*applause*] — strike together, vote together and, if necessary, fight together. [*Prolonged applause.*]

The capitalist and the leader of the pure and simple union do what they can to wipe out the class lines; they do not want you to recognize the *class* struggle; they contrive to keep you divided, and as long as you are divided, you will remain where you are, robbed and helpless.

When you unite and act together, the world is yours. [*Prolonged applause.*]

The fabled Samson, shorn of his locks, the secret of his power, was the sport and prey of the pygmies that tormented him. The modern working class, shorn of their tools, the secret of their power, are at the mercy of a small class who exploit them of what they produce and then hold them in contempt because of their slavery.

No master ever had the slightest respect for his slave, and no slave ever had the least real love for his master.

Between these two classes there is an irrepressible conflict, and we Industrial Workers are pointing it out that you may see it, that you may get on the right side of it, that you may get together and emancipate yourselves from every form of servitude.

It can be done in no other way; but a bit of sober reasoning will convince you workers of this fact.

It is so simple that a child can see it. Why can't you? You can if you will think for yourselves and see for yourselves. But you will not do this if you were taught in the old union school; you will still look to someone else to lead that you may follow: for you are trained to follow the blind leaders of the blind. You have been betrayed over and over again, and there will be no change until you make up your minds to think and see and act for yourselves.

I would not have you blindly walk into the Industrial Workers; if I had sufficient influence or power to draw

you into it, I would not do it. I would have you stay
where you are until you can see your way clear to join
it of your own accord. It is your organization; it is composed of your class; it is committed to the interests of your
class; it is going to fight for your class, for your whole
class, and continue the fight until your class is emancipated. [*Applause.*]

There is a great deal of opposition to this organization.
The whole capitalist class and all their labor lieutenants
are against it [*applause*]; and there is an army of them,
and all their names are on the payroll and expense account. They all hold salaried positions, and are looking
out for themselves.

When the working class unites, there will be a lot of job-
less labor leaders. [*Applause.*]

In many of these craft unions they have it so arranged
that the rank and file do not count for any more than if
they were so many sheep. In the railroad organizations,
for instance, if the whole membership vote to go out on
strike, they cannot budge without the official sanction of
the "Grand Chief." His word outweighs that of the entire
membership. In the light of this extraordinary fact, is it
strange that the workers are often betrayed? Is it strange
that they continue at the mercy of their exploiters?

Haven't they had quite enough of this? Isn't it time for
them to take an inventory of their own resources?

If you are a workingman, suppose you look yourself
over, just once; take an invoice of your mental stock and
see what you have. Do not accept my word; do not depend
upon anybody but yourself. Think it out for yourself; and
if you do, I am quite certain that you will join the organization that represents your class [*applause*]; the organization that has room for all your class; the organization
that appeals to you to develop your own brain, to rely
upon yourself and be a man among men. And that is
what the working class have to do, cultivate self-reliance
and think and act for themselves; and that is what they
are stimulated to do in the Industrial Workers.

We have great hope and abiding faith for we know that each day will bring us increasing numbers, influences and power; and this notwithstanding all the opposition that can be arrayed against us.

We know that the principles of the Industrial Workers are right and that its ultimate triumph is assured beyond the question of a doubt; and if you believe in its conquering mission, then we ask you to be true enough to yourselves and your class to join it; and when you join it you will have a duty to perform and that duty will be to go out among the unorganized and bring them into the ranks and help in this great work of education and organization, without which the working class is doomed to continued ignorance and slavery.

Karl Marx, the profound economic philosopher, who will be known in future as the great emancipator, uttered the inspiring shibboleth a half-century ago: "Workingmen of all countries unite; you have nothing to lose but your chains; you have a world to gain."

You workers are the only class essential to society; all others can be spared, but without you society would perish. You produce the wealth, you support government, you create and conserve civilization. You ought to be, can be and will be the masters of the earth. [*Great applause.*]

Why should you be dependent upon a capitalist? Why should this capitalist own a tool he cannot use? And why should not you own the tool you have to use?

Every cog in every wheel that revolves everywhere has been made by the working class, and is set and kept in operation by the working class; and if the working class can make and operate this marvelous wealth-producing machinery, they can also develop the intelligence to make themselves the masters of this machinery [*applause*], and operate it not to turn out millionaires, but to produce wealth in abundance for themselves.

You cannot afford to be contented with your lot; you have a brain to develop and a manhood to sustain. You ought to have some aspiration to be free.

Suppose you do have a job, and that you can get enough to eat and clothes enough to cover your body, and a place to sleep; you but exist upon the animal plane; your very life is suspended by a slender thread; you don't know what hour a machine may be invented to displace you, or you may offend your economic master, and your job is gone. You go to work early in the morning and you work all day; you go to your lodging at night, tired; you throw your exhausted body upon a bed of straw to recuperate enough to go back to the factory and repeat the same dull operation the next day, and the next, and so on and on to the dreary end; and in some respects you are not so well off as was the chattel slave.

He had no fear of losing his job; he was not blacklisted; he had food and clothing and shelter; and now and then, seized with a desire for freedom, he tried to run away from his master. You do not try to run away from yours. He doesn't have to hire a policeman to keep an eye on you. When you run, it is in the opposite direction, when the bell rings or the whistle blows.

You are as much subject to the command of the capitalist as if you were his property under the law. You have got to go to his factory because you have got to work; he is the master of your job, and you cannot work without his consent, and he only gives this on condition that you surrender to him all you produce except what is necessary to keep you in running order.

The machine you work with has to be oiled; you have to be fed; the wage is your lubricant, it keeps you in working order, and so you toil and sweat and groan and reproduce yourself in the form of labor power, and then you pass away like a silkworm that spins its task and dies.

That is your lot in the capitalist system and you have no right to aspire to rise above the dead level of wage slavery.

It is true that one in ten thousand may escape from his class and become a millionaire; he is the rare exception that proves the rule. The wage workers remain in the working class, and they never can become anything else in the capitalist system. They produce and perish, and their exploited bones mingle with the dust.

Every few years there is a panic, industrial paralysis, and hundreds of thousands of workers are flung into the streets; no work, no wages; and so they throng the highways in search of employment that cannot be found; they become vagrants, tramps, outcasts, criminals. It is in this way that the human being degenerates, and that crime graduates in the capitalist system, all the way from petty larceny to homicide.

The working millions who produce the wealth have little or nothing to show for it. There is widespread ignorance among them; industrial and social conditions prevail that defy all language properly to describe. The working class consists of a mass of human beings, men, women and children, in enforced competition with one another, in all of the circling hours of the day and night, for the sale of their labor power, and in the severity of the competition the wage sinks gradually until it touches the point of subsistence.

In this struggle more than five millions of women are engaged and about two millions of children, and the number of child laborers is steadily increasing, for in this system profit is important, while life has no value. It is not a question of male labor, or female labor, or child labor; it is simply a question of cheap labor without reference to the effect upon the working class; the woman is employed in preference to the man and the child in preference to the woman; and so we have millions of children, who, in their early, tender years, are seized in the iron clutch of capitalism, when they ought to be upon the playground, or at school; when they ought to be in the sunlight, when they ought to have wholesome food and enjoy the fresh atmosphere they are forced into the industrial dungeons and there they are riveted to the machines; they feed the insatiate monsters and become as living cogs in the revolving wheels. They are literally fed to industry to produce profits. They are dwarfed and deformed, mentally, morally and physically; they have no chance in life; they are the victims of the industrial system that the Industrial Workers is organized to abolish in the interest, not only of the working class, but in the higher interest of all humanity. [*Applause.*]

If there is a crime that should bring to the callous cheek of capitalist society the crimson of shame, it is the unspeakable crime of child slavery; the millions of babes that fester in the sweat shops, are the slaves of the wheel, and cry out in agony, but are not heard in the din and roar of our industrial infernalism.

Take that great army of workers, called coal miners, organized in a craft union that does nothing for them; that seeks to make them contented with their lot. These miners are at the very foundation of industry and without their labor every wheel would cease to revolve as if by the decree of some industrial Jehovah. [*Applause.*] There are 600,000 of these slaves whose labor makes possible the firesides of the world, while their own loved ones shiver in the cold. I know something of the conditions under which they toil and despair and perish. I have taken time enough to descend to the depths of these pits, that Dante never saw, or he might have improved upon his masterpiece. I have stood over these slaves and I have heard the echo of their picks, which sounded to me like muffled drums throbbing funeral marches to the grave, and I have said to myself, in the capitalist system, these wretches are simply following their own hearses to the potter's field.

In all of the horizon of the future there is no star that sheds a ray of hope for them.

Then I have followed them from the depth of these black holes, over to the edge of the camp, not to the home, they have no home; but to a hut that is owned by the corporation that owns them, and here I have seen the wife — Victor Hugo once said that the wife of a slave is not a wife at all; she is simply a female that gives birth to young — I have seen this wife standing in the doorway, after trying all day long to make a ten-cent piece do the service of a half-dollar, and she was ill-humored; this could not be otherwise, for love and abject poverty do not dwell beneath the same roof. Here there is no paper upon the wall and no carpet upon the floor; there is not a picture to appeal to the eye; there is no statue to challenge the soul, no strain of inspiring music to touch and quicken what Lincoln called the better angels of human nature. Here there is haggard poverty and want. And in this atmosphere the children of the future are being reared, many thousands of them, under conditions that make it morally certain that they will become paupers, or criminals, or both.

Man is the product, the expression of his environment. Show me a majestic tree that towers aloft, that challenges the admiration of man, or a beautiful rosebud that, under the influence of sunshine and shower, bursts into bloom and fills the common air with its fragrance; these are possible only because the soil and climate are adapted to the growth and culture. Transfer this flower from the sunlight and the atmosphere to a cellar filled with noxious gases, and it withers and dies. The same law applies to human beings; the industrial soil and the social climate must be adapted to the development of men and women, and then society will cease producing [*cry of "down with capitalism"*] the multiplied thousands of deformities that today are a rebuke to our much vaunted civilization, and, above all, an impeachment of the capitalist system. [*Applause.*]

What is true of the miners is true in a greater or less degree of all workers in all other departments of industrial activity. This system has about fulfilled its historic mission. Upon every hand there are the unerring signs of change, and the time has come for the education and organization of the working class for the social revolution [*applause*] that is to lift the workers from the depths of slavery and elevate them to an exalted plane of equality and fraternity. [*Applause.*]

At the beginning of industrial society men worked with hand tools; a boy could learn a trade, make himself the master of the simple tools with which he worked, and employ himself and enjoy what he produced; but that simple tool of a century ago has become a mammoth social instrument; in a word, that tool has been socialized. Not only this, but production has been socialized. As small a commodity as a pin or a pen or a match involves for its production all of the social labor of the land; but this evolution is not yet complete; the tool has been socialized, production has been socialized, and now ownership must also be socialized; in other words, those great social instruments that are used in modern industry for the production of wealth, those great social agencies that are socially made and socially used, must also be socially owned. [*Applause.*]

The Industrial Workers is the only economic organization that makes this declaration, that states this fact and is organized upon this foundation, that the workers must own their tools and employ themselves. This involves a revolution, and this means the end of the capitalist system, and the rearing of a working-class republic [*prolonged applause*], the first real republic the world has ever known; and it is coming just as certainly as I stand in your presence.

You can hasten it, or you can retard it, but you cannot prevent it.

This the working class can achieve, and if you are in that class and you do not believe it, it is because of your ignorance; it is because you got your education in the school of pure and simple unionism, or in a capitalist political party. This the working class can achieve and all that is required is that the working class shall be educated, that they shall unite, that they shall act together.

The capitalist politician and the labor lieutenant have always contrived to keep the working class divided, upon the economic field and upon the political field; and the workers have made no progress, and never will until they desert those false leaders and unite beneath the revolutionary standard of the Industrial Workers of the World. [*Applause.*]

The capitalists have the mills and the tools and the dollars, but you are an overwhelming majority; you have the men, you have the votes. There are not enough of them to continue this system an instant; it can only be continued by your consent and with your approval, and to the extent that you give it you are responsible for your slavery; and if you have your eyes opened, if you understand where you properly belong, it is still a fortunate thing that you cannot do anything for yourself until you have opened the eyes of those that are yet in darkness. [*Applause.*]

Now, there are many workers who have had their eyes opened and they are giving their time and energy to the revolutionary education of the working class [*applause*], and every day sees our minority increasing, and it is but a question of time until this minority will be converted into the triumphant majority [*applause*]; and so we wait and watch and work in all of the circling hours of the day and night.

We have just begun here in New York, and with a vim and an energy unknown in the circles of unionism. In six months from this night you will find that there is a very formidable organization of Industrial Workers in New York [*applause*]; and if you are a workingman and you have convictions of your own, it is your duty to join this union and take your place where you belong.

Don't hesitate because somebody else is falling back. Don't wait because somebody else is not yet ready. Act and act now and for yourself; and if you happen to be the only Industrial Workers in your shop, or in your immediate vicinity, you are simply monumental of the ignorance of your fellow workers, and you have got to begin to educate them. For a little while they may point you out with the finger of contempt, but you can stand this; you can bear it with patience; if they persecute you, because you are true to yourself, your latent powers will be developed, you will become stronger than you now dream, and then you will do the deeds that live, and you will write your name where it will stay.

Never mind what others may say, or think, or do. Stand erect in the majesty of your own manhood.

Listen for just once to the throbbing of your own heart, and you will hear that it is beating quickstep marches to Camp Freedom.

Stand erect! Lift your bowed form from the earth! The dust has long enough borne the impress of your knees.

Stand up and see how long a shadow you cast in the sunlight! [*Applause.*] Hold up your head and avow your convictions, and then accept, as becomes a man, the consequences of your acts!

We need you and you need us. We have got to have the workers united, and you have got to help us in the work. And so we make our appeal to you tonight, and we know that you will not fail. You can arrive at no other conclusion; you are bound to join the industrial workers, and become a missionary in the field of industrial unionism. You will then feel the ecstasy of a newborn aspiration. You will do your very best. You will wear the badge of the Industrial Workers, and you will wear it with pride and joy.

The very contempt that it invites will be a compliment to you; in truth, a tribute to your manhood.

Go out into the field and bring in the rest of the workers, that they may be fully equipped for their great mission. We will wrest what we can, step by step, from the capitalists, but with our eye fixed upon the goal; we will press forward, keeping step together with the inspiring music of the new emancipation; and when we have enough of this kind of organization, as Brother DeLeon said so happily the other day [*applause*], when we are lined up in battle array, and the capitalists try to lock us out, we will turn the tables on the gentlemen and lock them out. [*Applause.*]

We can run the mills without them but they cannot run them without us. [*Applause.*]

It is a very important thing to develop the economic

power, to have a sound economic organization. This has been the inherent weakness in the labor movement of the United States. We need, and sorely need, a revolutionary economic organization. We must develop this kind of strength; it is the kind that we will have occasion to use in due time, and it is the kind that will not fail us when the crisis comes. So we shall organize and continue to organize the political field; and I am of those who believe that the day is near at hand when we shall have one great revolutionary economic organization, and one great revolutionary political party of the working class. [*Cheers and prolonged applause.*] Then will proceed with increased impetus the work of education and organization that will culminate in emancipation.

This great body will sweep into power and seize the reins of government; take possession of industry in the name of the working class, and it can be easily done. All that will be required will be to transfer the title deeds from the parasites to the producers; and then the working class, in control of industry, will operate it for the benefit of all. The workday will be reduced in proportion to the progress of invention. Every man will work, or at least have a chance to work, and get the full equivalent of what he produces. He will work, not as a slave, but as a free man, and he will express himself in his work and work with joy. Then the badge of labor will be the only badge of aristocracy. The industrial dungeon will become a temple of science. The working class will be free, and all humanity disenthralled.

The workers are the saviors of society [*applause*]; the redeemers of the race; and when they have fulfilled their great historic mission, men and women can walk the highlands and enjoy the vision of a land without masters and without slaves, a land regenerated and resplendent in the triumph of freedom and civilization. [*Long, continued applause.*]

11

AROUSE, YE SLAVES!

Debs did not succeed in uniting the American working class in industrial unions of the IWW in 1905-1906. But he did play a leading role in uniting it in the broadest and most effective labor defense case the United States had ever seen.

On March 6, 1906, Charles H. Moyer, president, William D. Haywood, secretary-treasurer, and George A. Pettibone, Denver businessman and former active member of the Western Federation of Miners, were indicted in Idaho for murder.

Debs immediately recognized the charge as an attempt to destroy the Western Federation of Miners and the IWW, and blasted the action as "a foul plot; a damnable conspiracy; a hellish outrage."

The front page of the March 10, 1906, issue of Appeal to Reason, *in a special edition of four million copies, carried his flaming call to labor, "Arouse, Ye Slaves."*

The latest and boldest stroke of the plutocracy, but for the blindness of the people, would have startled the nation.

Murder has been plotted and is about to be executed in the name and under the forms of law.

Men who will not yield to corruption and browbeating must be ambushed, spirited away and murdered.

That is the edict of the Mine Owners' Association of the Western states and their Standard Oil backers and pals in Wall Street, New York.

These gory-beaked vultures are to pluck out the heart of resistance to their tyranny and robbery, that labor may be left stark naked at their mercy.

Charles Moyer and Wm. D. Haywood, of the Western Federation of Miners, and their official colleagues — men, all of them, and every inch of them — are charged with the assassination of ex-Governor Frank Steunenberg, of Idaho, who simply reaped what he had sown, as a mere subterfuge to pounce upon them in secret, rush them out of the state by special train, under heavy guard, clap them into the penitentiary, convict them upon the purchased perjured testimony of villains, and strangle them to death with the hangman's noose.

It is a foul plot; a damnable conspiracy; a hellish outrage.

The governors of Idaho and Colorado say they have the proof to convict. They are brazen falsifiers and venal villains, the miserable tools of the mine owners who, themselves, if anybody, deserve the gibbet.

Moyer, Haywood and their comrades had no more to do with the assassination of Steunenberg than I had; the charge is a ghastly lie, a criminal calumny, and is only an excuse to murder men who are too rigidly honest to betray their trust and too courageous to succumb to threat and intimidation.

Labor leaders that cringe before the plutocracy and do its bidding are apotheosized; those that refuse must be foully murdered.

Personally and intimately do I know Moyer, Haywood, Pettibone, St. John and their official coworkers, and I will stake my life on their honor and integrity; and that is precisely the crime for which, according to the words of the slimy sleuth who worked up the case against them, "they shall never leave Idaho alive."

Well, by the gods, if they don't the governors of Idaho

and Colorado and their masters from Wall Street, New York, to the Rocky Mountains had better prepare to follow them.

Nearly twenty years ago the capitalist tyrants put some innocent men to death for standing up for labor.

They are now going to try it again. Let them dare!

There have been twenty years of revolutionary education, agitation and organization since the Haymarket tragedy, and if an attempt is made to repeat it, there will be a revolution and I will do all in my power to precipitate it.

The crisis has come and we have got to meet it. Upon the issue involved the whole body of organized labor can unite and every enemy of plutocracy will join us. From the farms, the factories and stores will pour the workers to meet the redhanded destroyers of freedom, the murderers of innocent men and the archenemies of the people.

Moyer and Haywood are our comrades, staunch and true, and if we do not stand by them to the shedding of the last drop of blood in our veins, we are disgraced forever and deserve the fate of cringing cowards.

We are not responsible for the issue. It is not of our seeking. It has been forced upon us; and for the very reason that we deprecate violence and abhor bloodshed we cannot desert our comrades and allow them to be put to death. If they can be murdered without cause so can we, and so will we be dealt with at the pleasure of these tyrants.

They have driven us to the wall and now let us rally our forces and face them and fight.

If they attempt to murder Moyer, Haywood and their brothers, a million revolutionists, at least, will meet them with guns.

They have done their best and their worst to crush and enslave us. Their politicians have betrayed us, their courts have thrown us into jail without trial and their soldiers have shot our comrades dead in their tracks.

The worm turns at last, and so does the worker.

Let them dare to execute their devilish plot and every state in this Union will resound with the tramp of revolution.

Get ready, comrades, for action! No other course is left to the working class. Their courts are closed to us except to pronounce our doom. To enter their courts is simply to be mulcted of our meager means and bound hand and foot; to have our eyes plucked out by the vultures that fatten upon our misery.

Capitalist courts never have done, and never will do, anything for the working class.

Whatever is done we must do ourselves, and if we stand up like men from the Atlantic to the Pacific and from Canada to the Gulf, we will strike terror to their cowardly hearts and they will be but too eager to relax their grip upon our throats and beat a swift retreat.

We will watch every move they make and in the meantime prepare for action.

A special revolutionary convention of the proletariat at Chicago, or some other central point, would be in order, and, if extreme measures are required, a general strike could be ordered and industry paralyzed as a preliminary to a general uprising.

If the plutocrats begin the program, we will end it.

12

OPEN LETTER TO
PRESIDENT ROOSEVELT

Debs' threats in "Arouse, Ye Slaves!" did not halt the prosecution of Moyer, Haywood, and Pettibone, but his activity in helping to mobilize a massive defense campaign played an important part in winning a jury acquittal in July, 1907.

An example of one of the techniques employed to focus national attention on the case was Debs' challenge of President Theodore Roosevelt's intervention against the defendants. His open letter to the President was published in the Toledo Socialist *of April 21, 1906.*

Dear Mr. President:

The address delivered by you yesterday at the cornerstone ceremony at Washington has been carefully read and among other things I observe the following:

"We can no more and no less afford to condone evil in a man of capital than evil in a man of no capital. The wealthy man who exults because there is a failure of justice in the effort to bring some trust magnate to an account for his misdeeds is as bad, and no worse than, the so-called labor leader who clamorously strives to excite a foul class feeling on behalf of some other labor leader who is implicated in murder."

Obviously you have reference in this paragraph to the

149

leaders of labor in Colorado who were recently seized without warrant of law, forcibly taken from the state of which they are citizens, and incarcerated in the penitentiary of another state in which only convicted criminals are confined. I know of no other labor leaders to whom these remarks could apply, and it seems equally plain that I am one of the "so-called" leaders, if not the particular one, who is "striving to excite a foul class feeling in their behalf."

Permit me to ask you, Mr. President, how you know that these men are implicated in murder? Have they been tried and found guilty by due process of law?

Since when, Mr. President, are men charged with crime presumed and pronounced guilty until they are found innocent?

It is true that you do not name these men, but convict them by innuendo. Is this fair? Is it just? A square deal? Is it not, in fact, Mr. President, cowardly to take such an advantage of your high office to pronounce the guilt of three of your fellow citizens, who have as yet not been tried and against whom nothing has been proved?

These men, Mr. President, are workingmen; do you know of any capitalists who have ever been treated in the same way?

Suppose a lot of thugs were to seize a number of capitalists at the hour of midnight, put them in irons, hustle them aboard a special train, rush them into another state and throw them into the penitentiary. Would you take the same view of the case, coolly pronounce their guilt and proceed to deliver your homily upon good citizenship, the "square deal," and law and order?

If instead of Moyer, Haywood and Pettibone it had been Depew, Platt and Paul Morton—that is to say, if instead of innocent workingmen they had been criminal capitalists—would you have treated them in precisely the same manner?

You have told us over and over again, Mr. President, that rich and poor should be treated alike; that all are entitled to the equal protection of the law. That is what you say in substance in the paragraph above quoted. You have repeated this so often that it has become a stale platitude. You have also repeatedly stated that profession without practice is dishonest and hypocritical.

Very well, Mr. President, we will take you at your word; we will judge you by your acts.

I shall not now address myself to you as a "so-called" labor leader, but as your fellow citizen of the United States.

You, Mr. President, are the chief executive of the nation. You are the conservator of the Constitution of the United States and you have publicly sworn to support it.

Three citizens have been forcibly seized and deported from the state of their residence into another state in flagrant violation of the Constitution of the United States. These men now languish in prison cells.

Let me repeat the charge, Mr. President, without detail. Three citizens of the republic have been deprived of the protection vouchsafed to them under the Constitution of the United States. This fact is known of all men; denied by none, not even their accusers. There is not a shadow of doubt about it. It is a clear-cut case. All the country knows it. You, Mr. President, know it. Now, then, what are you going to do about it?

Will you make your acts square with your words; your practice with your profession?

It is up to you, Mr. President! You are reputed to have great moral courage and you certainly have great power. Under the Constitution, the one that has been violated, the one you have sworn to support, you have the power to redress the wrong that has been done. Will you do it?

All that I am asking is that you shall perform your sworn duty; you are not expected to do more, and you cannot do less without violating your oath of office and betraying your official trust.

If you do not believe, Mr. President, that the Constitution has been violated, or, if you have the least doubt about it, please call upon me to prove it.

I am not now handling a "muckrake"; not looking down, but up; up to you and awaiting your answer.

You are perhaps aware, Mr. President, that some of us are accused of advocating violence. It is not true. As a matter of fact we are resisting violence. In your address yesterday you quoted the commandment, "Thou shalt not steal!" Let me quote another, "Thou shalt not kill." This is precisely what we are trying to prevent, not lawful punishment, but cold-blooded murder.

In treating with Moyer, Haywood and Pettibone, our comrades, every law and all decency have been trampled under foot. The state in which these men have been stripped of their legal rights and treated as felons is notoriously in control of corporations whose absolute sway has been questioned by these leaders of the working class; and this, and this alone, constitutes their crime, and for this they have been marked for corporate vengeance.

These men, Mr. President, are our comrades, our brothers, and we propose to stand by them and see that justice is done them.

A fair trial will free and vindicate them as certain as the sun shines.

Knowing them as we do to be men of pure character, of absolute integrity and all other things of good report among men, we know that they are wholly incapable of committing the crime with which they have been charged.

It is not pretended that they were in the same state at the time the crime was committed. Not a shadow of crime rests upon them other than the alleged confession of a self-confessed criminal.

These are facts, Mr. President, and in view of these facts we would be craven indeed if we allowed our brothers to be made the victims of such an infamous conspiracy without doing all in our power to save them.

Every step thus far taken against these men has been in violation of law, and the purpose of the whole proceeding is so apparent that any man with eyes can see it.

In this connection, Mr. President, when the question of

law and order is raised, I beg of you to remember that we are dealing with corporations that have usurped the powers of state governments; that defy the legally expressed will of the people, as in Colorado, where a majority of forty-six thousand votes was overridden and treated with contempt; corporations whose crime-inciting shibboleths are: "To hell with the Constitution"; "To hell with habeas corpus."

These corporations rule the states and we have had evidence enough to know how they treat law when it interferes with their predatory program.

We are not in favor of violence, but seeking to avoid it. The facts prove it.

We are not objecting to a fair trial, but to a packed jury and a corporation court and the consummation of a criminal conspiracy.

"Thou shalt not kill!" This applies to capitalists as well as workingmen.

If Moyer, Haywood and Pettibone were capitalists instead of workingmen we should still do our utmost to see that they were given a "square deal."

Murder in any form is abhorrent, but most terribly so when committed under the forms and in the names of law and justice.

Wendell Phillips said that John Brown would have had twice as good a right to hang Governor Wise as Governor Wise had to hang John Brown.

All we are asking and insisting upon is that our accused brothers shall have the protection of the law, a fair hearing and just verdict, and upon that issue we are prepared to go before the American people.

Respectfully yours,
Eugene V. Debs

13

THOMAS McGRADY

While Debs' personal road to the socialist movement was through the struggles of organized labor, he opposed narrow, sectarian tendencies against recruiting revolutionists with other backgrounds.

One of his sharpest attacks against such tendencies in the Socialist Party is contained in this obituary for a Catholic priest who had left the church and joined the party. It appeared in the Appeal to Reason, *December 14, 1907.*

It is a strange and pathetic coincidence that almost at the very moment I completed the introduction to the brochure of Thomas McGrady on "The Catholic Church and Socialism," now in press, the sad news came that he had passed away, and the painful duty now devolves upon me to write the word "finis" at the close of his work and add a few words of obitual eulogy.

It is not customary among Socialists to pronounce conventional and meaningless panegyrics upon departed comrades; nor to pay fulsome tribute to virtues they never possessed. Mere form and ceremony have had their day — and a long and gloomy day it has been — and can have no place among Socialists when a comrade living pays his last reverent regards to a comrade dead.

Thomas McGrady was born at Lexington, Kentucky,

June 6, 1863. In 1887, at twenty-four years of age, he was ordained as a Catholic priest at the Cathedral of Galveston, Texas. His next pastorate was St. Patrick's Church, Houston, followed by his transfer to St. Patrick's Church, Dallas, Texas. In 1890 he returned to his Kentucky home, beginning his pastoral service there in Lexington, his native city. Later he went to St. Anthony's Church, Bellevue, Kentucky, and it was here, in 1896, that he began his first serious study of economic, political and social questions. He was first attracted by Henry George's single tax, but abandoned that as inadequate after some socialist literature fell into his hands, and he became convinced that nothing less than a social revolution, and the abolition of the capitalist competitive system would materially better the existing industrial and social condition of the people.

Father McGrady, who always had the lofty courage of his convictions, now avowed himself a Socialist. He drank deep at the fountain of socialist literature and mastered its classics. His library contained the works of the standard authors of all nations.

It was at this time that Father McGrady was at the very pinnacle of his priestly power and popularity. He was young, just past thirty, brilliant and scholarly. His magnetic personality was irresistible. . . .

Father McGrady soon began to feel that his new convictions did not fit his old conventicle. Honesty and candor being his predominant characteristics, the truth that dawned upon his brain found ready expression from his eloquent lips. He took his congregation into his confidence and told them frankly that he was a Socialist. Thenceforward every discourse attested that fact. He was warned by the bishop, threatened by the archbishop, but his flock closed around him, a living, throbbing citadel. He ministered to them in their suffering, comforted them in their sorrow, solemnized their nuptial vows, baptized their babes, tenderly laid to rest their dead, and they truly loved him.

But the conviction that the orthodox pulpit and the forum of freedom were irreconcilable, and that as a priest he was in the fetters of theology, grew upon him, and in spite of the pleadings and protestings of his followers he resigned his pastorate and withdrew from the priesthood. . . .

The formal abdication of the priesthood by Father McGrady created a great sensation. The dignitaries of the church affected pious rejoicing. The recreant priest had long been a thorn in their complacent flesh. It was well that the holy church was purged of his pernicious influence.

Columns of reports appeared in the daily papers, and the features of the converted priest, with which these accounts were embellished, became familiar to hundreds of thousands. A Socialist priest was indeed an anomaly. Vast concourses of people were attracted by the mere mention of his name. When he was announced to speak, standing room was always at a premium. . . .

It was in the midst of these oratorical triumphs that the first distinct shock of organized opposition was felt. The capitalist press as a unit, and as if by preconcerted action, cut him out of its columns. The sensation created by McGrady's leap from the Catholic pulpit to the Socialist platform had been fully exploited as far as its news value was concerned, and now the renegade priest, as his whilom paters in Christ, who profess to love their enemies, call him, must be relegated to oblivion by being totally ignored. The church he formerly served so faithfully now began to actively pursue him. Where he was announced to speak priests admonished the faithful, either openly from the pulpit or covertly through the confessional, not to stain their souls by venturing near the anti-Christ. But this form of opposition, however vexatious, trying and difficult to overcome, but aroused the latent spirit of the crusader and intensified his determination. In the fierce fires of persecution, fed and fanned by religious ignorance and fanaticism, he was tempered for the far greater work that spread out before him, rich and radiant as a field of promise. . . .

Notwithstanding that McGrady was attracting vast audiences, including many who had never before heard the philosophy of socialism expounded, the very ones most desired, and without whom progress is impossible; notwithstanding the door receipts almost uniformly recouped the treasury of the local Socialists by a substantial net balance, certain "leaders," whose narrow prejudices were inflamed by the new agitator's success and increasing popularity in the movement, began to turn upon him, and sting him with venomous innuendo or attack him openly through the Socialist press.

Paradoxical as it may seem, he was denied the right to serve the Socialist movement — by Socialists.

Among the first charges brought against him — not by capitalists; they were too wise, if not too decent, to utter such a palpable untruth, but by men calling themselves Socialists — was that he had joined the movement as a "grafter," and was making Socialist speeches for "the money there was in it."

A baser falsehood, a more atrocious slander was never uttered.

Had McGrady been a miserable grafter instead of a great white soul, he would have remained in the pulpit. His people worshiped him and his "superiors" held out the most glittering inducements if he would only abandon his wicked and abominable "economic heresies." The eloquence and power of the young priest were widely recognized in church circles. A brilliant future spread out before him. He could easily become the petted and pampered favorite of the fathers. But he spurned the life of ease and luxury at the price of his self-respect. The positions of eminence he might attain by stifling his convictions sank to degradation from his lofty point of view.

Turning his back upon the wealth and luxury of the capitalist class he cast his lot with the proletariat, the homeless and hungry, the ragged and distressed, and this he did, according to some Socialists, to "graft" on them, and the cry was raised, "The grafter must go!"

It was this that shocked his tender sensibilities, silenced his eloquent tongue, and broke his noble and generous heart.

Those Socialists who vilified him as a "sky pilot," and as a "grafter," who declared him to be "unsound," "unscientific," and who indulged in similar tirade and twaddle, ought now to be satisfied. Their ambition has been realized. They scourged the "fakir" from the platform with whips of asps into a premature grave and he will trouble them no more. May they find it in their consciences to forgive themselves.

There is a deep lesson in the melancholy and untimely death of Comrade Thomas McGrady. Let us hope that so much good may result from it that the cruel sacrifice may be softened by the atonement and serve the future as a noble and inspiring example.

While it is the duty of every member to guard the movement against the impostor, the chronic suspicion that a man who has risen above the mental plane of a scavenger is a "grafter" is a besetting sin, and has done incalculable harm to the movement. The increasing cry from the same source that only the proletariat is revolutionary and that "intellectuals" are middle class reactionaries is an insult to the movement, many of whose staunchest supporters are of the latter type. Moreover, it would imply by its sneering allusion to the "intellectuals" that the proletariat are a brainless rabble, revelling in their base degeneracy and scorning intellectual enlightenment.

Many a fine spirit who would have served the movement as an effective agitator and powerful advocate, stung to the quick by the keen lash in the hands of a "comrade," has dropped into silence and faded into obscurity.

Fortunately the influence of these self-appointed censors is waning. The movement is no longer a mere fanatical sect. It has outgrown that period in spite of its sentinels and doorkeepers.

Between watchful devotion, which guards against impostors, and chronic heresy-hunting, which places a premium upon dirt and stupidity and imposes a penalty upon brains and self-respect, there is a difference wide as the sea. The former is a virtue which cannot be too highly commended, the latter a vice which cannot be too severely condemned.

Thomas McGrady was an absolutely honest man. Almost ten years of intimate and varied relations with him enables the writer to conscientiously pay him this tribute — to place this perennial flower where he sleeps.

No attempt is made to convert our deceased comrade into a saint. Could he speak he would not be shorn of his foibles. Like all great souls he had his faults — the faults that attested his humanity and brought into more perfect relief the many virtues which adorned his manly character and enriched his noble life.

Thomas McGrady found joy in social service and his perfect consecration to his social ideals was the crowning glory of his life and the bow of promise at his death.

THE RED SPECIAL: Debs leans out window; man standing second from right is Tom Mooney.

14

THE SOCIALIST PARTY'S APPEAL
(1908)

The depression of 1907 was the background of the 1908 presidential election campaign. Debs, again the Socialist candidate, addressed himself to the problems of the unemployed, the unorganized and unskilled workers, and the poor farmers.

Travelling from coast to coast in the Red Special, a locomotive with a coach, a sleeper and a baggage car packed with campaign literature, buttons, posters and leaflets, Debs reached more thousands than ever before.

The recorded vote was 420,973, not much more than in 1904, but the campaign was a success. Debs had spoken to some 500,000 persons and 50,000 new subscribers had been secured for Appeal to Reason, *the most popular socialist weekly.*

This article by Debs from The Independent, *July-December 1908, is typical of the message by voice and pen.*

At a public meeting in New York City some months ago the present presidential candidate of the Republican Party was asked this question: "What is a man to do who is out of work in a financial panic and is starving?"

This is an intensely human as well as a very practical question. It epitomizes the problem of the unemployed and places it in bold relief. It is not too much to say that the

future welfare and progress of our country — aye, the fate
of civilization itself — depends upon a correct solution of
this problem. In view of the supreme importance of the
question it might naturally be expected that the Republican
Party would offer some practical and well-defined method
of dealing with it, and one might suppose that the party's
standard-bearer would be in a position clearly to expound
that method in making reply to his interrogator. But how
pitifully inadequate was the answer! It is at least creditable
to Mr. Taft's honesty that he frankly replied, "God knows!"

When Mr. Kern, the vice-presidential candidate of the
Democratic Party, was asked recently what his party proposed to do for the relief of the unemployed, he is reported
to have answered, "Nothing directly, nothing socialistic.
We hope that carrying out the general ideas in our platform will so restore confidence that industry will start up
again. But that's about all. In fact, that's enough."

These answers are not cited for any partisan purpose,
but because they serve admirably to illustrate the really
essential difference between the Socialist Party and its most
formidable political rivals. The Socialist Party does not
refer this important problem to the Deity for solution. It
recognizes the fact that it is of human creation and must
be solved by human effort. It proposes to do something
"directly," something "socialistic," for the relief of the unemployed. The Socialist Party recognizes the serious nature
of the unemployed problem and aims to solve it in the
only way it can be solved, namely, by removing its cause.
As means of temporary relief, applicable during the period
of transition to a collective system of industry, the party
proposes "immediate government relief for the unemployed
workers by building schools, by reforesting of cut-over and
waste lands, by reclamation of arid tracts and the building of canals, and by extending all other useful public
works." Both from the standpoint of effectiveness and that
of practicability this program may be offered without comment in lieu of Mr. Taft's "God knows!" and Mr. Kern's
"hope" of restored confidence.

As a matter of fact, it is an entire impossibility for either the Republican or the Democratic Party to offer any practicable solution for our industrial ills, because those ills are the inevitable and perfectly natural outgrowth of the wage system of industry, which system both parties are alike pledged to support and defend. That the economic policy of the Republican Party is impotent to stay the periodic recurrence of industrial and financial crises is proved by the existing depression, and as the party's platform utterance in relation to labor pledges it to a continuance of what is denominated "the same wise policy," there is certainly no hope of relief from that quarter. With regard to the Democratic Party, the country already has had sufficient experience with its methods of dealing with important economic problems to justify the suspicion that Mr. Kern's "hope" may prove somewhat elusive.

The Socialist Party of the United States is part of a great international movement which far overshadows any other movement recorded in history. Its basic idea is the complete and permanent emancipation of labor all over the world. To quote from a recent article by George Allan England:

"First of all, the fact should be made quite clear that the Socialist Party is far and away the largest political unit not only of today but of any time. To the uninformed who conceive of Socialists as a rather obscure and fantastic sect of Utopians — of 'dreamers' — the discovery must come as something of a shock that the world's Socialist vote now stands between 8,000,000 and 9,000,000, representing about 30,000,000 adult Socialists. This latter number includes, of course, women and disfranchised persons, who in the Socialist concept of government, in the 'state within a state' which Socialism is building up, enjoy equal rights with present voters. There is something peculiarly disconcerting to the present governments of, by, and for plutocracy in those 30,000,000 of 'dreamers,' all so active in propaganda, all so terribly in earnest — in that ever widening acceptance of the visionary axiom that 'without rights there shall be no duties; without duties no rights.'

"In the second place, it should be definitely understood that the movement is already breaking into legislative bodies all over the civilized world, to an extent hardly realized by the casual critic. The United States is practically the only large country of modern type in which the party has no national representation — a state of affairs, be it said in passing, which will soon be remedied. . . . Prophecy is dangerous, but 1908 should for many reasons hold in store a great surprise for the old-party politicians. From now on there is 'a new Richmond in the field.'"

The Socialist Party is the political expression of what is known as "the class struggle." This struggle is an economic fact as old as history itself, but it is only within the past generation that it has become a thoroughly conscious and well-organized political fact. As long as this struggle was confined to its economic aspect the ruling classes had nothing to fear, as, being in control of all the means and agencies of government, they were always able to use their power effectively to suppress uprisings either of chattel slaves, feudal serfs, or freeborn and politically equal capitalist wage workers. But now that the struggle has definitely entered the political field it assumes for the present ruling class a new and sinister aspect. With the whole power of the state — the army, the navy, the courts, the police — in possession of the working class by virtue of its victory at the polls, the death knell of capitalist private property and wage slavery is sounded.

This does not mean, however, that the workers will wrest control of government from the capitalist class simply for the purpose of continuing the class struggle on a new plane, as has been the case in all previous political revolutions when one class has superseded another in the control of government. It does not mean that the workers and capitalists will merely change places, as many poorly informed persons undoubtedly still believe. It means the inauguration of an entirely new system of industry, in which the exploitation of man by man will have no place. It means the establishment of a new economic motive for production and distribution. Instead of profit being the ruling motive of industry, as at present, all production and distribution will be for use. As a consequence, the class struggle and economic class antagonisms as we now know them will entirely disappear. Did the Socialist Party have no higher political ideal than the victory of one class over another it would not be worthy of a moment's support from any right-thinking individual. It would, indeed, be impossible for the party to gain any considerable strength or prestige. It is the great moral worth of its ideals that attracts adherents to the Socialist movement even from the ranks of the capitalist class, and holds them to their allegiance with an enthusiasm that suggests a close parallel with the early days of Christianity; and it is the mathematical certainty with which its conclusions are stated that enables the Socialist Party to expand and advance with irresistible force to the goal it has in view, in spite of the appalling opposition it has had to encounter. It is this certainty, and the moral worth of its ideals, which moved Mommsen, the venerable German historian, to say that "this is the only great party which has a claim to political respect."

The capitalist was originally a socially useful individual, but the evolution of our industrial system has rendered him a parasite, an entirely useless functionary that must be eliminated if civilization is to endure. It is a leading thought in modern philosophy that in its process of development each institution tends to cancel itself. Born out of social necessity, its progress is determined by repulsions and attractions arising in society, which produce effects tending to negate its original function. Now, that is what has happened to the capitalist. He is no longer useful. He is merely a clog to social progress and must be abolished, just as the feudal lord and chattel slaveholder has been abolished.

The capitalist was originally a manager who worked hard at his business and received what economists call the "wages of superintendence." So long as he occupied that position the capitalist might be restrained and controlled in various ways, but he could not be got rid of. He performed real functions, and as society was not yet prepared to take those functions upon itself, it could not afford to discharge him. But now the capitalist proper has become absolutely useless. Finding it easier to combine with others of his class in a large undertaking, he has abdicated his position of overseer and has put in a salaried manager to act for him. This salaried manager now performs the only social function of the capitalist, while the capitalist himself has become a mere rent or interest receiver. The rent or interest he receives is paid for the use of a monopoly which not he, but a vast multitude of people, created by their joint efforts.

This differentiation between manager and capitalist is a necessary part of the process of capitalistic evolution due to machine industry. As competition led to waste in production, so it also led to the cutting of profits among capitalists. To prevent this the concentration of capital was necessary, by which the large capitalist could undersell his small rivals in the marketing of goods produced by machinery and distributed by agencies initially too costly for any individual competitor to purchase or set on foot. For such massive capitals the contributions of several capitalists are necessary. Hence the joint stock company, the corporation, and finally the trust. Through the medium of such agencies a person in the United States can own stock in an enterprise in Africa or South America which he has never visited and never intends to visit, and which, therefore, he cannot "superintend" in any way. He and the other stockholders put in a manager with injunctions to be economical. The manager's business is to earn the largest possible dividends for his employers. If he does not do so he is dismissed. To secure high dividends the manager will lower wages. If that is resisted there will probably be either a strike or a lockout. Cheap labor will be imported by the manager, and if the workers resist by intimidation or organized boycotting the forces of the state will be used against them, and in the end they must submit. The old personal relation between the workers and the employer is gone. From the point of view of the corporation owners the workers are simply an extension of the machine of profit production. The workers are not regarded as having human attributes. Their labor is trafficked in as a commodity, like iron and steel, and the only interest the capitalist retains in production is his interest as an idle dividend receiver. Society can get along without the capitalist; it refuses longer to support him in idleness and luxury.

The process of industrial evolution that has rendered the capitalist a useless functionary has at the same time evolved an organization, cooperative in character, whereby industry may be carried on without friction for the benefit of the whole people instead of for the profit of the individual capitalist. The conduct of industry will be entrusted to men who are technically familiar with its processes, precisely as it is now entrusted to managers by the stockholders of a corporation; in short, the whole industry will represent a giant corporation in which all citizens are stockholders, and the state will represent a board of directors acting for the whole people. Details of organization and performance may well be left to the experts to whose direction the matter will be given when the time comes. It is not the mission of the Socialist Party to speculate concerning the manner in which the workers will conduct their affairs when they have come into possession of their inheritance which the ages have prepared for them. Standards of right and justice under the *new regime*, however, may well be indicated.

"Without rights there shall be no duties; without duties no rights." What will be the practical interpretation of this socialist axiom? Obviously, social parasitism must cease; every man must be a producer, or perform some socially useful function, in order to procure title to any share in the product of the collective industry. The only citizenship held honorable will be economic citizenship, or comradeship in production and in the sharing of product.

The spectacle of strong men walking the streets idle and hungry, vainly begging for a chance to work for the pittance that will suffice to ward off starvation from themselves and their loved ones, will be no more. The cruelty of children of tender years being forced hungry to school in a great city like New York will disappear. No longer will there be a problem of the unemployed, and the capitalist will be elevated from his present condition of parasitism to that of a worker and producer of wealth. The class struggle must necessarily cease, for there will be no classes. Each individual will be his own economic master, and all will be servants of the collectivity. Human brotherhood, as taught by Christ nineteen centuries ago, will for the first time begin to be realized.

The struggle for working-class emancipation, which finds its expression through the Socialist Party, must continue, and will increase in intensity until either the ruling class completely subjugates the working class, or until the working class entirely absorbs the capitalist class. There is no middle ground possible, and it is this fact that makes ludicrous those sporadic reform movements typified by the Populist and Independence Parties.

But the subjugation of the working class is out of the question. Intelligence has gone too far for that; it is the capitalist class that is doomed. Hence the only possible outcome of the present struggle is victory for the working class and the absorption by that class of all other classes.

When the present Socialist Party has accomplished its mission of uniting the workers of the world into a solid political phalanx the end of capitalist domination is at hand, and the era of industrial peace so long wished for by philanthropists and seers will dawn upon the world.

15

TWO LETTERS ON PARTY POLICY

Debs generally avoided involvement in the internal strug-
gles over policy in the Socialist Party. He did take posi-
tions on questions of principles and tactics that divided
the party into right- and left-wing factions. He expressed
his views in letters to comrades and in articles which were
published in the International Socialist Review, *which had*
become the organ of the left wing.

However, he did not participate in the conventions or
committee meetings where policies were debated and acted
on, and this limited his effectiveness in winning majority
support of the delegates for his views.

The first of the two letters reprinted here was written to
William English Walling, a Socialist writer, on December
7, 1909, opposing the opportunist tendency of the right
wing in the party. It was published in the January 1910
issue of the Review.

The second, written to another comrade, attacked the
proposal of the party's Committee on Immigration which
advocated the exclusion of Orientals from the United
States. Debs' letter arrived too late for the May 1910
convention and was published in the July 1910 Review.
The convention had adopted a compromise resolution.

Dear Walling:

. . . *I am with you* thoroughly, and thank you for bringing the matter to my attention.

I have been watching the situation closely and especially the tendencies to *reaction* to which we are so unalterably opposed. The Socialist Party has already *catered far too much* to the American Federation of Labor, and there is no doubt that *a halt will have to be called.*

The *revolutionary* character of our party and our movement *must* be preserved in all its integrity *at all cost*, for if that be compromised, it had better cease to exist.

I have no fear that any great number will be deflected when it comes to a showdown. Wish I could have an hour or two with you. Believe me always,

Yours faithfully,
Eugene V. Debs

P. S. I am more than gratified with your uncompromising spirit and attitude. If the trimmers had their way, we should degenerate into bourgeois reform. But *they will not have their way.*

On Immigration

My Dear Brewer:

Have just read the majority report of the Committee on Immigration. It is utterly unsocialistic, reactionary and in truth outrageous, and I hope you will oppose with all your power. The plea that certain races are to be excluded because of tactical expediency would be entirely consistent in a bourgeois convention of self-seekers, but should have no place in a proletarian gathering under the auspices of an international movement that is calling on the oppressed and exploited workers of all the world to unite for their emancipation. . . .

Away with the "tactics" which require the exclusion of the oppressed and suffering slaves who seek these shores with the hope of bettering their wretched condition and are driven back under the cruel lash of expediency by those who call themselves Socialists in the name of a movement whose proud boast it is that it stands uncompromisingly for the oppressed and downtrodden of all the earth. These poor slaves have just as good a right to enter here as even the authors of this report who now seek to exclude them. The only difference is that the latter had the advantage of a little education and had not been so cruelly ground and oppressed, but in point of principle there is no difference, the motive of all being precisely the same, and if the convention which meets in the name of socialism should discriminate at all it should be in favor of the miserable races who have borne the heaviest burdens and are most nearly crushed to the earth.

Upon this vital proposition I would take my stand against the world and no specious argument of subtle and sophistical defenders of the Civic Federation unionism, who do not hesitate to sacrifice principle for numbers and jeopardize ultimate success for immediate gain, could move me to turn my back upon the oppressed, brutalized and despairing victims of the old world, who are lured to these shores by some faint glimmer of hope that here their crushing burdens may be lightened, and some star of promise rise in their darkened skies.

The alleged advantages that would come to the Socialist movement because of such heartless exclusion would all be swept away a thousand times by the sacrifice of a cardinal principle of the international Socialist movement, for well might the good faith of such a movement be questioned by intelligent workers if it placed itself upon record as barring its doors against the very races most in need of relief, and extinguishing their hope, and leaving them in dark despair at the very time their ears were first attuned to the international call and their hearts were beginning to throb responsive to the solidarity of the oppressed of all lands and all climes beneath the skies.

In this attitude there is nothing of maudlin sentimentality, but simply a rigid adherence to fundamental principles of the international proletarian movement. If socialism, international revolutionary socialism, does not stand staunchly, unflinchingly, and uncompromisingly for the working class and for the exploited and oppressed masses of all lands, then it stands for none and its claim is a false pretense and its profession a delusion and a snare.

Let those desert us who will because we refuse to shut the international door in the faces of their own brethren; we will be none the weaker but all the stronger for their going, for they evidently have no clear conception of the international solidarity, are wholly lacking in the revolutionary spirit, and have no proper place in the Socialist movement while they entertain such aristocratic notions of their own assumed superiority.

Let us stand squarely on our revolutionary, working-class principles and make our fight openly and uncompromisingly against all our enemies, adopting no cowardly tactics and holding out no false hopes, and our movement will then inspire the faith, arouse the spirit, and develop the fiber that will prevail against the world.

Yours without compromise,

Eugene V. Debs.

16

WORKING CLASS POLITICS

A major issue in dispute at the Socialist Party convention of 1910 was the old one of craft versus industrial unionism. Debs was not present and the right wing was able to win a majority vote not to take a position on the question.

In this article in the November 1910 International Socialist Review, *Debs explained why working-class politics must combine industrial and political organization and why socialists should take a position in favor of industrial unionism.*

We live in the capitalist system, so-called because it is dominated by the capitalist class. In this system the capitalists are the rulers and the workers the subjects. The capitalists are in a decided minority and yet they rule because of the ignorance of the working class.

So long as the workers are divided, economically and politically, they will remain in subjection, exploited of what they produce and treated with contempt by the parasites who live out of their labor.

The economic unity of the workers must first be effected before there can be any progress toward emancipation. The interests of the millions of wage workers are identical, regardless of nationality, creed or sex, and if they will only open their eyes to this simple, self-evident fact, the greatest obstacle will have been overcome and the day of victory will draw near.

The primary need of the workers is industrial unity and by this I mean their organization in the industries in which they are employed as a whole instead of being separated into more or less impotent unions according to their crafts. Industrial unionism is the only effective means of economic organization and the quicker the workers realize this and unite within one compact body for the good of all, the sooner will they cease to be the victims of ward-heeling labor politicians and accomplish something of actual benefit to themselves and those dependent upon them. In Chicago where the labor grafters, posing as union leaders, have so long been permitted to thrive in their iniquity, there is especially urgent need of industrial unionism, and when this is fairly under way it will express itself politically in a class-conscious vote of and for the working class.

So long as the workers are content with conditions as they are, so long as they are satisfied to belong to a craft union under the leadership of those who are far more interested in drawing their own salaries and feathering their own nests with graft than in the welfare of their followers, so long, in a word, as the workers are meek and submissive followers, mere sheep, they will be fleeced, and no one will hold them in greater contempt than the very grafters and parasites who fatten out of their misery.

It is not Gompers, who banquets with Belmont and Carnegie, and Mitchell, who is paid and pampered by the plutocrats, who are going to unite the workers in their struggle for emancipation. The Civic Federation, which was organized by the master class and consists of plutocrats, politicians and priests, in connivance with so-called labor leaders, who are used as decoys to give that body the outward appearance of representing both capital and labor, is the staunch supporter of trade unions and the implacable foe of industrial unionism and socialism, and this in itself should be sufficient to convince every intelligent worker that the trade union under its present leadership and, as now used, is more beneficial to the capitalist class than it is to the workers, seeing that it is the means of keeping them disunited and pitted against each other, and as an inevitable result, in wage slavery.

The workers themselves must take the initiative in uniting their forces for effective economic and political action; the leaders will never do it for them. They must no longer suffer themselves to be deceived by the specious arguments of their betrayers, who blatantly boast of their unionism that they may traffic in it and sell out the dupes who blindly follow them. I have very little use for labor leaders in general and none at all for the kind who feel their self-importance and are so impressed by their own wisdom that where they lead, their dupes are expected to blindly follow without a question. Such "leaders" lead their victims to the shambles and deliver them over for a consideration and this is possible only among craft-divided wage slaves who are kept apart for the very purpose that they may feel their economic helplessness and rely upon some "leader" to do something for them.

Economic unity will be speedily followed by political unity. The workers once united in one great industrial union will vote a united working-class ticket. Not only this, but only when they are so united can they fit themselves to take control of industry when the change comes from wage slavery to economic freedom. It is precisely because it is the mission of industrial unionism to unite the workers in harmonious cooperation in the industries in which they are employed, and by their enlightened interdependence and self-imposed discipline prepare them for industrial mastery and self-control when the hour strikes, thereby backing up with their economic power the verdict they render at the ballot box, it is precisely because of this fact that every Socialist, every class-conscious worker should be an industrial unionist and strive by all the means at his command to unify the workers in the all-embracing bonds of industrial unionism.

The Socialist Party is the party of the workers, organized to express in political terms their determination to break their fetters and rise to the dignity of free men. In this party the workers must unite and develop their political power to conquer and abolish the capitalist political state and clear the way for industrial and social democracy.

But the new order can never be established by mere votes alone. This must be the result of industrial development and intelligent economic and political organization, necessitating both the industrial union and the political party of the workers to achieve their emancipation.

In this work, to be successfully accomplished, woman must have an equal part with man. If the revolutionary movement of the workers stands for anything it stands for the absolute equality of the sexes and when this fact is fully realized and the workingwoman takes her place side by side with the workingman all along the battlefront the great struggle will soon be crowned with victory.

17

DANGER AHEAD

*The Socialist Party experienced its greatest growth in
membership and votes between 1908 and 1912. From
an estimated 10,000 members when it was founded in
1901, it grew to 20,763 in 1904, 41,751 in 1908 and
117,984 in 1912.*

*The Socialist electoral activity was not only increasing
the number of votes for its candidates, but was winning
local elections. By 1911 there were 33 cities and towns
with Socialist administrations, including such cities as
Milwaukee, Wisconsin; Berkeley, California; Butte, Montana; and Flint and Jackson, Michigan.*

In the January 1911 International Socialist Review,
*Debs warned of the danger that the party would be de-
stroyed as a revolutionary organization by its opportunist and reformist electoral policies and practices.*

The large increase in the Socialist vote in the late national
and state elections is quite naturally hailed with elation
and rejoicing by party members, but I feel prompted to
remark in the light of some personal observations during
the campaign, that it is not entirely a matter for jubila-
tion. I am not given to pessimism, or captious criticism,
and yet I cannot but feel that some of the votes placed
to our credit this year were obtained by methods not con-

sistent with the principles of a revolutionary party, and in the long run will do more harm than good.

I yield to no one in my desire to see the party grow and the vote increase, but in my zeal I do not lose sight of the fact that healthy growth and a substantial vote depend upon efficient organization, the self-education and self-discipline of the membership, and that where these are lacking, an inflated vote secured by compromising methods can only be hurtful to the movement.

The danger I see ahead is that the Socialist Party at this stage, and under existing conditions, is apt to attract elements which it cannot assimilate, and that it may be either weighted down, or torn asunder with internal strife, or that it may become permeated and corrupted with the spirit of bourgeois reform to an extent that will practically destroy its virility and efficiency as a revolutionary organization.

To my mind the working-class character and the revolutionary integrity of the Socialist Party are of first importance. All the votes of the people would do us no good if our party ceased to be a revolutionary party, or only incidentally so, while yielding more and more to the pressure to modify the principles and program of the party for the sake of swelling the vote and hastening the day of its expected triumph.

It is precisely this policy and the alluring promise it holds out to new members with more zeal than knowledge of working-class economics that constitutes the danger we should guard against in preparing for the next campaign. The truth is that we have not a few members who regard vote-getting as of supreme importance, no matter by what method the votes may be secured, and this leads them to hold out inducements and make representations which are not at all compatible with the stern and uncompromising principles of a revolutionary party. They seek to make the Socialist propaganda so attractive — eliminating whatever may give offense to bourgeois sensibilities — that it serves as a bait for votes rather than as a means of education, and votes thus secured do not properly belong to us and do injustice to our party as well as to those who cast them.

These votes do not express socialism and in the next ensuing election are quite as apt to be turned against us, and it is better that they be not cast for the Socialist Party, registering a degree of progress the party is not entitled to and indicating a political position the party is unable to sustain.

Socialism is a matter of growth, of evolution, which can be advanced by wise methods, but never by obtaining for it a fictitious vote. We should seek only to register the actual vote of socialism, no more and no less. In our propaganda we should state our principles clearly, speak the truth fearlessly, seeking neither to flatter nor to offend, but only to convince those who should be with us and win them to our cause through an intelligent understanding of its mission.

There is also a disposition on the part of some to join hands with reactionary trade unionists in local emergencies and in certain temporary situations to effect some specific purpose, which may or may not be in harmony with our revolutionary program. No possible good can come from any kind of a political alliance, express or implied, with trade unions or the leaders of trade unions who are opposed to socialism and only turn to it for use in some extremity, the fruit of their own reactionary policy.

Of course we want the support of trade unionists, but only of those who believe in socialism and are ready to vote and work with us for the overthrow of capitalism.

The American Federation of Labor, as an organization, with its Civic Federation to determine its attitude and control its course, is deadly hostile to the Socialist Party and to any and every revolutionary movement of the working class. To kowtow to this organization and to join hands with its leaders to secure political favors can only result in compromising our principles and bringing disaster to the party.

Not for all the vote of the American Federation of Labor and its labor-dividing and corruption-breeding craft unions should we compromise one jot of our revolutionary principles; and if we do we shall be visited with the contempt we deserve by all real Socialists, who will scorn to remain in a party professing to be a revolutionary party of the working class while employing the crooked and disreputable methods of ward-heeling and politicians to attain their ends.

Of far greater importance than increasing the vote of the Socialist Party is the economic organization of the working class. To the extent, and only to the extent, that the workers are organized and disciplined in their respective industries can the Socialist movement advance and the Socialist Party hold what is registered by the ballot. The election of legislative and administrative officers, here and there, where the party is still in a crude state and the members economically unprepared and politically unfit to assume the responsibilities thrust upon them as the result of popular discontent, will inevitably bring trouble and set the party back, instead of advancing it, and while this is to be expected and is to an extent unavoidable, we should court no more of that kind of experience than is necessary to avoid a repetition of it. The Socialist Party has already achieved some victories of this kind which proved to be defeats, crushing and humiliating, and from which the party has not even now, after many years, entirely recovered.

We have just so much socialism that is stable and dependable, because securely grounded in economics, in discipline, and all else that expresses class-conscious solidarity, and this must be augmented steadily through economic and political organization, but no amount of mere votes can accomplish this in even the slightest degree.

Voting for socialism is not socialism any more than a menu is a meal.

Socialism must be organized, drilled, equipped and the place to begin is in the industries where the workers are employed. Their economic power has got to be developed through sufficient organization, or their political power, even if it could be developed, would but react upon them, thwart their plans, blast their hopes, and all but destroy them.

Such organization to be effective must be expressed in terms of industrial unionism. Each industry must be organized in its entirety, embracing all the workers, and all working together in the interest of all, in the true spirit of solidarity, thus laying the foundation and developing the superstructure of the new system within the old, from which it is evolving, and systematically fitting the workers, step by step, to assume entire control of the productive forces when the hour strikes for the impending organic change.

Without such economic organization and the economic power with which it is clothed, and without the industrial cooperative training, discipline and efficiency which are its corollaries, the fruit of any political victories the workers may achieve will turn to ashes on their lips.

Now that the capitalist system is so palpably breaking down, and in consequence its political parties breaking up, the disintegrating elements with vague reform ideas and radical bourgeois tendencies will head in increasing numbers toward the Socialist Party, especially since the greatly enlarged vote of this year has been announced and the party is looming up as a possible dispenser of the spoils of office. There is danger, I believe, that the party may be swamped by such an exodus and the best possible means, and in fact the only effectual means of securing the party against such a fatality is the economic power of the industrially organized workers.

The votes will come rapidly enough from now on without seeking them and we should make it clear that the Socialist Party wants the votes only of those who want socialism, and that, above all, as a revolutionary party of the working class, it discountenances vote-seeking for the sake of votes and holds in contempt office-seeking for the sake of office. These belong entirely to capitalist parties with their bosses and their boodle and have no place in a party whose shibboleth is emancipation.

With the workers efficiently organized industrially, bound together by the common tie of their enlightened self-interest, they will just as naturally and inevitably express their economic solidarity in political terms and cast a united vote for the party of their class as the forces of nature express obedience to the laws of gravitation.

18

THE CRISIS IN MEXICO

*In this remarkable document Debs speaks directly on the
question of program and tactics for the revolution in un-
derdeveloped, semicolonial countries in our epoch.*

*His brief comment on the problems and tasks of Mexican
revolutionists following the overthrow of the Diaz regime
in November 1910 was printed in the July 1911* International Socialist Review.

Now that Diaz is overthrown and his administration is a
thing of the past, what of the Mexican revolution and the
future? Will the substitution of Madero or some other
landed aristocrat and bourgeois political reformer placate
the people and end the revolution? Let us hope not, and
yet it takes but very little in the way of concession to satisfy the ignorant and oppressed masses.

The mere overthrow of Diaz of itself means little to the
Mexican people. Their condition will remain substantially
the same under the new regime, and yet this change of
administration with its attendant circumstances marks an
epoch in the history of the Mexican nation. Certain political reforms will be instituted as concessions to the people
and while economic conditions will remain substantially
as they have been the people have been inspirited by the
revolutionary movement and the concessions made to

them will but stimulate their ardor in the struggle to overthrow not merely their political dictators but their economic exploiters, and they will never cease their agitation until they have achieved their emancipation.

The real crisis in Mexico, as it seems to me, is now at hand. What the results of the approaching election may be or what the successor of Diaz may or may not do in the way of political reform are of little consequence compared to what the revolutionists will do in this crisis. Will they be able to keep their forces intact and unite in carrying on the fight along lines leading most directly to their emancipation? Most earnestly do I hope so and yet it is almost too much to expect. Already there are signs of dissension among the revolutionists themselves which threaten grave results to their movement.

As one who realizes in some measure the gravity of the situation our comrades are facing in Mexico and the vital concern of the entire working class of America in that situation, and as one whose whole heart has been with the Mexican revolutionary movement since its inception, I feel moved to declare what I believe to be the only safe course for our Mexican comrades to pursue to reach the end they have in view. It is with no desire to obtrude myself and in no spirit of dictation that I now speak, but solely from a desire to do my duty toward our Mexican comrades as I understand that duty.

First of all, the masses of Mexican workers and producers, like those of other countries, are ignorant, superstitious, unorganized and all but helpless in their slavish subjugation. In their present demoralized state economic emancipation is simply out of the question. They must first be reached and aroused, educated and organized, and until this work is accomplished to at least some extent all hope of successful revolution is doomed to disappointment.

It is well enough for the leaders of the Mexican Liberal Party to declare that this is an "economic revolution," but do the masses so understand it, and are they consciously aiming at such an end? And until they are in some degree class conscious and fitted by training and discipline for economic mastery, is not the success of such a revolution utterly out of the question?

If I read aright the manifesto recently issued by the Mexican Liberal Party all political action is tabooed. "Direct action," so-called, is relied upon for results. Reading between the lines I can see nothing but anarchism in this program and if that is what the leaders mean they should frankly say so that there may be no misunderstanding as to their attitude and program. Of course they have the right to take any position they may think proper, the same right that I have to disagree with them, and frankly, if I correctly understand their position it is not calculated to promote but rather to put off the revolutionary end they have in view.

The anarchistic attitude the leaders seem to have assumed and the "direct action" they contemplate, if persisted in, will eventuate, in my opinion, in a series of Haymarket sacrifices and the useless shedding of their noblest blood.

The battle cry of the Mexican Liberal Party is, "Land and Liberty," and its leaders declare that "the taking away of the land from the hands of the rich must be accomplished during the present insurrection." If the land can be taken from the rich in this insurrection so can also the mills, factories, mines, railroads, and the machinery of production, and the question is, what would the masses in their present ignorant and unorganized state do with them after having obtained them? It would simply add calamity to their calamities, granting that this impossible feat were capable of achievement.

It seems to me that the leaders of the Mexican Liberal Party, whose honesty is unquestioned and whose ability and attainments are of a high order, underestimate the magnitude and malignity of the power they are dealing with. They propose to take the lands from the rich, dispossess them at one swoop, when they are scarcely organized, while the rich control all the armies and navies of the world. The present insurrection has accomplished much but it cannot be expected to accomplish everything, least of all economic revolution overnight.

When the leaders of the Mexican Liberal Party undertake to transfer the lands from the rich to the poor, that hour they attack the armed forces of capitalism, which means the United States as well as Mexico. The lands in Mexico belong in large part to American capitalists and they will fight for them to the last ditch and with all the powerful resources at their command.

Let not the Mexican revolutionists depend too much on the "International Committee of the Mexican Liberal Party Junta" which they propose organizing "in all the principal cities of the United States and Europe." That some effective cooperation may thus be secured is entirely probable, but our Mexican comrades who saw their own leaders thrown into American prisons with scarcely a protest except among the Socialists are apt to be disappointed if they rely to any great extent upon the enslaved working classes of other countries whose energies are all absorbed in their own struggle for existence.

The right course for the Mexican revolutionists to pursue in this crisis, in my opinion, is to lay the foundation for economic and political organization of the dispossessed and enslaved masses, throughout the republic. This may seem to be too painfully slow in such an extreme exigency, but it will prove in the end to be not only the most direct road but the only road out of the wilderness.

The historic process must be taken into account by our Mexican comrades. There is no short cut to economic freedom. Power is necessary to achieve it, the power that springs from right education and organization, and this power in the present struggle is both economic and political, and to refuse to develop and exercise either is folly that is certain to end in disaster.

When the Mexican revolutionary leaders renounce all political action as unclean and demoralizing and when they express their abhorrence of all class-conscious political activity as simply vicious illusion "dreamed of in the opium den of politics," they align themselves with the anarchists and virtually repudiate and renounce the international Socialist movement.

If this is not their attitude I must confess I do not understand it; if it is their attitude, their dream of establishing anarchist-communism in Mexico at this stage of its industrial and social development will be rudely dispelled before many days.

The workers of all other countries are turning to the international Socialist movement and developing their economic and political power to carry out its program of emancipation and that is what they will have to do in Mexico. Other countries have had their insurrections and revolutions, their dreams and hopes of sudden emancipation, but they have all had to settle down at last to the education and organization of the masses as the only possible means of attaining that end.

The overthrow of Diaz will mean at least, I take it, the right to organize the working class and this is the work that should be taken in hand with all the energy that can be brought to bear upon it.

Here is virgin soil for industrial unionism and all the workers should be organized as speedily as possible within one great industrial organization and at the same time united politically within the Socialist Party. This is the most direct action I know and I have had experience enough to be satisfied at least in my own mind that what is now so urgently advocated by some as direct action is the most indirect and fruitless action that could possibly be taken.

If the leaders of the Mexican revolution will in this crisis align themselves with the international working-class movement, accept its principles, adopt its program, and then proceed with all their energy to educate and organize, economically and politically, the masses of Mexican peons and wage slaves, they will mark the most important era in Mexican history and blaze the way direct to emancipation.

19

SOUND SOCIALIST TACTICS

In this "preconvention discussion article" published in the February 1912 Review, *Debs deals with the differences that were sharpening for a showdown at the May convention of the Socialist Party.*

Many of the same issues are again being debated in the radical movement today: the attitude of revolutionists toward "capitalist property rights"; "direct action" and the "propaganda of the deed" versus political action; secret guerrilla warfare versus mass organization with open, free discussion of differences; bureaucracy versus democracy within the movement.

Socialists are practically all agreed as to the fundamental principles of their movement. But as to tactics there is wide variance among them. The matter of sound tactics, equally with the matter of sound principles, is of supreme importance. The disagreements and dissensions among Socialists relate almost wholly to tactics. The party splits which have occurred in the past have been due to same cause, and if the party should ever divide again, which it is to be hoped it will not, it will be on the rock of tactics.

Revolutionary tactics must harmonize with revolutionary principles. We could better hope to succeed with reactionary principles and revolutionary tactics than with revolutionary principles and reactionary tactics.

The matter of tactical differences should be approached with open mind and in the spirit of tolerance. The freest discussion should be allowed. We have every element in every shade of capitalist society in our party, and we are in for a lively time at the very best before we work out these differences and settle down to a policy of united and constructive work for socialism instead of spending so much time and energy lampooning one another.

In the matter of tactics we cannot be guided by the precedents of other countries. We have to develop our own and they must be adapted to the American people and to American conditions. I am not sure that I have the right idea about tactics; I am sure only that I appreciate their importance, that I am open to correction, and that I am ready to change whenever I find myself wrong.

It seems to me there is too much rancor and too little toleration among us in the discussion of our differences. Too often the spirit of criticism is acrid and hypercritical. Personal animosities are engendered, but opinions remain unchanged. Let us waste as little as possible of our militant spirit upon one another. We shall need it all for our capitalist friends.

There has recently been some rather spirited discussion about a paragraph which appears in the pamphlet on "Industrial Socialism," by William D. Haywood and Frank Bohn. The paragraph follows:

"When the worker, either through experience or study of Socialism, comes to know this truth, he acts accordingly. *He retains absolutely no respect for the property 'rights' of the profit-takers. He will use any weapon which will win his fight.* He knows that the present laws of property are made by and for the capitalists. *Therefore he does not hesitate to break them."*

The sentences which I have italicized provoked the controversy.

We have here a matter of tactics upon which a number of comrades of ability and prominence have sharply disagreed. For my own part I believe the paragraph to be entirely sound.

Certainly all Socialists, knowing how and to what end capitalist property "rights" are established, must hold such "rights" in contempt. In the *Manifesto* Marx says: "The Communist (Socialist) revolution is the most radical rupture with traditional property relations; no wonder that its development involves the most radical rupture with traditional ideas."

As a revolutionist I can have no respect for capitalist property laws, nor the least scruple about violating them. I hold all such laws to have been enacted through chicanery, fraud and corruption, with the sole end in view of dispossessing, robbing and enslaving the working class. But this does not imply that I propose making an individual lawbreaker of myself and butting my head against the stone wall of existing property laws. That might be called force, but it would not be that. It would be mere weakness and folly.

If I had the force to overthrow these despotic laws I would use it without an instant's hesitation or delay, but I haven't got it, and so I am law-abiding under protest — not from scruple — and bide my time.

Here let me say that for the same reason I am opposed to sabotage and to "direct action." I have not a bit of use for the "propaganda of the deed." These are the tactics of anarchist individualists and not of socialist collectivists. They were developed by and belong exclusively to our anarchist friends and accord perfectly with their philosophy. These and similar measures are reactionary, not revolutionary, and they invariably have a demoralizing effect upon the following of those who practice them. If I believed in the doctrine of violence and destruction as party policy; if I regarded the class struggle as guerrilla warfare, I would join the anarchists and practice as well as preach such tactics.

It is not because these tactics involve the use of force

that I am opposed to them, but because they do not. The physical forcist is the victim of his own boomerang. The blow he strikes reacts upon himself and his followers. The force that implies power is utterly lacking, and it can never be developed by such tactics.

The foolish and misguided, zealots and fanatics, are quick to applaud and eager to employ such tactics, and the result is usually hurtful to themselves and to the cause they seek to advance.

There have been times in the past and there are countries today where the frenzied deed of a glorious fanatic like old John Brown seems to have been inspired by Jehovah himself, but I am now dealing with the twentieth century and with the United States.

There may be, too, acute situations arising and grave emergencies occurring, with perhaps life at stake, when recourse to violence might be justified, but a great body of organized workers, such as the Socialist movement, cannot predicate its tactical procedure upon such exceptional instances.

But my chief objection to all these measures is that they do violence to the class psychology of the workers and cannot be successfully inculcated as mass doctrine. The very nature of these tactics adapts them to guerrilla warfare, to the bomb planter, the midnight assassin; and such warfare, in this country, at least, plays directly into the hands of the enemy.

Such tactics appeal to stealth and suspicion, and cannot make for solidarity. The very teaching of sneaking and surreptitious practices has a demoralizing effect and a tendency to place those who engage in them in the category of "Black Hand" agents, dynamiters, safeblowers, holdup men, burglars, thieves and pickpockets.

If sabotage and direct action, as I interpret them, were incorporated in the tactics of the Socialist Party, it would at once be the signal for all the *agents provocateurs* and police spies in the country to join the party and get busy. Every solitary one of them would be a rabid "direct actionist," and every one would safely make his "getaway" and secure his reward, a la McPartland, when anything was "pulled off" by their dupes, leaving them with their necks in the nooses.

With the sanctioning of sabotage and similar practices the Socialist Party would stand responsible for the deed of every spy or madman, the seeds of strife would be subtly sown in the ranks, mutual suspicion would be aroused, and the party would soon be torn into warring factions to the despair of the betrayed workers and the delight of their triumphant masters.

If sabotage or any other artifice of direct action could be successfully employed, it would be wholly unnecessary, as better results could be accomplished without it. To the extent that the working class has power based upon class consciousness, force is unnecessary; to the extent that power is lacking, force can only result in harm.

I am opposed to any tactics which involve stealth, secrecy, intrigue, and necessitate acts of individual violence for their execution.

The work of the Socialist movement must all be done out in the broad open light of day. Nothing can be done by stealth that can be of any advantage to it in this country.

The workers can be emancipated only by their own collective will, the power inherent in themselves as a class, and this collective will and conquering power can only be the result of education, enlightenment and self-imposed discipline.

Sound tactics are constructive, not destructive. The collective reason of the workers repels the idea of individual violence where they are free to assert themselves by lawful and peaceable means.

The American workers are law-abiding and no amount of sneering or derision will alter that fact. Direct action will never appeal to any considerable number of them while they have the ballot and the right of industrial and political organization.

Its tactics alone have prevented the growth of the Industrial Workers of the World. Its principles of industrial
unionism are sound, but its tactics are not. Sabotage repels the American worker. He is ready for the industrial
union, but he is opposed to the "propaganda of the deed,"
and as long as the I. W. W. adheres to its present tactics
and ignores political action, or treats it with contempt by
advising the workers to "strike at the ballot box with an
ax," they will regard it as an anarchist organization, and
it will never be more than a small fraction of the labor
movement.

The sound education of the workers and their thorough
organization, both economic and political, on the basis
of the class struggle, must precede their emancipation.
Without such education and organization they can make
no substantial progress, and they will be robbed of the
fruits of any temporary victory they may achieve, as
they have been through all the centuries of the past.

For one, I hope to see the Socialist Party place itself
squarely on record at the coming national convention
against sabotage and every other form of violence and
destructiveness suggested by what is known as "direct action."

It occurs to me that the Socialist Party ought to have a
standing committee on tactics. The art or science of proletarian party tactics might well enlist the serious consideration of our clearest thinkers and most practical propagandists.

To return for a moment to the paragraph above quoted
from the pamphlet of Haywood and Bohn. I agree with
them that in their fight against capitalism the workers
have a right to use any weapon that will help them to
win. It should not be necessary to say that this does not
mean the blackjack, the dirk, the leadpipe or the sawed-
off shotgun. The use of these weapons does not help the
workers to win, but to lose, and it would be ridiculous
to assume that they were in the minds of the authors when
they penned that paragraph.

The sentence as it reads is sound. It speaks for itself and requires no apology. The workers will use any weapon which will help them *win* their fight.

The most powerful and the all-sufficient weapons are the industrial union and the Socialist Party, and they are not going to commit suicide by discarding these and resorting to the slingshot, the dagger and the dynamite bomb.

Another matter of party concern is the treatment of so-called "intellectuals" in the Socialist movement. Why the term "intellectual" should be one of reproach in the Socialist Party is hard to understand, and yet there are many Socialists who sneer at a man of intellect as if he were an interloper and out of place among Socialists. For myself I am always glad to see a man of brains, of intellect, join the movement. If he comes to us in good faith he is a distinct acquisition and is entitled to all the consideration due to any other comrade.

To punish a man for having brains is rather an anomalous attitude for an educational movement. The Socialist Party, above every other, should offer a premium on brains, intellectual capacity, and attract to itself all the mental forces that can be employed to build up the Socialist movement, that it may fulfill its emancipating mission.

Of course the Socialist movement is essentially a working-class movement, and I believe that as a rule party officials and representatives, and candidates for public office, should be chosen from the ranks of the workers. The intellectuals in office should be the exceptions, as they are in the rank and file.

There is sufficient ability among the workers for all official demands, and if there is not, it should be developed without further delay. It is their party, and why should it not be officered and represented by themselves?

An organization of intellectuals would not be officered and represented by wage earners; neither should an organization of wage earners be officered by intellectuals.

There is plenty of useful work for the intellectuals to do

without holding office, and the more intellectual they are the greater can their service be to the movement. Lecturers, debaters, authors, writers, artists, cartoonists, statisticians, etc., are in demand without number, and the intellectuals can serve to far better advantage in those capacities than in official positions.

I believe, too, in rotation in office. I confess to a prejudice against officialism and a dread of bureaucracy. I am a thorough believer in the rank and file, and in *ruling* from the *bottom up* instead of *being ruled* from the *top down*. The natural tendency of officials is to become bosses. They come to imagine that they are indispensable and unconsciously shape their acts to keep themselves in office.

The officials of the Socialist Party should be its servants, and all temptation to yield to the baleful influence of officialism should be removed by constitutional limitation of tenure.

There is a tendency in some states to keep the list of locals a solemn secret. The sheep have got to be protected against the wolves. No one must know what locals there are, or who its officials, for fear they may be corrupted by outside influences. This is an effective method for herding sheep, but not a good way to raise men. If the locals must be guarded against the wolves on the outside, then someone is required to guard them, and that someone is a boss, and it is the nature of the boss to be jealous of outside influences.

If our locals and the members who compose them need the protection of secrecy, they are lacking in the essential revolutionary fiber which can be developed only in the play of the elements surrounding them, and with all the avenues of education and information, and even of miseducation and misinformation, wide open for their reception. They have got to learn to distinguish between their friends and their enemies and between what is wise and what is otherwise and until the rank and file are so educated and enlightened their weakness will sooner or later deliver them as the prey of their enemies.

Still another matter about which there has been not a little ill-natured discussion is the proposed investigation of the Kerr publishing house. I cannot help wondering what business the national committee has making such an investigation. It would be quite as proper, in my opinion, to order an investigation of a building and loan association in which members have their savings invested.

It is true, without a doubt, that the *International Socialist Review* has published articles with which many of us disagreed, but why should it be investigated on that account? Are we Socialists who are constantly protesting against the suppression of free speech now going to set an example of what we propose doing by putting a gag on the lips of our own publications?

I don't agree with a good deal that appears in the *Review*, and I like it all the better on that account. That is the reason, in fact, why I subscribe for it and read it, and I cannot for the life of me understand why anyone would want to suppress it on that account.

If the *Review* and the concern which publishes it belonged to the national party it would be different, but it does not belong to the party, and the party is in no wise responsible for it, and if I were a stockholder I should regard the action of the national committee as the sheerest impertinence and treat it accordingly.

I do not know if the house of Kerr & Co. needs investigating or not. I am satisfied that it does not, but it is none of my business.

The Kerr company consists, as I understand it, of some fifteen hundred stockholders, nearly all of whom are Socialists and none of whom, as far as I am advised, are feebleminded and in need of a guardian. They have paid in all the money, they own all the stock and they are responsible for the concern; and if they want their publishing business investigated that is their affair and not the affair of the national committee of the Socialist Party.

If the object aimed at is to punish Kerr & Co. and cripple the *Review* for its advocacy of industrial unionism and for opposing pure and simple craftism, and for keeping open columns and exercising the right of free speech, then it will be found in due time that the uncalled-for investigation of the national committee and the uncomradely spirit which prompted it will have produced the opposite effect.

I cannot close without appealing for both the industrial and political solidarity of the workers.

I thoroughly believe in economic as well as political organization, in the industrial union and in the Socialist Party.

I am an industrial unionist because I am a Socialist and a Socialist because I am an industrial unionist.

I believe in making every effort within our power to promote industrial unionism among the workers and to have them all united in one economic organization. To accomplish this I would encourage industrial independent organization, especially among the millions who have not yet been organized at all, and I would also encourage the "boring from within" for all that can be accomplished by the industrial unionists in the craft unions.

I would have the Socialist Party recognize the historic necessity and inevitability of industrial unionism, and the industrial union reciprocally recognize the Socialist Party, and so declare in the respective preambles to their constitutions.

The Socialist Party cannot be neutral on the union question. It is compelled to declare itself by the logic of evolution, and as a revolutionary party it cannot commit itself to the principles of reactionary unionism. Not only must the Socialist Party declare itself in favor of economic unionism, but the kind of unionism which alone can complement the revolutionary action of the workers on the political field.

I am opposed under all circumstances to any party alliances or affiliations with reactionary trade unions and to compromising tactics of every kind and form, excepting alone in event of some extreme emergency. While the "game of politics," as it is understood and as it is played under capitalist rules, is as repugnant to me as it can possibly be to anyone, I am a thorough believer in political organization and political action.

Political power is essential to the workers in their struggle, and they can never emancipate themselves without developing and exercising that power in the interests of their class.

It is not merely in a perfunctory way that I advocate political action, but as one who has faith in proletarian political power and in the efficacy of political propaganda as an educational force in the Socialist movement. I believe in a constructive political program and in electing all the class-conscious workers we can, especially as mayors, judges, sheriffs and as members of the state legislatures and the national Congress.

The party is now growing rapidly and we are meeting with some of the trials which are in store for us and which will no doubt subject us to the severest tests. We need to have these trials, which are simply the fires in which we have to be tempered for the work before us.

There will be all kinds of extremists to deal with, but we have nothing to fear from them. Let them all have their day. The great body of the comrades, the rank and file, will not be misled by false teachings or deflected from the true course.

We must put forth all our efforts to control our swelling ranks by the use of wise tactics and to assimilate the accessions to our membership by means of sound education and party discipline.

The new year has opened auspiciously for us, and we have never been in such splendid condition on the eve of a national campaign. Let us all buckle on our armor and go forth determined to make this year mark an epoch in the social revolution of the United States.

20

THIS IS OUR YEAR

As usual, Debs did not attend the 1912 convention. In hard-fought struggle, the left wing won endorsement of industrial unionism by the delegates. The right wing won passage of an amendment to the party constitution (Article II, Section 6) providing expulsion for any member "who opposes political action or advocates crime, sabotage or other methods of violence as a weapon of the working class to aid in its emancipation."

The right wing also made a determined but unsuccessful attempt to substitute one of their tendency for Debs as the party's candidate in the presidential election that year.

Debs' views of the meaning of the convention's action and the next tasks of the party were printed in the July 1912 Review.

It is now thirty-seven years since I became active in the labor movement. These years have all been crowded with struggle, with defeat and disappointment, but there has never been an hour when there was any thought of surrender. Now at last the labors of all these years are coming to fruition. We have a real labor movement and its power was never so great, nor its promise so bright as it is today.

When we first began to organize the workers the em-

ploying class stamped out the unions with an iron heel.
Later they began to realize that the unions were bound to
come, and they then began to patronize them. They could
not crush them and so they resolved to control them in
their interests. We have passed through these stages of
union progress and have now reached a point where the
workers are organized and control their organization in
their own interests.

It is true that this work of organization is far from
complete, but it is also true that it is in a healthier and
more promising state than ever before since it was first
begun.

The workers now realize that they have got to *build
their organization themselves*, that it has got to be built
from the bottom up, and that it must include them all.
This knowledge had to come to them through painful
and costly experience, but they have it and it is of priceless value to them. In proportion as they have lost faith
in their former "leaders" they have acquired faith in themselves. And faith is what the workers now need most of
all, faith in each other, faith in the working class, and
faith in the coming triumph that is to rid the world of
wage slavery and usher in the full-orbed day of freedom
and social justice.

The late national convention of the Socialist Party did
more to renew and vitalize the faith of the organized workers in themselves and in the future than any similar gathering ever held in this country. The delegates met under
difficulties which threatened to divide if not disrupt the
party. There were those who freely predicted another split.
But the convention proved that it had the capacity to deal
wisely with the gravest questions which confronted it, and
that however great the differences might be, or how acute-
ly factional feeling might become, the genius of revolutionary solidarity was triumphant and henceforth the
workers were united for the great struggle and no power
on earth could ever tear them asunder.

The Indianapolis convention proved that the Socialists

are now united on a solid basis and there will never be another split in the Socialist Party in the United States.

On the whole the work of the convention was all that could be expected. All things considered there is reason for mutual congratulation among us all. Some things, doubtless, many of us would have had different. But they are of a minor nature. The spirit of the convention was perfectly revolutionary. There was never any danger of getting off the main track or of following after any of the many gods of opportunism. A very great majority of the delegates were red-blooded, clear-eyed, straight-out and uncompromising. The last thing they thought of, if they thought of it at all, was trimming or trading, or setting traps to catch votes.

There were some things, of course, I could wish had turned out otherwise. But I shall not point them out now further than to say that I would limit as few matters as possible to constitutional prohibition and reduce to the minimum the offenses punishable by expulsion from the party. I am opposed to anarchistic tactics and would have the party so declare itself on moral ground rather than oppose such tactics by prohibition and expulsion. I believe in the fullest freedom of speech and action consistent with the fundamental principles of our movement.

Following the Indianapolis convention and taking inspiration from its splendid example, the workers all over the country are going to get into closer touch, clearer understanding, and more harmonious cooperation, industrially and politically, than ever before. Let us do all in our power to encourage this tendency and to really unite the workers in the bonds of class solidarity for the revolutionary struggle and the overthrow of industrial slavery.

Let us make this our year! Let us make the numerals *1912* appear in flaming red in the calendar of this century!

We have had enough of controversial engagement to satisfy us all. Let differences of all kinds be subordinated to the demand for unity and concord, solidarity and victory. And let us make our acts conform to our words.

We all believe in industrial unity, and in political unity. Now let us join in a supreme endeavor to unite the workers in one great economic organization and one great political party. We need not be agreed over nonessentials. We are one fundamentally, our goal is the same, and while we may as individuals, or as groups, work at varying angles and according to our light and the means at our command, we need not clash, nor come in conflict with each other, nor resort to epithets and personal detraction, but on the contrary we can work to far better advantage and accomplish vastly more by preserving a unity of spirit and temper and keeping uppermost in mind the one great thing we are all working for and subordinating to this the ten thousand little things over which we are bound to be more or less divided.

We shall accomplish more in bending our energies getting together than we shall in columns of discussion as to how it is to be done. Let us get rid of our differences by engaging in the actual fight of the workers. At San Diego there are now no differences among Socialists or unionists, from the most revolutionary to the most reactionary of them. In the heat of actual conflict these differences we are so prone to magnify melt away and disappear.

Let us get into the fight as completely as we can and we shall solve the problem of industrial and political unity without any more vain and rancorous discussion about the precise lines along which it is to be done.

It does not matter whose fight it is, whether it be that of the I. W. W. or the A. F. of L., the S. P. or the S. L. P., if it is a working-class fight it is our fight, and if we all get into it we shall be united in it and emerge from it cemented together and triumphant.

Let us back up the workers who are waging such a splendid fight in San Diego, in Aberdeen and Gray's

Harbor; let us rally solidly to the support of Ettor and Giovannitti, the staunch industrial leaders, whose persecution by the mill owners is an outrage and whose imprisonment is a reproach to us all; let us resent the infamous sentence of Rudolph Katz and give united aid and encouragement to the strikers at Paterson; let us stand behind the striking pressmen at Chicago, against the scabs, union and otherwise, which have been pitted against them; let us give our support to the railroad workers who are on strike on the Harriman lines, to the striking motormen and conductors in Boston and to strikers everywhere, and before this year closes we will accomplish more in the way of building up a revolutionary industrial organization and a conquering working-class political party than the most sanguine and optimistic of us now imagine to be possible.

Let us all join in one supreme effort to get together this year; let bickering and strife be put aside and let the "dear love of comrades" prevail among us and bind our hearts together into one great heart that shall throb for the emancipation of all the workers of the world!

21

A PLEA FOR SOLIDARITY

Early in 1914 Debs felt that the objective basis existed for unifying the revolutionary movement—the two sections of the IWW, the industrial unionists in the IWW and the AFL, the socialists and the industrial unionists, and the Socialist Party and Socialist Labor Party.

His appeal for a realignment in the revolutionary movement based on a proletarian class struggle program was published in the March 1914 issue of the International Socialist Review. *Of particular interest is the analysis it contains of the strengths and weaknesses of the IWW.*

["Solidarity—a word we owe to the French Communists and which signifies a community in gain and loss, in honor and dishonor, a being (so to speak) all in the same bottom—is so convenient that it will be in vain to struggle against its reception."— *Trench.*]

To the foregoing Webster adds the following definition: "An entire union, or consolidation of interests and responsibilities; fellowship."

The future of labor, the destiny of the working class,

depends wholly upon its own solidarity. The extent to which this has been achieved or is lacking, determines the strength or weakness, the success or failure of the labor movement.

Solidarity, however, is not a matter of sentiment, but of fact, cold and impassive as the granite foundation of a skyscraper. If the basic elements, identity of interest, clarity of vision, honesty of intent, and oneness of purpose, or any of these is lacking, all sentimental pleas for solidarity and all efforts to achieve it will be alike barren of results.

The identity of interest is inherent in the capitalist system and the machine process, but the remaining elements essential to solidarity have to be developed in the struggle necessary to achieve it, and it is this struggle in which our unions and parties have been torn asunder and ourselves divided and pitted against each other in factional warfare so bitter and relentless as to destroy all hope of solidarity if the driving forces of capitalism did not operate to make it ultimately inevitable. This struggle has waxed with increasing bitterness and severity during the years since the I. W. W. came upon the scene to mark the advent of industrial unionism to supplant the failing craft unionism of a past age.

But there is reason to believe, as it appears to me, that, as it is "darkest just before the dawn," so the factional struggle for solidarity waxes fiercest just before its culmination. The storm of factional contention, in which diverse views and doctrines clashed and were subjected to the ordeal of fire, in which all the weapons of the revolution must be forged and tempered, has largely spent itself, and conditions which gave rise to these contentions have so changed, as was pointed out by the editor in the February *Review*, that unity of the revolutionary forces now seems near at hand.

Industrial unionism is now, theoretically at least, universally conceded. Even Gompers himself now acknowledges himself an industrial unionist. The logic of industrial development has settled that question and the dissension it gave rise to is practically ended.

For the purpose of this writing the proletariat and the working class are synonymous terms. I know of no essential distinction between skilled and unskilled salary and wage workers. They are all in the same economic class and in their aggregate constitute the proletariat or working class, and the hairsplitting attempts that are made to differentiate them in the class struggle give rise to endless lines of cleavage and are inimical if not fatal to solidarity.

Webster describes a proletaire as a "low person," "belonging to the commonalty; hence, mean, vile, vulgar." This is a sufficiently explicit definition of the proletaire by his bourgeois master which at the same time defines his status in capitalist society, and it applies to the entire working and producing class; hence the *lower class.*

Such distinction between industrial workers as still persists the machine is reducing steadily to narrower circles and will eventually blot out entirely.

It is now about a century since a few of the skilled and more intelligent workers in the United States began to dimly perceive their identity of interest, and to band themselves together for their mutual protection against the further encroachments of their employers and masters. From that time to this there has been continuous agitation among the workers, now open and pronounced and again under cover and in whispers, according to conditions and opportunities, but never has the ferment ceased and never can it cease until the whole mass has been raised to manhood's level by the leaven of solidarity.

The net result of a hundred years of agitation, education and unification, it must be confessed, is hardly calculated to inspire one with an excess of optimism and yet, to the keen observer, there is abundant cause for satisfaction with the past and for confidence in the future.

After a century of unceasing labors to organize the workers, about one in fourteen now belongs to a union.

To put it in another way, fourteen out of every fifteen who are eligible to membership are still outside of the labor movement. At the same relative rate of growth it would require several centuries more to organize a majority of the working class in the United States.

But there are sound reasons for believing that a new era of labor unionism is dawning and that in the near future organized labor is to come more rapidly to fruition and expand to proportions and develop power which will compensate in full measure for the slow and painful progress of the past and for all its keen disappointments and disastrous failures; and chief of these reasons is the disintegration and impending fall of reactionary craft unionism and the rise and spread of the revolutionary industrial movement.

Never has the trade union of the past given adequate recognition to the vast army of common laborers, and in its narrow and selfish indifference to these unorganized masses it has weakened its own foundations, played into the hands of its enemies, and finally sealed its own doom.

The great mass of common, unskilled labor, steadily augmented by the machine process, is the granite foundation of the working class and of the whole social fabric, and to ignore or slight this proletarian mass, or fail to recognize its essentially fundamental character, is to build without a foundation and rear a house of scantlings instead of a fortress of defense.

That the I. W. W. recognized this fundamental fact and directed its energies to the awakening and stimulation of the unskilled masses which had until then lain dormant, was the secret of its spread and power and likewise of the terror it inspired in the ruling class, and had it continued as it began, a revolutionary industrial union, recognizing the need of political as well as industrial action, instead of being hamstrung by its own leaders and converted, officially at least, into an antipolitical machine, it would today be the most formidable labor organization in America, if not the world. But the time has not yet come, seemingly, for the organic change from craft segregation to industrial solidarity. There must needs be further industrial evolution and still greater economic pressure brought to bear upon the workers in the struggle with their masters, to force them to disregard the dividing lines of their craft unions and make common cause with their fellow workers.

The inevitable split in the I. W. W. came and a bitter factional fight followed. The promising industrial organization was on the rocks. Industrial unionism, which had begun to spread in all directions, came almost to a halt. Fortunately about this time the mass strikes broke out, first in the steel and next in the textile industries. Thousands of unskilled and unorganized workers struck, and for a time both factions of the I. W. W. grew apace and waged the warfare against the mill bosses with an amazing display of power and resources. The important part taken by the Socialist Party and its press and speakers in raising funds for the strikers, giving publicity to the issues involved, creating a healthy public sentiment, bringing their political power to bear in forcing a congressional investigation and backing up the I. W. W. and the strikers in every possible way, had much to do with the progress made and the success achieved during this period.

The victory at Lawrence, one of the most decisive and far-reaching ever won by organized workers, triumphantly demonstrated the power and invincibility of industrial unity backed by political solidarity. Without the cooperation and support of the Socialist Party the Lawrence victory would have been impossible, as would also that at Schenectady which followed some time later.

For reasons which came to light after the Lawrence strike, this solidarity was undermined to a considerable extent when the Paterson strike came, and still more so when the Akron strike of the rubber workers followed, both resulting disastrously to the strikers. Both of these strikes were fought with marvelous loyalty and endurance and could and should have been won.

Now again followed the inevitable. The ranks of the I. W. W. were depleted as suddenly as they had filled up. What is there now left of it at McKee's Rocks, at Lawrence, at Paterson, at Akron in the east; or at Goldfield, Spokane, and San Diego in the west?

Of course the experience is not lost and if only the workers are wise enough to profit by its lessons it will be worth all its terrible cost to its thousands of victims.

These important events have been rapidly sketched for the reason that just now I am more interested in the future than in the past. The conditions under which the I. W. W. was organized almost a decade ago and which soon afterward disrupted its forces and gave rise to the bitter factional feud and the threatening complications which followed, have undergone such changes that now, unless all the signs of today are misleading, there is a solid economic foundation for the merging of the hitherto conflicting elements into a great industrial organization.

The essential basis of such organization must, as I believe, be the same as it was when the I. W. W. was first launched, and to which the Detroit faction of that body still adheres. This faction is cornerstoned in the true principle of unionism in reference to political action.

In the past the political party of the workers has been disrupted because of disagreement about the labor union and the labor union has been disrupted because of disagreement about the political party. It is that rock upon which we have been wrecked in the past and must steer clear of in the future.

Like causes produce like results. Opponents of political action split the I. W. W. and they will split any union that is not composed wholly of antipolitical actionists or in which they are not in a hopeless minority. I say this in no hostile spirit. They are entitled to their opinion the same as the rest of us.

At bottom all antipolitical actionists are to all intents anarchists, and anarchists and Socialists have never yet pulled together and probably never will.

Now the industrial organization that ignores or rejects

political action is as certain to fail as is the political party that ignores or rejects industrial action. Upon the mutually recognized unity and cooperation of the industrial and political powers of the working class will both the union and the party have to be built if real solidarity is to be achieved.

To deny the political equation is to fly in the face of past experience and invite a repetition of the disruption and disaster which have already wrecked the organized forces of industrialism.

The antipolitical unionist and the antiunion Socialist are alike illogical in their reasoning and unscientific in their economics. The one harbors the illusion that the capitalist state can be destroyed and its police powers, court injunctions and gatling guns — in short its political institutions — put out of business by letting politics alone, and the other that the industries can be taken over and operated by the workers without being industrially organized and that the Socialist republic can be created by a majority of votes and by political action alone.

It is beyond question, I think, that an overwhelming majority of industrial unionists favor independent political action and that an overwhelming majority of Socialists favor industrial unionism. Now it seems quite clear to me that these forces can and should be united and brought together in harmonious and effective economic and political cooperation.

There is no essential difference between the Chicago and Detroit factions of the I. W. W. except that relating to political action and if I am right in believing that a majority of the rank and file of the Chicago faction favor political action, then there is no reason why this majority should not consolidate with the Detroit faction and thus put an end to the division of these forces. This accomplished, a fresh start for industrial unionism would undoubtedly be made, and with competent organizers to go out into the field among the unorganized, the reunited I. W. W. would grow by leaps and bounds.

The rumblings of revolt in the A. F. of L. prove conclusively that the leaven of industrialism is also doing its work in the trade unions. The miners at their recent Indianapolis convention, in their scathing indictment of Gompers and his ossified "executive council," disclosed their true attitude toward the reactionary and impotent old federation. When Duncan MacDonald declared that Gompers and his official inner circle slaughtered every progressive measure and that the federation under their administration was reactionary to the core and boss-ridden and worse than useless, the indictment was confirmed by a roar of applause.

At the same convention Charles Moyer, president of the Western Federation of Miners, charged that if the strike of the copper miners in Michigan was lost the responsibility would rest upon Gompers and his "executive council." Gompers, notwithstanding this grave charge, left the convention without waiting to face Moyer. He had to catch a train. He remained long enough, however, to solemnly warn the delegates that the two-cent assessment asked for by the W. F. of M. to support the copper strikers would break up his powerful federation.

Almost eighteen years ago the W. F. of M. withdrew from the A. F. of L. in disgust because the financial support (?) it gave to the Leadville strikers did not amount to enough to cover the postage required to mail the appeal to the local unions. Today, when the W. F. of M. is again fighting for its life, the copper miners are told that a two-cent assessment to keep them and their families from starving would "bust" the Federation.

And this is the mighty American Federation of Labor, boasting a grand army of more than two million organized workers!

What has the A. F. of L., Gompers and his "executive council," done for the desperately struggling miners of Colorado and Michigan? Practically nothing.

Then why should the miners put up their scanty and hard-earned wages to support Gompers and the A. F. of L.?

The boasted power of this Civic Federationized, Militia of Christified body of reactionary craft union apostles of the Brotherhood of Capital and Labor turns to ashes always when the test comes, and a two-cent assessment, according to its national president, would kill it stone dead.

The United Mine Workers and the Western Federation of Miners, becoming more and more revolutionary in the desperate fight they are compelled to wage for their existence, are bound to merge soon into one great industrial organization, and the same forces that are driving them together will also drive them out of Gompers' federation of craft unions. There are other progressive unions in the A. F. of L. that will follow the secession of the miners and augment the forces of revolutionary unionism.

The consolidated miners and the reunited I. W. W. would draw to themselves all the trade unions with industrial tendencies, and thus would the reactionary federation of craft unions be transformed, from both within and without, into a revolutionary industrial organization.

On the political field there is no longer any valid reason why there should be more than one party. I believe that a majority of both the Socialist Party and the Socialist Labor Party would vote for consolidation, and I hope to see the initiative taken by the rank and file of both at an early day. The unification of the political forces would tend to clear the atmosphere and promote the unification of the forces of the industrial field.

This article is already longer than I intended, but before closing, I want to say that in my opinion, Section 6 of Article II ought to be stricken from the Socialist Party's constitution. I have not changed my opinion in regard to sabotage, but I am opposed to restricting free speech under any pretense whatsoever, and quite as decidedly opposed to our party seeking favor in bourgeois eyes by protesting that it does not countenance violence and is not a criminal organization.

I believe our party attitude toward sabotage is right,

and this attitude is reflected in its propaganda and need not be enforced by constitutional penalties of expulsion. If there is anything in sabotage we should know it, and free discussion will bring it out; if there is nothing in it we need not fear it, and even if it is lawless and hurtful, we are not called upon to penalize it any more than we are theft or any other crime.

The conditions of today, the tendency and the outlook are all that the most ardent Socialists and industrialists could desire, and if all who believe in a united party backed by a united union and a united union backed by a united party, will now put aside the prejudices created by past dissensions, sink all petty differences, strike hands in comradely concord, and get to work in real earnest, we shall soon have the foremost proletarian revolutionary movement in the world.

We need not only a new alignment and a better mutual understanding, but we need above all the real Socialist spirit, which expresses itself in boundless enthusiasm, energetic action, and the courage to dare and do all things in the service of the cause. We need to *be* comrades in all the term implies and to help and cheer and strengthen one another in the daily struggle. If the "love of comrades" is but a barren ideality in the Socialist movement, then there is no place for it in the heart of mankind.

I appeal to all Socialist comrades and all industrial unionists to join in harmonizing the various elements of the revolutionary movement and in establishing the economic and political solidarity of the workers. If this be done a glorious new era will dawn for the working class in the United States.

22

HOMESTEAD AND LUDLOW

On April 20, 1914, a tent-colony of striking miners and their families near Ludlow, Colorado, was raked with machine-gun fire and burned to the ground by militia in the service of the Rockefeller coal interests. Eleven children and two women died in the fire. Three strikers were taken prisoner by the militia and shot while unarmed and under custody.

Debs wrote this article in the International Socialist Review *of August 1914 for "those who have been shocked by Ludlow and are students of the system and of the struggle in which such atrocious crimes against the working class are possible."*

The twenty-two years which lie between Homestead and Ludlow embrace a series of bloody and historic battles in the class war in the United States.

The battle between the organized steel workers and the Carnegie-Pinkerton thugs which stirred the whole nation occurred on July 1, 1892; the Rockefeller massacre at Ludlow, which shocked the world, on April 20, 1914.

In recalling Homestead I have been struck by the similarity of methods employed there and at Ludlow to crush the strikers, and by some other features common to both that have suggested a review of Homestead in the light of

Ludlow, that we may the better understand their historic connection and at the same time see Ludlow in the light of Homestead.

As Ludlow is so recent and so vivid in the public memory and its horrors still so fresh in the minds of all, I need not review this appalling industrial massacre here, but will occupy the space in reviewing the essential facts about Homestead for the purpose of study and comparison.

Andrew Carnegie incarnated triumphant and despotic capitalism at Homestead in July, 1892, just as John D. Rockefeller did at Ludlow in April, 1914.

Carnegie, reducing the wages of the 4,000 employees in his steel mills from 15 to 40 percent, transforming his mills into forts, with 300 Pinkerton hirelings armed with Winchester rifles in command, fled to his castle in Scotland to escape the storm about to break. In vain was he appealed to by the whole country to cable the word that would end the bloody conflict, exactly as John D. Rockefeller, twenty-two years later, refused to utter the word that would have prevented the massacre at Ludlow.

That was and is Carnegie, who, with Rockefeller, is famed as a philanthropist, but whom history will pillory as cold-blooded murderers.

Homestead will haunt Carnegie and Ludlow will damn Rockefeller to the last hour of their lives and the memory of their basely murdered victims will load their names with infamy to the end of time.

It was in 1889, after he had become a plutocrat, that Carnegie began to write and preach about the "Gospel of Wealth," which was being exploited as oracular wisdom and as the quintessence of philanthropy by the grovelling and sycophantic capitalist press, purely because it was the gush and outpouring of a pompous plutocrat.

Carnegie deliberately plotted and prepared for the Homestead massacre, but was too cowardly to face it. He placed Henry C. Frick, then his lieutenant, in charge and then put the wide Atlantic between himself and Homestead before the fuse was lighted that set off the destructive battery.

At the time of this historic conflict I was editing the *Locomotive Firemen's Magazine* and I shall here reproduce from its columns what I had to say about this event at the time of its occurrence. I remember the intense excitement as if it had been but yesterday, but there was no class-conscious labor movement or press, such as we have today, to interpret Homestead in the light of the class struggle. I myself had not yet become a Socialist, although I was heart and soul with the steel workers, did all in my power to support them, and to that extent was alive to the nature of the struggle in which they were engaged.

The Amalgamated Association of Iron and Steel Workers, the most powerful union then in existence, was the union then involved and almost identically the same brutal method was employed to crush that organization that is now being employed to wipe out the United Mine Workers in Colorado.

Carnegie used an army of Pinkerton hirelings and Rockefeller an army of Baldwin-Feltz thugs. The only difference was that at Homestead, twenty-two years ago, the plutocrats had not yet learned how to murder pregnant women and roast babes to death in the exemplification of their "Gospel of Wealth."

The following, quoted from my article reviewing Homestead in the *Locomotive Firemen's Magazine* for August, 1892, will, I venture to believe, be of interest to those who have been shocked by Ludlow and are students of the system and of the struggle in which such atrocious crimes against the working class are possible:

"The 4,000 employees of Carnegie & Co., at Homestead, Pennsylvania, have been engaged for years in pouring capital into the lap of capital, content if they could build for themselves humble homes, obtain the necessities of life, rear their children as becomes American citizens, and save a few dollars for a rainy day, for sickness and old age, and secure for themselves a decent burial.

"By virtue of their brain and brawn, their skill and muscle, their fidelity to duty, Homestead grew in importance. It obtained a world-wide fame. The chief proprietor, Andrew Carnegie, a Scotchman by birth, an aristocrat by inclination, and a Christian with Christ omitted, waxed fat in wealth while the men toiled on. The works spread out, area expanded, buildings and machinery increased, night and day the forges blazed and roared, the anvils rang, wheels revolved, and still Carnegie grew in opulence. Taking his place among the millionaires of the world, he visits his native land and sensation follows sensation as he dazzles lords and ladies, dukes and dudes by the display of his wealth in highland and lowland.

"All the while 4,000 or more of the hardy sons of toil keep the machinery at Homestead in operation. The Monongahela is not more ceaseless in its flow than are Carnegie's workingmen in their devotion to his interests. Suddenly Carnegie, to use a phrase, 'gets religion,' and begins to blubber about the duty of rich men to the poor. He out-phariseed all the pharisees who made broad their phylacteries and made long prayers on the corners of the streets in Jerusalem that they might be seen of men, while they were 'devouring widows' houses' and binding burdens on the backs of men grievous to be borne, for Carnegie, bent on show and parade, seeking applause, ambitious of notoriety, concluded to bestow a portion of his plunder to build libraries bearing his name to perpetuate his fame.

"This Andrew Carnegie, in 1889, began to preach his 'Gospel of Wealth,' the purpose of which was to demonstrate that wealth creates 'rigid castes,' not unlike those that exist in India among the followers of the Brahmin religion, the Carnegies being the priests and the workingmen the pariahs, and this Brahminism of wealth being established, Carnegie, the author of the 'gospel,' lays back on his couch of down and silk and writes, this condition 'is best for the race because it insures the survival of the fittest.'

"Andrew Carnegie, who for a quarter of a century has coined the sweat and blood and the life of thousands into wealth until his fortune exceeds many times a million, proclaims 'that upon the sacredness of property civilization itself depends.' This Carnegie, a combination of flint and steel, plutocrat and pirate, Scotch terrier and English bulldog, rioting in religious rascality, attempts to show that he is animated by 'Christ's spirit,' and remembering that when Christ wanted 'tribute money' to satisfy Caesar, He told Peter to go to the sea and cast a hook, catch a fish and in its mouth the required funds would be found, Carnegie and his Phipps and Frick, wanting cash wherewith to pay tribute to Mammon, have cast hooks into the sea of labor and securing from 5,000 to 10,000 bites a day, have hauled in that number of workingmen and taken from their mouths such sums as their greed demanded wherewith to enlarge their fortunes and enable them with autocratic pomp and parade, to take the place of Jumbos in the procession.

"Under the influence of his 'Gospel of Wealth,' Carnegie, having prospered prodigiously, having millions at his command, concluded that the time had arrived for him to array himself in purple and parade before the people of Great Britain. He was ambitious of applause. He wanted to sit in an open carriage drawn by a half dozen spanking high steppers and hear the roar of the groundlings as the procession moved along the streets. In the United States Carnegie was not held in much higher esteem than

Robert Kidd as he sailed

Indeed, the freebooter never robbed as many men as Andrew Carnegie, though their methods were somewhat different. Kidd never wrote a 'Gospel of Wealth.' He never played the role of hypocrite. When he struck a rich prize on the high seas, captured the valuables, killed the crew and sunk the ship, he did not go ashore and bestow his booty to build a church or found a library; but, like Carnegie, he was influenced by a 'Gospel of Wealth,' which was to get all he could and live luxuriously while he lived and then, like the rich man spoken of in the New Testament, go to 'hell.'

"Kidd had heartless lieutenants, cold-blooded villains, but it is to be doubted if he had one equal to H. C. Frick, into whose hands Carnegie, when he left home for his triumphal march through Scotland, committed all power over the Homestead workingmen. The fellow Frick was not long in laying his plans to reduce the workingmen at Homestead to the condition of serfs.

"To do this wages must be reduced from 15 to 40 percent. Having less wages, the workingmen must have less of the necessities and comforts of life, they must be subjected to privations, must begin the downward road of degradation. Their homes must be darkened. Contentment must give way to unrest, harmony to discord. Regard for the employer must be transformed into hate, and the once smiling, joyous, happy Homestead be transformed into pandemonium.

"It is just here that Carnegie's 'Gospel of Wealth' has its practical application. The Carnegie steel works at Homestead employ, say, 4,000 men: that is the current estimate. The fellow Frick proposes to reduce the wages of these men from 15 to 40 percent, an average of 27.5 percent, and this reduction, whatever it may amount to, is sheer robbery, unadulterated villainy. It is an exhibition of the methods by which Christless capitalists rob labor, and this is done while the brazen pirates prate of religion and the 'Spirit of Christ'; who plunder labor that they may build churches, endow universities and found libraries. Is it required to say that hell is full of such blatherskites?

"But direct and immediate robbery on the part of these plutocratic pharisees is not the only purpose they have in view, nor, perhaps, the chief purpose. They have in view the abolition, the annihilation of labor organizations. This purpose, on the part of the fellow Frick, is now openly avowed. It was the Order of the Amalgamated Iron Workers that antagonized the reduction of wages from 15 to 40 percent. The men would not submit to robbery. They comprehended the intent of Carnegie's 'Gospel of Wealth.' They knew it to be a gospel of piracy rather than of peace. They saw Frick's operations to transform the Homestead steel works into a fort. They saw the murderous devices perfected to kill by electricity and scalding water. Carnegie's gospel was finding expression in numerous plans for wholesale murder. But the workingmen were not intimidated. They saw the shadows of coming events but their courage did not desert them. They themselves had built these steel works. From their toil had flowed a ceaseless stream of wealth into the coffers of Carnegie and his associates. Around these works they had built their cottages and had hoped to live in them the remainder of their days. They made no unusual demand for wages. It was the same old 'scale.' There was no good reason for its change. Still they were willing to concede something to the greedy capitalists. They were willing to make some concession in the interest of peace. Having done this they resolved to stand by their rights and to resist oppression and degradation.

"What is the plea of Frick? By virtue of the capital these workingmen have created Carnegie had been able to introduce new machinery, whereby it was claimed the men could make better wages, and it was resolved that the men should not be the beneficiaries of the improved machinery; only Carnegie & Co. should pocket the proceeds. Such was the teaching of the 'Gospel of Wealth.' The pariahs were to remain pariahs forever.

"The day of the lockout came, July 1, 1892. The steel works at Homestead were as silent as a cemetery. The workingmen were remanded to idleness. Their offense was that they wanted fair wages—the old scale—and that they were members of a powerful labor organization, created to resist degradation.

"Between July 1 and the morning of July 6, unrest was universal; excitement increased with every pulsebeat. The workingmen had charge of Homestead. Frick was in exile, but he was not quiet. He wanted possession of the steel works. His purpose was to introduce scabs, to man Fort Frick; to get his dynamos to work and send streams of electricity along his barbed wires, to touch which was death. He wanted to have seas of hot water to be sent on its scalding, death-dealing mission if a discharged workingman approached the works. He wanted the muzzle of a Winchester rifle at every porthole in the fence, and behind it a thug to send a quieting bullet through the head or the heart of any man who deemed it prudent to resist oppression.

"What was the scheme? To introduce Pinkerton thugs armed with Winchester rifles, a motley gang of vagabonds mustered from the slums of the great cities: pimps and parasites, outcasts, abandoned wretches of every grade; a class of characterless cutthroats who murder for hire; creatures in the form of humans but as heartless as stones. Frick's reliance was upon an army of Christless whelps to carry into effect Carnegie's 'Gospel of Wealth.'

"Oh, men, who wear the badge of labor! Now is the time for you in fancy at least to go to Homestead. You need to take in the picture of this little town on the bank of the Monongahela. You peer through the morning mists and behold the Frick flotilla approaching, bearing to the landing 300 armed Pinkertons, each thug with a Winchester and all necessary ammunition to murder Homestead workingmen. The plot of Frick was hellish from its inception. There is nothing to parallel it in conflicts labor has had since Noah built his ark. No man with a heart in him can contemplate Frick's scheme without a shudder.

"The alarm had been sounded. The Homestead workingmen were on the alert. They were the 'minute men' such as resisted the British troops at Concord and Lexington in 1775. The crisis had come. Nearer and nearer approached Frick's thugs. Four thousand workingmen are on guard. Now, for Carnegie's 'Gospel of Wealth.' In quick succession rifle reports ring out from the 'Model Barges' and workingmen bite the dust. Homestead is now something more than the seat of the Carnegie steel works. It is a battlefield, and from Thermopylae to Waterloo, from Concord to Yorktown, from Bull's Run to Appomattox there is not one which to workingmen is so fraught with serious significance.

"Amidst fire and smoke, blood and dying groans, the workingmen stood their ground with Spartan courage. It was shot for shot, and the battle continued until Frick's thugs surrendered and left the workingmen at Homestead masters of the field. A number of the thugs were killed, others were wounded and the remainder, demoralized, were glad to surrender and return to the slums from which they were hired by Frick.

"Rid of the gang of mercenary murderers, the workingmen proceeded to bury their dead comrades, the gallant men who preferred death to degradation, and who are as deserving of monuments as was ever a soldier who died in defense of country, flag or home. Of these, there were ten who were killed outright on the morning of the battle.

"The fiend Frick, of coke region infamy, is the man directly responsible for the Homestead tragedies, and the blood of the murdered men are blotches upon his soul, which the fires of hell will only make more distinct, and still this monster simply represents a class of Christless capitalists who are now engaged in degrading workingmen for the purpose of filching from them a portion of their earnings that they may roll in the luxuries which wealth purchases.

"Carnegie wires from his triumphal march through Scotland that he has no word of advice to give, and constitutes Frick the Nero of Homestead, consenting thereby to the employment of Pinkertons to murder his old and trusted employees.

"It would be easy to reproduce here the arguments pro and con, showing the underlying causes which led to the murder of workingmen at Homestead. But we do not care to introduce them here, except in so far as the fact is brought out that the country has a class of capitalists who conduct vast industrial enterprises and who, not content with honest dividends upon honest investments, are ceaselessly seeking to rob labor of its legitimate rewards, and the better to accomplish their nefarious designs are determined to break up, if possible, labor organizations, the one barrier that keeps them from accomplishing their purpose.

"The Homestead slaughter of workingmen must serve to remind the armies of labor of what is in store for them if the Carnegies, the Phippses and the Fricks can, by the aid of Pinkertons, come out victorious.

It occurs to us that the Homestead tragedies will serve to bind labor organizations in closer union. If not, then the blood of workingmen, as it calls from the ground, exhorting the living to emulate the courage of the men who fell at Homestead, might as well call upon a herd of 'dumb, driven cattle.'

"Ralph Waldo Emerson wrote of the first shot at Concord and Lexington on the 20th of April, 1775, as 'The Shot Heard Round the World.' The first shot of the Pinkertons at Homestead has been heard around the world, and its reverberations ought to continue until the statutes of all the states make the employment of Pinkerton thugs murder in the first degree.

"It required Lexington, Concord and Bunker Hill to arouse the colonies to resistance, and the battle of Homestead should serve to arouse every workingman in America to a sense of the dangers which surround them."

It will be seen by the foregoing, written twenty-two years ago, that there is much in Homestead to remind us of

Ludlow and much in both to emphasize the absolute necessity for the economic and political solidarity of the working class.

It is interesting to note that Lexington and Ludlow occurred on the same day. The shot that was "heard around the world" and was the signal for the American political revolution was fired on April 20, 1775, and 139 years later, to a day, on April 20, 1914, the shot was fired that made Ludlow more historic than Lexington and that will prove, as we believe, the signal for the American industrial revolution.

There is much more in the way of striking analogy between Homestead and Ludlow that appeals for comment, but space forbids further review at this time.

Homestead, although finally lost, put an end to Pinkertonism as it was known twenty-two years ago and Ludlow, before it is over, will put an end not only to government by gunmen and assassination, but to the infamous system under which these hideous crimes against the working class have been perpetrated.

23

THE GUNMEN AND THE MINERS

Debs did not limit himself to explaining Homestead and Ludlow as part of "a series of bloody and historic battles in the class war in the United States." He intervened in the struggles. He advocated armed struggle in self-defense by the working class.

In this article in the Review *of September 1914 he called on the miners' unions to create a Gunmen Defense Fund to arm their members with the latest high-powered rifles and machine guns equal to the equipment of the private armies of the corporations.*

As a matter of fact, the embattled miners were already defending themselves with weapons and Debs was arming them ideologically.

The time has come for the United Mine Workers and the Western Federation of Miners to levy a special monthly assessment to create a Gunmen Defense Fund.

This fund should be sufficient to provide each member with the latest high-power rifle, the same as used by the corporation gunmen, and 500 rounds of cartridges.

In addition to this every district should purchase and equip and man enough Gatling and machine guns to match the equipment of Rockefeller's private army of assassins.

This suggestion is made advisedly and I hold myself responsible for every word of it.

If the corporations have the right to recruit and maintain private armies of thieves, thugs and ex-convicts to murder striking workingmen, sack their homes, insult their wives, and roast their babes, then labor unions not only have the right but it is their solemn duty to arm themselves to resist these lawless attacks and defend their homes and loved ones.

To the miners especially do these words apply, and to them in particular is this message addressed.

Paint Creek, Calumet and Ludlow are of recent occurrence.

You miners have been forced out on strike, and you have been made the victims of every conceivable method of persecution.

You have been robbed, insulted and treated with contempt; you have seen your wives and babes murdered in cold blood before your eyes.

You have been thrown into foul dungeons where you have lain for months for daring to voice your protest against these cruel outrages, and many of you are now cold in death with the gaping bullet wounds in your bodies to bear mute testimony to the efficacy of government by gunmen as set up in the mining camps by the master class during the last few years.

Under government by gunmen you are literally shorn of the last vestige of liberty and you have absolutely no protection under the law. When you go out on strike, your master has his court issue the injunction that strips you of your power to resist his injustice, and then has his private army of gunmen invade your camp, open fire on your habitations and harass you and your families until the strike is broken and you are starved back into the pits on your master's terms. This has happened over and over again in all the mining states of this union.

Now the private army of gunmen which has been used

to break your strikes is an absolutely lawless aggregation.

If you miners were to arm a gang of thugs and assassins with machine guns and repeating rifles and order them to march on the palatial residences of the Rockefellers, riddle them with bullets, and murder the inmates in cold blood, not sparing even the babes, if there happened to be any, how long would it be before your officials would be in jail and your unions throttled and put out of business by the law?

The Rockefellers have not one particle more lawful right to maintain a private army to murder you union men than you union men would have to maintain a private army to murder the Rockefellers.

And yet the law does not interfere with the Rockefellers when they set up government by gunmen, and have their private army of man-killers swoop down on a mining camp, turn loose their machine guns, kill without mercy, and leave death, agony and desolation in their wake, and therefore it becomes your solemn duty to arm yourselves in defense of your homes and in driving out these invading assassins, and putting an end to government by gunmen in the United States.

In a word, the protection the government owes you and fails to provide, you are morally bound to provide for yourselves.

You have the unquestioned right, under the law, to defend your life and to protect the sanctity of your fireside. Failing in either, you are a coward and a craven and undeserving of the name of man.

If a thief or thug attacks you or your wife or child and threatens to take your life, you have a lawful right to defend yourself and your loved ones, even to the extent of slaying the assailant. This right is quite as valid and unimpaired — in fact it is even more inviolate — if the attack is made by a dozen or a hundred, instead of only one.

Rockefeller's gunmen are simply murderers at large, and you have the same right to kill them when they attack you that you have to kill the burglar who breaks into your house at midnight or the highwayman who holds you up at the point of his pistol.

Rockefeller's hired assassins have no lawful right that you miners are bound to respect. They are professional man-killers, the lowest and vilest on earth. They hire out to break your strike, shoot up your home and kill you, and you should have no more compunction in killing them than if they were so many mad dogs or rattlesnakes that menaced your homes and your community.

Recollect that in arming yourselves, as you are bound to do unless you are willing to be forced into abject slavery, you are safely within the spirit and letter of the law.

The Constitution of the United States guarantees to you the right to bear arms, as it does to every other citizen, but there is not a word in this instrument, nor in any United States statute, state law, or city ordinance, that authorizes the existence of a private army for purposes of cold-blooded murder and assassination.

"Mine guard" is simply a master-class term for a working-class assassin.

Let the United Mine Workers and the Western Federation of Miners take note that a private army of gunmen is simply a gang of outlaws and butchers and that:

they have not a solitary right an honest workingman is bound to respect!

Let these unions and all other organized bodies of workers that are militant and not subservient to the masters, declare war to the knife on these lawless and criminal hordes and swear relentless hostility to government by gunmen in the United States.

Murderers are no less murderers because they are hired by capitalists to kill workingmen than if they were hired by workingmen to kill capitalists.

Mine guards, so-called, are murderers pure and simple, and are to be dealt with accordingly. The fact that they are in uniform, as in Colorado, makes them even more loathsome and repulsive than the common reptilian breed.

A "mine guard" in the uniform of a state militiaman is

a copperhead in the skin of a rattlesnake, and possibly only because an even deadlier serpent has wriggled his slimy way into the executive chair of the state.

It remains only to be said that we stand for peace, and that we are unalterably opposed to violence and bloodshed if by any possible means, short of absolute degradation and self-abasement, these can be prevented. We believe in law, the law that applies equally to all and is impartially administered, and we prefer reason infinitely to brute force.

But when the law fails, and in fact, becomes the bulwark of crime and oppression, then an appeal to force is not only morally justified, but becomes a patriotic duty.

The Declaration of Independence proclaims this truth in words that burn with the patriotic fervor the revolutionary fathers must have felt when they rose in revolt against the red-coated gunmen of King George and resolved to shoot king rule out of existence.

Wendell Phillips declared that it was the glory of honest men to trample bad laws under foot with contempt, and it is equally their glory to protect themselves in their lawful rights when those who rule the law fail to give them such protection.

Let the unions, therefore, arm their members against the gunmen of the corporations, the gangs of criminals, cutthroats, women-ravishers and baby-burners that have absolutely no lawful right to existence!

Let organized labor, from one end of the country to the other, declare war on these privately licensed assassins, and let the slogan of every union man in the land be

Down with Government by Gunmen and Assassination in the United States!

24

THE PROSPECT FOR PEACE

Debs was a consistent socialist opponent of capitalist war. In the Appeal to Reason *of September 11, 1915, he had written:*

"I am not a capitalist soldier; I am a proletarian revolutionist . . . I am opposed to every war but one; I am for that war with heart and soul, and that is the worldwide war of the social revolution. In that war I am prepared to fight in any way the ruling class may make necessary, even to the barricades. That is where I stand and where I believe the Socialist Party stands, or ought to stand, on the question of war."

As the leading American socialist and a participant in the antiwar movement opposed to U. S. involvement in the war in Europe, he was asked by the Scripps League of 117 newspapers to express his opinion on the prospect for peace. His answer was this article, reprinted in the American Socialist *of February 19, 1916.*

There is no doubt that the belligerent nations of Europe are all heartily sick of war and that they would all welcome peace even if they could not dictate all its terms.

But it should not be overlooked that this frightful upheaval is but a symptom of the international readjustment which the underlying economic forces are bringing about, as well as of the fundamental changes which are being wrought in our industrial and political institutions. Still, every war must end and so must this. The destruction of both life and property has been so appalling during the eighteen months that the war has been waged that we may well conclude that the fury of the conflict is largely spent and that, with bankruptcy and ruin such as the world never beheld staring them in the face, the lords of capitalist misrule are about ready to sue for peace.

From the point of view of the working class, the chief sufferers in this as in every war, the most promising indication of peace is the international conference recently held in Zimmerwald, Switzerland, attended by representatives of all European neutral nations and some of the belligerent powers. This conference, consisting wholly of representatives of the working class, issued a ringing manifesto in favor of international reorganization on a permanent and uncompromising antiwar basis and of putting forth all possible efforts to end the bloody conflict which for a year and a half has shocked Christendom and outraged the civilization of the world.

The manifesto above referred to has been received with enthusiasm by the workers of all of the belligerent nations and the sentiment in favor of its acceptance and of the program of procedure it lays down is spreading rapidly in labor circles in the nations at war as well as in those at peace.

It would no doubt do much to clear the situation and expedite peace overtures if a decisive battle were fought and the indications are that such a battle, or series of battles, will be fought between now and spring. But the opportune moment for pressing peace negotiations can be determined only by the logic of events and when this comes the people of the United States should be ready to help in every way in their power to terminate this unholy massacre and bring peace to the world.

As to the terms upon which peace is to be restored these will no doubt be determined mainly by the status of the several belligerent powers when the war is ended. A program of disarmament looking to the prevention of another such catastrophe would seem to be suggested by the present heartbreaking situation but as experience has demonstrated that capitalist nations have no honor and that the most solemn treaty is but a "scrap of paper" in their mad rivalry for conquest and plunder, such a program, even if adopted, might prove abortive and barren of results.

The matter of the conquered provinces will no doubt figure largely in the peace negotiations and the only way to settle that in accordance with the higher principles of civilized nations is to allow the people of each province in dispute to decide for themselves by popular vote what nation they desire to be annexed to, or to remain, if they prefer, independent sovereignties.

Permanent peace, however, peace based upon social justice, will never prevail until national industrial despotism has been supplanted by international industrial democracy. The end of profit and plunder among nations will also mean the end of war and the dawning of the era of "Peace on Earth and Good Will among Men."

25

LETTER OF ACCEPTANCE

In 1916 Debs was 60 years old and had been in poor health for some time. He had asked his comrades not to nominate him to head the Socialist Party election campaign that year. But when he was drafted to serve as the candidate of the Socialist Party for Congress from the Fifth District of Indiana, he accepted the assignment and proceeded with a local campaign against the war and U. S. preparation for involvement that held the attention and won the support of socialists throughout the world.

His letter of acceptance of the nomination was published in the American Socialist *of April 2, 1916.*

By the unanimous voice of my comrades I have been chosen as the candidate of the Socialist Party for Congress for the Fifth District of Indiana.

When I first became a Socialist and a member of the party it was with the determination to serve the cause with such zeal and ardor as to consume all selfish desire, and to avoid even the appearance of self-seeking by declining to be a candidate for any public office. Later there came a time when I was made to realize that my comrades had an equal voice with myself in deciding such matters and that their collective will was the supreme law by which the party was governed. I was nominated for office notwithstanding my protest; and I could not have refused to serve under the circumstances without disregarding my obligation to my comrades and forfeiting my allegiance to the party.

This year I had hoped for immunity and asked the comrades in advance of their convention to place some other candidate in nomination. They did not agree with me but chose me as their candidate by acclamation, and I now accept their decision and shall stand as their candidate in the present campaign, and serve the party and the cause with all the strength and ability at my command.

I do not deem that any personal honor has been conferred upon me by this nomination. The Socialist Party could not nominate one of its members for a high public office to honor him personally without discrediting itself. I have simply been commanded by the party to perform a certain duty in the interest of the party and the cause it represents, and whatever of honor or dishonor may ensue will depend entirely upon the fidelity with which that duty is discharged and will be shared by the entire party.

The Socialist Party will be the only party which follows in the wake of economic exploitation.

The Socialist Party recognizes the fact that there is nothing in common between the exploiting and exploited classes; that there is in truth a conflict between them old as the centuries and that this conflict must continue with ever-increasing education and organization on the part of the working class until they have developed the power, economic, political and otherwise, to abolish the prevailing system and establish the world-wide industrial democracy and commonwealth of comrades.

The Socialist Party voices with unrelaxing devotion to its ideals and unconquerable faith in its mission the interests, hopes and aspirations of the toiling and producing millions and their sympathizers; it is their party, sprung from their loins and consecrated to their cause, and it stands uncompromisingly for their education, their organization, and their emancipation. It appeals to all workers to unite industrially and politically, recognize their common kinship, and make common cause in the great struggle to overthrow the system that robs and degrades them and win the world for democracy and peace, for freedom and self-government. It knows no race or nationality; no creed, no color, no sex. It stands loyally, unflinchingly for equal rights, equal freedom, and equal opportunity for all.

The mission of the Socialist Party is to destroy industrial despotism and establish industrial democracy; to abolish class rule and inaugurate true freedom and self-government; wipe out rent, interest and profit and produce wealth for the use of all instead of for the benefit of the few; stop producing parasites and paupers; grant to women all the rights that men have; liberate the children from the slave pens in which they are dwarfed, diseased and deformed; proclaim the emancipation of the toiling masses, and make the world fit for human beings to live in. All other parties stand for the present system, for wage slavery, poverty, unemployment and the whole brood of social ills.

The terrible war now raging in Europe which has transformed nation after nation boasting of their civilization and Christianity into hideous slaughterhouses, where millions of our brothers have turned brutes and been shot like dogs; where king and kaiser and czar rule and bureaucracy and aristocracy and plutocracy, all rotten to the core and buttressed by dead men's bones are supreme; where honest toilers are fit only to slave in peace and die in war for the profit and glory of the parasites who hold the title deeds to their so-called "Fatherland"; where the lamentations of widows are borne on every breeze, where orphaned children by thousands are dying like insects, where there is wreck and ruin, desolation, agony, curses, misery — horrors untold and untellable — all crying to heaven in the name of God who has been denied and blasphemed and in the name of humanity that has been betrayed and slaughtered, insulted, sold, spat upon, and crushed beneath the iron hoof of triumphant militarism — these appalling, indescribable atrocities, made ghastlier by the shriek and glare of the midnight bomb, typify our vaunted civilization and place international capitalism, supported by every political party save the Socialist Party alone, on exhibition before the world — a lurid scene of crime and horror to be chronicled by history and handed down to remotest generations.

And this is the true meaning of "preparedness" for which the ruling class, its press, its pulpit, its college professors and its menial hirelings and mercenaries in general are now clamoring in the United States.

Preparedness is one of the cardinal principles of the Socialist Party but it is diametrically opposed to the preparedness advocated by the organs of predatory, plundering capitalism.

The preparedness that the Socialist Party stands for is for the education and organization of the working class, for universal democracy, for mutual interests and good will among men, for the prosperity and peace of all — for a free people and a happy world.

26

THE IWW BOGEY

With the declaration of war by the United States on April 6, 1917, all stops were removed in the campaign to crush the opposition on the home front. All the legal and extra-legal agencies of the Establishment were unleashed for a wave of atrocities against pacifists, socialists and militant unionists.

Debs wrote this article in the February 1918 International Socialist Review *calling for solidarity in defense of the IWW against the most concentrated government attack.*

The morning paper I have just read contains an extended press dispatch from Washington, under screaming head-lines, making the startling disclosure that a world-wide conspiracy to overthrow the existing social order has been unearthed by the secret service agents of the government. The basis of the conspiracy is reported to have been the discovery of some guns and ammunition in the hold of a Russian freighter just arrived at a Pacific port in charge of a Bolsheviki crew, from which it has been deduced that the guns must have been sent by the Russian revolution-ists to the I. W. W. of the United States in pursuance of a conspiracy of the Russian reds, the Sinn Fein leaders of

Ireland, and the American I. W. W.s to overthrow all the governments of the civilized world.

This is really too much!

We are not told how the Sinn Feiners happen to get in on this universal conspiracy, but as their name, like that of the Bolsheviki and the I. W. W., has great potency as a bogey to frighten the feebleminded, the inventors of this wonderful cock-and-bull story may well be allowed this additional license to their perfervid imagination.

Everything that happens nowadays that the ruling classes do not like and everything that does not happen that they do like is laid at the door of the I. W. W. Its name is anathema wherever capitalism wields the lash and drains the veins of its exploited victims.

It is a wonderful compliment! Is the working class wise to its significance? Unfortunately not or the leaders and moving spirits of this persecuted industrial organization would not now be in jail waiting month after month to be tried for criminal offenses charged against them which they never dreamed of committing.

I think I may claim to be fairly well informed as to the methods and tactics of the I. W. W. — with some of which I am not at all in agreement — and I have no hesitancy in branding the sweeping criminal charges made against them since the war was declared as utterly false and malicious and without so much as a shadow of foundation in fact.

Repeatedly the sensational charge has been spread broadcast through the capitalist press that the I. W. W. were in conspiracy to blow up the mills and factories in the East, to burn the crops and destroy the orchards in the West, poison the springs and wells in the North, paralyze the cotton and rice industries in the South, and spread ruin and desolation everywhere for the profit and glory of the crazy Teuton Kaiser and his atrocious junker plunderbund and the overthrow of democracy and freedom in the United States.

Was a more stupendous lie or a more stupid one ever hatched in a human brain?

Look at the I. W. W. and then at the government and the more than one hundred million people of the United States! Is the lie not apparent on the very face of this absurd and malicious charge? Would any but an idiot or madman ever dream of the slaughter and destruction of an entire nation by a comparative handful of its population? Would any but a fool be deceived by such glaringly self-evident lies and calumnies?

Oh, the ghastly joke of it all! And the stark tragedy, too, when one thinks of the many simple-minded people whose attitude of fierce hostility toward the I. W. W. and its leaders is determined by these inspired fabrications!

Why should the I. W. W., organized for the very purpose of destroying despotism and establishing democracy, go across seas to lend its aid to the most brutal autocracy on the face of the earth?

Ah, but the autocracy within our own borders know how to play upon the prejudice and credulity of the unthinking and turn them against the men who at the peril of their freedom and their very lives are battling for the liberation of the people!

It is from Wall Street, the money center of the American plutocracy, that the campaign of falsehood and slander against the I. W. W. is directed; from there that the orders are issued to raid its national and state offices, jail its leaders, break up its meetings, and tar and feather and lacerate with whips and finally lynch and assassinate its speakers and organizers.

Wall Street mortally fears the I. W. W. and its growing menace to capitalist autocracy and misrule. The very name of the I. W. W. strikes terror to Wall Street's craven soul.

But Wall Street does not fear Sammy Gompers and the A. F. of L.

Every plutocrat, every profiteering pirate, every food vulture, every exploiter of labor, every robber and oppressor of the poor, every hog under a silk tie, every vampire in human form, will tell you that the A. F. of L. under Gompers is a great and patriotic organization and that the I. W. W. under Haywood is a gang of traitors in the pay of the bloody Kaiser.

Which of these, think you, Mr. Wage Slave, is your friend and the friend of your class?

It is interesting to note that at the very time the plutocracy and its hirelings are charging the I. W. W. with treason and cramming the jails with its members they are also driving union labor out into the desert to perish under armed vigilantes as at Bisbee and Bingham, while in the same hour their Supreme Court outlaws picketing and legalizes and protects strike-breaking as in the cases of the union miners in West Virginia and the southwestern states.

There is one thing in this situation that is clear to every union man, to every sympathizer with the working class, and every believer in justice and fair play, and that is that the hundreds of I. W. W.s and Socialists now in jail are entitled to be fairly tried. Upon that question there can be no difference among decent men, whatever may be their attitude toward the union and its principles. The Socialist Party, through its national executive committee — to its supreme credit — has taken this position and in a ringing declaration and appeal has expressed its determination that the accused I. W. W. leaders and members receive a fair trial and a square deal.

To this end money will be needed, all that can be raised, and as the Captain Kidd Kaiser and his pirate crew of junkers have not yet come across with that cargo of gold covering the purchase price of the I. W. W., it becomes the duty of every one who is with us to forthwith send his contribution to the defense of our shamelessly persecuted comrades.

This is our fight! We of the working class are all vitally interested in the outcome.

The war within the war and beyond the war in which

the I. W. W. is fighting—the war of the workers of all countries against the exploiters of all countries—is our war, the war of humanity against its oppressors and despoilers, the holiest war ever waged since the race began.

Let there be no mistake. The guerrilla warfare of Wall Street is not against the I. W. W. alone but against the labor movement in general except insofar as union labor suffers itself to be emasculated and crawls on its belly at the feet of its despotic masters.

A spineless and apologetic union bearing the official seal of the Civic Federation is the noblest specimen of working-class patriotism in the eyes of our Wall Street rulers.

Now is the time to meet the attack; to resist the assault; to turn the guns on the real conspirators. The inevitable reaction will swiftly follow and instead of smashing the revolutionary labor movement this dastardly conspiracy will prove the making of it.

Now is the time for the fighting union men of America to stand together. The situation is the grimmest that ever confronted the working class but every such crisis bears with it the golden opportunity to the workers to strike the decisive blow and to forge ahead to a higher level of life. To take advantage of this supreme opportunity and profit by it to the limit, the workers must be united and act together like a well-disciplined army.

Solidarity must be the watchword!

As we stand upon the threshold of the year 1918 let us resolve to make it the most luminous one in the annals of proletarian achievement.

Industrial unity and political unity, the revolutionary solidarity of the working class, will give us the power to conquer capitalism and emancipate the workers of the world.

27

THE CANTON, OHIO, SPEECH

Of the thousands of speeches Eugene V. Debs gave in his lifetime, this one is the most famous for a number of reasons. It was a socialist antiwar speech at a public meeting when the United States was at war with Germany. It was given at a time when many Socialists and IWW members had been persecuted and jailed for their opposition to the war and others were discouraged and demoralized by the public defection of prominent American Socialists and all the European Socialist parties except the Bolsheviks.

It expressed solidarity with Lenin and Trotsky, the leaders of the Russian Revolution, who had unilaterally made peace with Germany when their appeal for an international peace conference was rejected. It reaffirmed Debs' revolutionary socialist internationalism.

Finally, it was the speech for which he was sentenced to ten years in prison.

Debs delivered this speech Sunday afternoon, June 16, 1918, at the state convention of the Socialist Party of Ohio held at Nimisilla Park, Canton, to a crowd of 1,200 persons. He came to the park directly from the Stark County Jail nearby, where he had visited three Cleveland Socialists, Charles E. Ruthenberg, Alfred Wagenknecht and Charles Baker, imprisoned for their opposition to the war.

The speech published here was recorded by a govern-

ment stenographer in the crowd and was submitted in evidence by the prosecution.

Comrades, friends and fellow workers, for this very cordial greeting, this very hearty reception, I thank you all with the fullest appreciation of your interest in and your devotion to the cause for which I am to speak to you this afternoon. [*Applause.*]

To speak for labor; to plead the cause of the men and women and children who toil; to serve the working class, has always been to me a high privilege [*applause*]; a duty of love.

I have just returned from a visit over yonder [*pointing to the workhouse*] [*laughter*], where three of our most loyal comrades [*applause*] are paying the penalty for their devotion to the cause of the working class. [*Applause.*] They have come to realize, as many of us have, that it is extremely dangerous to exercise the constitutional right of free speech in a country fighting to make democracy safe in the world. [*Applause.*]

I realize that, in speaking to you this afternoon, there are certain limitations placed upon the right of free speech. I must be exceedingly careful, prudent, as to what I say, and even more careful and prudent as to how I say it. [*Laughter.*] I may not be able to say all I think [*Laughter and applause*]; but I am not going to say anything that I do not think. [*Applause.*] I would rather a thousand times be a free soul in jail than to be a sycophant and coward in the streets. [*Applause and shouts.*] They may put those boys in jail — and some of the rest of us in jail — but they can not put the Socialist movement in jail. [*Applause and shouts.*] Those prison bars separate their bodies from ours, but their souls are here this afternoon. [*Applause and cheers.*] They are simply paying the penalty that all men have paid in all the ages of history for standing erect, and for seeking to pave the way to better conditions for mankind. [*Applause.*]

If it had not been for the men and women who, in the past, have had the moral courage to go to jail, we would still be in the jungles. [*Applause.*]

This assemblage is exceedingly good to look upon. I wish it were possible for me to give you what you are giving me this afternoon. [*Laughter.*] What I say here amounts to but little; what I see here is exceedingly important. [*Applause.*] You workers in Ohio, enlisted in the greatest cause ever organized in the interest of your class, are making history today in the face of threatening opposition of all kinds — history that is going to be read with profound interest by coming generations. [*Applause.*]

There is but one thing you have to be concerned about, and that is that you keep foursquare with the principles of the international Socialist movement. [*Applause.*] It is only when you begin to compromise that trouble begins. [*Applause.*] So far as I am concerned, it does not matter what others may say, or think, or do, as long as I am sure that I am right with myself and the cause. [*Applause.*] There are so many who seek refuge in the popular side of a great question. As a Socialist, I have long since learned how to stand alone. [*Applause.*]

For the last month I have been traveling over the Hoosier State; and, let me say to you that, in all my connection with the Socialist movement, I have never seen such meetings, such enthusiasm, such unity of purpose; never have I seen such a promising outlook as there is today, notwithstanding the statement published repeatedly that our leaders have deserted us. [*Laughter.*] Well, for myself, I never had much faith in leaders. [*Applause and laughter.*] I am willing to be charged with almost anything, rather than to be charged with being a leader. I am suspicious of leaders, and especially of the intellectual variety. [*Applause.*] Give me the rank and file every day in the week. If you go to the city of Washington, and you examine the pages of the Congressional Directory, you will find that almost all of those corporation lawyers and cowardly politicians, members of Congress, and misrepresentatives of the masses — you will find that almost all of them claim, in glowing terms, that they have risen from the ranks to places of eminence and distinction. I am very glad I cannot make that claim for myself. [*Laughter.*] I would be ashamed to admit that I had risen from the ranks. When I rise it will be with the ranks, and not from the ranks. [*Applause.*]

When I came away from Indiana, the comrades said: "When you cross the line and get over into the Buckeye State, tell the comrades there that we are on duty and doing duty. Give them for us, a hearty greeting, and tell them that we are going to make a record this fall that will be read around the world." [*Applause.*]

The Socialists of Ohio, it appears, are very much alive this year. The party has been killed recently [*laughter*], which, no doubt, accounts for its extraordinary activity. [*Laughter.*] There is nothing that helps the Socialist Party so much as receiving an occasional deathblow. [*Laughter and cheers.*] The oftener it is killed the more active, the more energetic, the more powerful it becomes.

They who have been reading the capitalist newspapers realize what a capacity they have for lying. We have been reading them lately. They know all about the Socialist Party — the Socialist movement, except what is true. [*Laughter.*] Only the other day they took an article that I had written — and most of you have read it — most of you members of the party, at least — and they made it appear that I had undergone a marvelous transformation. [*Laughter.*] I had suddenly become changed — had in fact come to my senses; I had ceased to be a wicked Socialist, and had become a respectable Socialist [*laughter*], a patriotic Socialist — as if I had ever been anything else. [*Laughter.*]

What was the purpose of this deliberate misrepresentation? It is so self-evident that it suggests itself. The purpose was to sow the seeds of dissension in our ranks; to have it appear that we were divided among ourselves; that we were pitted against each other, to our mutual undoing. But Socialists were not born yesterday. [*Applause.*]

They know how to read capitalist newspapers [*laughter and applause*]; and to believe exactly the opposite of what they read. [*Applause and laughter.*]

Why should a Socialist be discouraged on the eve of the greatest triumph in all the history of the Socialist movement? [*Applause.*] It is true that these are anxious, trying days for us all — testing days for the women and men who are upholding the banner of labor in the struggle of the working class of all the world against the exploiters of all the world [*applause*]; a time in which the weak and cowardly will falter and fail and desert. They lack the fiber to endure the revolutionary test; they fall away; they disappear as if they had never been. On the other hand, they who are animated by the unconquerable spirit of the social revolution; they who have the moral courage to stand erect and assert their convictions; stand by them; fight for them; go to jail or to hell for them, if need be [*applause and shouts*] — they are writing their names, in this crucial hour — they are writing their names in fadeless letters in the history of mankind. [*Applause.*]

Those boys over yonder — those comrades of ours — and how I love them! Aye, they are my younger brothers [*laughter and applause*]; their very names throb in my heart, thrill in my veins, and surge in my soul. [*Applause.*] I am proud of them; they are there for us [*applause*]; and we are here for them. [*Applause, shouts and cheers.*] Their lips, though temporarily mute, are more eloquent than ever before; and their voice, though silent, is heard around the world. [*Great applause.*]

Are we opposed to Prussian militarism? [*Laughter.*] [*Shouts from the crowd of "Yes. Yes."*] Why, we have been fighting it since the day the Socialist movement was born [*applause*]; and we are going to continue to fight it, day and night, until it is wiped from the face of the earth. [*Thunderous applause and cheers.*] Between us there is no truce — no compromise.

But, before I proceed along this line, let me recall a little history, in which I think we are all interested.

In 1869 that grand old warrior of the social revolution,

the elder Liebknecht, was arrested and sentenced to prison for three months, because of his war, as a Socialist, on the Kaiser and on the junkers that rule Germany. In the meantime the Franco-Prussian war broke out. Liebknecht and Bebel were the Socialist members in the Reichstag. They were the only two who had the courage to protest against taking Alsace-Lorraine from France and annexing it to Germany. And for this they were sentenced two years to a prison fortress charged with high treason; because, even in that early day, almost fifty years ago, these leaders, these forerunners of the international Socialist movement were fighting the Kaiser and fighting the junkers of Germany. [*Great applause and cheers.*] They have continued to fight them from that day to this. [*Applause.*] Multiplied thousands of Socialists have languished in the jails of Germany because of their heroic warfare upon the despotic ruling class of that country. [*Applause.*]

Let us come down the line a little farther. You remember that, at the close of Theodore Roosevelt's second term as President, he went over to Africa [*laughter*] to make war on some of his ancestors. [*Laughter, continued shouts, cheers, laughter and applause.*] You remember that, at the close of his expedition, he visited the capitals of Europe; and that he was wined and dined, dignified and glorified by all the Kaisers and Czars and Emperors of the Old World. [*Applause.*] He visited Potsdam while the Kaiser was there; and, according to the accounts published in the American newspapers, he and the Kaiser were soon on the most familiar terms. [*Laughter.*] They were hilariously intimate with each other, and slapped each other on the back. [*Laughter.*] After Roosevelt had reviewed the Kaiser's troops, according to the same accounts, he became enthusiastic over the Kaiser's legions and said: "If I had that kind of an army, I could conquer the world." [*Laughter.*] He knew the Kaiser then just as well as he knows him now. [*Laughter.*] He knew that he was the Kaiser, the Beast of Berlin. And yet, he permitted himself to be entertained by that Beast of Berlin [*applause*]; had his feet under the mahogany of the Beast of Berlin; was cheek by jowl with the Beast of Berlin. [*Applause.*] And, while Roosevelt was being entertained royally by the German Kaiser, that same Kaiser was putting the leaders of the Socialist Party in jail for fighting the Kaiser and the junkers of Germany. [*Applause.*] Roosevelt was the guest of honor in the white house of the Kaiser, while the Socialists were in the jails of the Kaiser for fighting the Kaiser. [*Applause.*] Who then was fighting for democracy? Roosevelt? [*Shouts of "no."*] Roosevelt, who was honored by the Kaiser, or the Socialists who were in jail by order of the Kaiser? [*Applause.*]

"Birds of a feather flock together." [*Laughter.*]

When the newspapers reported that Kaiser Wilhelm and ex-President Theodore recognized each other at sight, were perfectly intimate with each other at the first touch, they made the admission that is fatal to the claim of Theodore Roosevelt, that he is the friend of the common people and the champion of democracy; they admitted that they were kith and kin; that they were very much alike; that their ideas and ideals were about the same. If Theodore Roosevelt is the great champion of democracy [*laughter*] — the arch foe of autocracy [*laughter*], what business had he as the guest of honor of the Prussian Kaiser? And when he met the Kaiser, and did honor to the Kaiser, under the terms imputed to him, wasn't it pretty strong proof that he himself was a Kaiser at heart? [*Applause*] Now, after being the guest of Emperor Wilhelm, the Beast of Berlin, he comes back to this country, and wants you to send ten million men over there to kill the Kaiser [*applause and laughter*]; to murder his former friend and pal. [*Laughter*] Rather queer, isn't it? And yet, he is the patriot, and we are the traitors. [*Applause.*] I challenge you to find a Socialist anywhere on the face of the earth who was ever the guest of the Beast of Berlin [*applause*], except as an inmate of his prison — the elder Liebknecht and the younger Liebknecht, the heroic son of his immortal sire.

A little more history along the same line. In 1902 Prince
Henry paid a visit to this country. Do you remember
him? [*Laughter.*] I do, exceedingly well. Prince Henry
is the brother of Emperor Wilhelm. Prince Henry is another Beast of Berlin, an autocrat, an aristocrat, a junker
of junkers — very much despised by our American patriots. He came over here in 1902 as the representative
of Kaiser Wilhelm; he was received by Congress and by
several state legislatures — among others, by the state legislature of Massachusetts, then in session. He was invited
there by the capitalist captains of that so-called commonwealth. And when Prince Henry arrived, there was one
member of that body who kept his self-respect, put on
his hat, and as Henry, the Prince, walked in, that member of the body walked out. And that was James F. Carey,
the Socialist member of that body. [*Applause.*] All the
rest — all the rest of the representatives in the Massachusetts legislature — all, all of them — joined in doing honor,
in the most servile spirit, to the high representative of
the autocracy of Europe. And the only man who left
that body, was a Socialist. And yet [*applause*], and yet
they have the hardihood to claim that they are fighting
autocracy and that we are in the service of the German
government. [*Applause.*]

A little more history along the same line. I have a
distinct recollection of it. It occurred fifteen years ago
when Prince Henry came here. All of our plutocracy,
all of the wealthy representatives living along Fifth Av-
enue — all, all of them — threw their palace doors wide
open and received Prince Henry with open arms. But
they were not satisfied with this; they got down and grov-
elled in the dust at his feet. Our plutocracy — women and
men alike — vied with each other to lick the boots of Prince
Henry, the brother and representative of the "Beast of
Berlin." [*Applause.*] And still our plutocracy, our junkers,
would have us believe that all the junkers are confined
to Germany. It is precisely because we refuse to believe
this that they brand us as disloyalists. They want our

eyes focused on the junkers in Berlin so that we will not see those within our own borders.

I hate, I loathe, I despise junkers and junkerdom. I have no earthly use for the junkers of Germany, and not one particle more use for the junkers in the United States. [*Thunderous applause and cheers.*]

They tell us that we live in a great free republic; that our institutions are democratic; that we are a free and self-governing people. [*Laughter.*] This is too much, even for a joke. [*Laughter.*] But it is not a subject for levity; it is an exceedingly serious matter.

To whom do the Wall Street junkers in our country marry their daughters? After they have wrung their countless millions from your sweat, your agony and your life's blood, in a time of war as in a time of peace, they invest these untold millions in the purchase of titles of broken-down aristocrats, such as princes, dukes, counts and other parasites and no-accounts. [*Laughter.*] Would they be satisfied to wed their daughters to honest workingmen? [*Shouts from the crowd, "No!"*] To real democrats? Oh, no! They scour the markets of Europe for vampires who are titled and nothing else. [*Laughter.*] And they swap their millions for the titles, so that matrimony with them becomes literally a matter of money. [*Laughter.*]

These are the gentry who are today wrapped up in the American flag, who shout their claim from the housetops that they are the only patriots, and who have their magnifying glasses in hand, scanning the country for evidence of disloyalty, eager to apply the brand of treason to the men who dare to even whisper their opposition to junker rule in the United Sates. No wonder Sam Johnson declared that "patriotism is the last refuge of the scoundrel." He must have had this Wall Street gentry in mind, or at least their prototypes, for in every age it has been the tyrant, the oppressor and the exploiter who has wrapped himself in the cloak of patriotism, or religion, or both to deceive and overawe the people. [*Applause.*]

They would have you believe that the Socialist Party consists in the main of disloyalists and traitors. It is true in a sense not at all to their discredit. We frankly admit that we *are* disloyalists and traitors to the real traitors of this nation [*applause*]; to the gang that on the Pacific coast are trying to hang Tom Mooney and Warren Billings in spite of their well-known innocence and the protest of practically the whole civilized world. [*Applause, shouts and cheers.*]

I know Tom Mooney intimately—as if he were my own brother. He is an absolutely honest man. [*Applause.*] He had no more to do with the crime with which he was charged and for which he was convicted than I had. [*Applause.*] And if he ought to go to the gallows, so ought I. If he is guilty every man who belongs to a labor organization or to the Socialist Party is likewise guilty.

What is Tom Mooney guilty of? I will tell you. I am familiar with his record. For years he has been fighting bravely and without compromise the battles of the working class out on the Pacific coast. He refused to be bribed and he could not be browbeaten. In spite of all attempts to intimidate him he continued loyally in the service of the organized workers, and for this he became a marked man. The henchmen of the powerful and corrupt corporations, concluding finally that he could not be bought or bribed or bullied, decided he must therefore be murdered. That is why Tom Mooney is today a life prisoner, and why he would have been hanged as a felon long ago but for the world-wide protest of the working class. [*Applause.*]

Let us review another bit of history. You remember Francis J. Heney, special investigator of the state of California, who was shot down in cold blood in the courtroom in San Francisco. You remember that dastardly crime, do you not? The United Railways, consisting of a lot of plutocrats and highbinders represented by the Chamber of Commerce, absolutely control the city of San Francisco. The city was and is their private reservation. Their will is the supreme law. Take your stand against them and question their authority, and you are doomed. They do not hesitate a moment to plot murder or any other crime to perpetuate their corrupt and enslaving regime. Tom Mooney was the chief representative of the working class they could not control. [*Applause.*] They own the railways; they control the great industries; they are the industrial masters and the political rulers of the people. From their decision there is no appeal. They are the autocrats of the Pacific coast — as cruel and infamous as any that ever ruled in Germany or any other country in the old world. [*Applause.*] When their rule became so corrupt that at last a grand jury indicted them and they were placed on trial, and Francis J. Heney was selected to assist in their prosecution, this gang, represented by the Chamber of Commerce; this gang of plutocrats, autocrats and highbinders, hired an assassin to shoot Heney down in the courtroom. Heney, however, happened to live through it. But that was not their fault. The same identical gang that hired the murderer to kill Heney also hired false witnesses to swear away the life of Tom Mooney and, foiled in that, they have kept him in a foul prison-hole ever since. [*Applause.*]

Every solitary one of these aristocratic conspirators and would-be murderers claims to be an arch-patriot; every one of them insists that the war is being waged to make the world safe for democracy. What humbug! What rot! What false pretense! These autocrats, these tyrants, **these red-handed robbers and murderers,** the "patriots," while the men who have the courage to stand face to face with them, speak the truth, and fight for their exploited victims — they are the disloyalists and traitors. If this be true, I want to take my place side by side with the traitors in this fight. [*Great applause.*]

The other day they sentenced Kate Richards O'Hare to the penitentiary for five years. Think of sentencing a woman to the penitentiary simply for talking. [*Laughter.*] The United States, under plutocratic rule, is the only country that would send a woman to prison for five years for exercising the right of free speech. [*Applause.*] If this be treason, let them make the most of it. [*Applause.*]

Let me review a bit of history in connection with this case. I have known Kate Richards O'Hare intimately for twenty years. I am familiar with her public record. Personally I know her as if she were my own sister. All who know Mrs. O'Hare know her to be a woman of unquestioned integrity. [*Applause.*] And they also know that she is a woman of unimpeachable loyalty to the Socialist movement. [*Applause.*] When she went out into North Dakota to make her speech, followed by plain-clothes men in the service of the government intent upon effecting her arrest and securing her prosecution and conviction — when she went out there, it was with the full knowledge on her part that sooner or later these detectives would accomplish their purpose. She made her speech, and that speech was deliberately misrepresented for the purpose of securing her conviction. The only testimony against her was that of a hired witness. And when the farmers, the men and women who were in the audience she addressed — when they went to Bismarck where the trial was held to testify in her favor, to swear that she had not used the language she was charged with having used, the judge refused to allow them to go upon the stand. This would seem incredible to me if I had not had some experience of my own with federal courts.

Who appoints our federal judges? The people? In all the history of the country, the working class have never named a federal judge. There are 121 of these judges and every solitary one holds his position, his tenure, through the influence and power of corporate capital. The corporations and trusts dictate their appointment. And when they go to the bench, they go, not to serve the people, but to serve the interests that place them and keep them where they are.

Why, the other day, by a vote of five to four — a kind of craps game — come seven, come 'leven [*laughter*] — they declared the child labor law unconstitutional — a law secured after twenty years of education and agitation on the part of all kinds of people. And yet, by a majority of one, the Supreme Court, a body of corporation lawyers, with just one exception, wiped that law from the statute books, and this in our so-called democracy, so that we may continue to grind the flesh and blood and bones of puny little children into profits for the junkers of Wall Street. [*Applause.*] And this in a country that boasts of fighting to make the world safe for democracy! [*Laughter.*] The history of this country is being written in the blood of the childhood the industrial lords have murdered.

These are not palatable truths to them. They do not like to hear them; and what is more they do not want you to hear them. And that is why they brand us as undesirable citizens [*laughter and applause*], and as disloyalists and traitors. If we were actual traitors — traitors to the people and to their welfare and progress, we would be regarded as eminently respectable citizens of the republic; we would hold high office, have princely incomes, and ride in limousines; and we would be pointed out as the elect who have succeeded in life in honorable pursuit, and worthy of emulation by the youth of the land. It is precisely because we are disloyal to the traitors that we are loyal to the people of this nation. [*Applause.*]

Scott Nearing! You have heard of Scott Nearing. [*Applause.*] He is the greatest teacher in the United States. [*Applause.*] He was in the University of Pennsylvania until the Board of Trustees, consisting of great capitalists, captains of industry, found that he was teaching sound economics to the students in his classes. This sealed his fate in that institution. They sneeringly charged — just as the same usurers, money-changers, pharisees, hypocrites charged the Judean Carpenter some twenty centuries ago — that he was a false teacher and that he was stirring up the people.

The Man of Galilee, the Carpenter, the workingman who became the revolutionary agitator of his day soon found himself to be an undesirable citizen in the eyes of the ruling knaves and they had him crucified. And now their lineal descendants say of Scott Nearing, "He is preaching false economics. We cannot crucify him as we did his elder brother but we can deprive him of employment and so cut off his income and starve him to death or into submission. [*Applause.*] We will not only discharge him but place his name upon the blacklist and make it impossible for him to earn a living. He is a dangerous man for he is teaching the truth and opening the eyes of the people." And the truth, oh, the truth has always been unpalatable and intolerable to the class who live out of the sweat and misery of the working class. [*Applause.*]

Max Eastman [*applause*] has been indicted and his paper suppressed, just as the papers with which I have been connected have all been suppressed. What a wonderful compliment they pay us! [*Laughter and applause.*] They are afraid that we may mislead and contaminate you. You are their wards; they are your guardians and they know what is best for you to read and hear and know. [*Laughter.*] They are bound to see to it that our vicious doctrines do not reach your ears. And so in our great democracy, under our free instituions, they flatter our press by suppression; and they ignorantly imagine that they have silenced revolutionary propaganda in the United States. What an awful mistake they make for our benefit! As a matter of justice to them we should respond with resolutions of thanks and gratitude. Thousands of people who had never before heard of our papers are now inquiring for and insisting upon seeing them. They have succeeded only in arousing curiosity in our literature and propaganda. And woe to him who reads Socialist literature from curiosity! He is surely a goner. [*Applause.*] I have known of a thousand experiments but never one that failed.

John M. Work! You know John, now on the editorial staff of the *Milwaukee Leader*! When I first knew him he was a lawyer out in Iowa. The capitalists out there became alarmed because of the rapid growth of the Socialist movement. So they said: "We have to find some able fellow to fight this menace." They concluded that John Work was the man for the job and they said to him: "John, you are a bright young lawyer; you have a brilliant future before you. We want to engage you to find out all you can about socialism and then proceed to counteract its baneful effects and check its further growth."

John at once provided himself with Socialist literature and began his study of the red menace, with the result that after he had read and digested a few volumes he was a full-fledged Socialist and has been fighting for socialism ever since.

How stupid and shortsighted the ruling class really is! Cupidity is stone blind. It has no vision. The greedy, profit-seeking exploiter cannot see beyond the end of his nose. He can see a chance for an "opening"; he is cunning enough to know what graft is and where it is, and how it can be secured, but vision he has none — not the slightest. He knows nothing of the great throbbing world that spreads out in all directions. He has no capacity for literature; no appreciation of art; no soul for beauty. That is the penalty the parasites pay for the violation of the laws of life. The Rockefellers are blind. Every move they make in their game of greed but hastens their own doom. Every blow they strike at the Socialist movement reacts upon themselves. Every time they strike at us they hit themselves. It never fails. [*Applause.*] Every time they strangle a Socialist paper they add a thousand voices proclaiming the truth of the principles of socialism and the ideals of the Socialist movement. They help us in spite of themselves.

Socialism is a growing idea; an expanding philosophy. It is spreading over the entire face of the earth: It is as vain to resist it as it would be to arrest the sunrise on the morrow. It is coming, coming, coming all along the line. Can you not see it? If not, I advise you to consult an oculist. There is certainly something the matter with your vision. It is the mightiest movement in the history of mankind. What a privilege to serve it! I have regretted a thousand times that I can do so little for the movement that has done so much for me. [*Applause.*] The little that I am, the little that I am hoping to be, I owe to the Socialist movement. [*Applause.*] It has given me my ideas and ideals; my principles and convictions, and I would not exchange one of them for all of Rockefeller's bloodstained dollars. [*Cheers.*] It has taught me how to serve — a lesson to me of priceless value. It has taught me the ecstasy in the handclasp of a comrade. It has enabled me to hold high communion with you, and made it possible for me to take my place side by side with you in the great struggle for the better day; to multiply myself over and over again, to thrill with a fresh-born manhood; to feel life truly worthwhile; to open new avenues of vision; to spread out glorious vistas; to know that I am kin to all that throbs; to be class-conscious, and to realize that, regardless of nationality, race, creed, color or sex, every man, every woman who toils, who renders useful service, every member of the working class without an exception, is my comrade, my brother and sister — and that to serve them and their cause is the highest duty of my life. [*Great applause.*]

And in their service I can feel myself expand; I can rise to the stature of a man and claim the right to a place on earth — a place where I can stand and strive to speed the day of industrial freedom and social justice.

Yes, my comrades, my heart is attuned to yours. Aye, all our hearts now throb as one great heart responsive to the battle cry of the social revolution. Here, in this alert and inspiring assemblage [*applause*] our hearts are with the Bolsheviki of Russia. [*Deafening and prolonged applause.*] Those heroic men and women, those unconquerable comrades have by their incomparable valor and sacrifice added fresh luster to the fame of the international movement. Those Russian comrades of ours have made greater sacrifices, have suffered more, and have shed more heroic blood than any like number of men and women anywhere on earth; they have laid the foundation of the first real democracy that ever drew the breath of life in this world. [*Applause.*] And the very first act of the triumphant Russian revolution was to proclaim a state of peace with all mankind, coupled with a fervent moral appeal, not to kings, not to emperors, rulers or diplomats but to *the people* of all nations. [*Applause.*] Here we have the very breath of democracy, the quintessence of the dawning freedom. The Russian revolution proclaimed its glorious triumph in its ringing and inspiring appeal to *the peoples* of all the earth. In a humane and fraternal spirit new Russia, emancipated at last from the curse of the centuries, called upon all nations engaged in the frightful war, the Central Powers as well as the Allies, to send representatives to a conference to lay down terms of peace that should be just and lasting. Here was the supreme opportunity to strike the blow to make the world safe for democracy. [*Applause.*] Was there any response to that noble appeal that in some day to come will be written in letters of gold in the history of the world? [*Applause.*] Was there any response whatever to that appeal for universal peace? [*From the crowd, "No!"*] No, not the slightest attention was paid to it by the Christian nations engaged in the terrible slaughter.

It has been charged that Lenin and Trotsky and the leaders of the revolution were treacherous, that they made a traitorous peace with Germany. Let us consider that proposition briefly. At the time of the revolution Russia had been three years in the war. Under the Czar she had lost more than four million of her ill-clad, poorly-equipped, half-starved soldiers, slain outright or disabled on the field of battle. She was absolutely bankrupt. Her soldiers were mainly without arms. This was what was bequeathed to the revolution by the Czar and his regime; and for this condition Lenin and Trotsky were not responsible, nor the Bolsheviki. For this appalling state of affairs the Czar and his rotten bureaucracy were solely responsible. When the Bolsheviki came into power and went through the archives they found and exposed the secret treaties — the treaties that were made between the Czar and the French government, the British government and the Italian government, proposing, after the victory was achieved, to dismember the German Empire and destroy the Central Powers. These treaties have never been denied nor repudiated. Very little has been said about them in the American press. I have a copy of these treaties, showing that the purpose of the Allies is exactly the purpose of the Central Powers, and that is the conquest and spoliation of the weaker nations that has always been the purpose of war.

Wars throughout history have been waged for conquest and plunder. In the Middle Ages when the feudal lords who inhabited the castles whose towers may still be seen along the Rhine concluded to enlarge their domains, to increase their power, their prestige and their wealth they declared war upon one another. But they themselves did not go to war any more than the modern feudal lords, the barons of Wall Street go to war. [*Applause.*] The feudal barons of the Middle Ages, the economic predecessors of the capitalists of our day, declared all wars. And their miserable serfs fought all the battles. The poor, ignorant serfs had been taught to revere their masters; to believe that when their masters declared war upon one another, it was their patriotic duty to fall upon one another and to cut one another's throats for the profit and glory of the lords and barons who held them in contempt. And that is war in a nutshell. The master class has always declared the wars; the subject class has always fought the battles. The master class has had all to gain and nothing to lose, while the subject class has had nothing to gain and all to lose — especially their lives. [*Applause.*]

They have always taught and trained you to believe it to be your patriotic duty to go to war and to have yourselves slaughtered at their command. But in all the history of the world you, the people, have never had a voice in declaring war, and strange as it certainly appears, no war by any nation in any age has ever been declared by the people.

And here let me emphasize the fact — and it cannot be repeated too often — that the working class who fight all the battles, the working class who make the supreme sacrifices, the working class who freely shed their blood and furnish the corpses, have never yet had a voice in either declaring war or making peace. It is the ruling class that invariably does both. They alone declare war and they alone make peace.

> Yours not to reason why;
> Yours but to do and die.

That is their motto and we object on the part of the awakening workers of this nation.

If war is right let it be declared by the people. You who have your lives to lose, you certainly above all others have the right to decide the momentous issue of war or peace. [*Applause.*]

Rose Pastor Stokes! And when I mention her name I take off my hat. [*Applause.*] Here we have another heroic and inspiring comrade. She had her millions of dollars at command. Did her wealth restrain her an instant? On the contrary her supreme devotion to the cause outweighed all considerations of a financial or social nature. She went out boldly to plead the cause of the working class and they rewarded her high courage with a ten years' sentence to the penitentiary. Think of it! Ten years! What atrocious crime had she committed? What frightful things had she said? Let me answer candidly. She said nothing more than I have said here this afternoon. [*Laughter*] I want to admit — I want to admit without reservation that if Rose Pastor Stokes is guilty of crime, so am I. If she is guilty for the brave part she has taken in this testing time of human souls I would not be cowardly enough to plead my innocence. And if she ought to be sent to the penitentiary for ten years, so ought I without a doubt.

What did Rose Pastor Stokes say? Why, she said that a government could not at the same time serve both the profiteers and the victims of the profiteers. Is it not true? Certainly it is and no one can successfully dispute it.

Roosevelt said a thousand times more in the very same paper, the *Kansas City Star*. Roosevelt said vauntingly the other day that he would be heard if he went to jail. He knows very well that he is taking no risk of going to jail. He is **shrewdly laying his wires** for the Republican nomination in 1920 and he is an adept in making the appeal of the demagogue. He would do anything to discredit the Wilson administration that he may give himself and his party all credit. That is the only rivalry there is between the two old capitalist parties — the Republican Party and the Democratic Party — the political twins of the master class. They are not going to have any friction between them this fall. They are all patriots in this campaign, and they are going to combine to prevent the election of any disloyal Socialist. I have never heard anyone tell of any difference between these corrupt capitalist parties. Do you know of any? I certainly do not. The situation is that one is in and the other trying to break in, and that is substantially the only difference between them. [*Laughter.*]

Rose Pastor Stokes never uttered a word she did not have a legal, constitutional right to utter. But her message to the people, the message that stirred their thoughts and opened their eyes — that must be suppressed; her voice must be silenced. And so she was promptly subjected to a mock trial and sentenced to the penitentiary for ten years. Her conviction was a foregone conclusion. The trial of a Socialist in a capitalist court is at best a farcical affair. What ghost of a chance had she in a court with a packed jury and a corporation tool on the bench? Not the least in the world. And so she goes to the penitentiary for ten years if they carry out their brutal and disgraceful program. For my part I do not think they will. In fact I feel sure they will not. If the war were over tomorrow the prison doors would open to our people. They simply mean to silence the voice of protest during the war.

What a compliment it is to the Socialist movement to be thus persecuted for the sake of the truth! The truth alone will make the people free. [*Applause.*] And for this reason the truth must not be permitted to reach the people. The truth has always been dangerous to the rule of the rogue, the exploiter, the robber. So the truth must be ruthlessly suppressed. That is why they are trying to destroy the Socialist movement; and every time they strike a blow they add a thousand new voices to the hosts proclaiming that socialism is the hope of humanity and has come to emancipate the people from their final form of servitude. [*Applause.*] [*Here Mr. Debs is handed a drink of water.*]

How good this sip of cool water from the hand of a comrade! It is as refreshing as if it were out on the desert waste. And how good it is to look into your glowing faces this afternoon! [*Applause.*] You are really good looking [*laughter*] to me, I assure you. And I am glad there are so many of you. Your tribe has increased amazingly since first I came here. [*Laughter.*] You used to be so few and far between. A few years ago when you struck a town the first thing you had to do was to see if you could locate a Socialist; and you were pretty lucky if you struck the trail of one before you left town. If he happened to be the only one and he is still living, he is now regarded as a pioneer and pathfinder; he holds a place of honor in your esteem, and he has lodgment in the hearts of all who have come after him. It is far different now. You can hardly throw a stone in the dark without hitting a Socialist. [*Laughter.*] They are everywhere in increasing numbers; and what marvelous changes are taking place in the people!

Some years ago I was to speak at Warren in this state. It happened to be at the time that President McKinley was assassinated. In common with all others I deplored that tragic event. There is not a Socialist who would have been guilty of that crime. We do not attack individuals. We do not seek to avenge ourselves upon those opposed to our faith. We have no fight with individuals as such. We are capable of pitying those who hate us. [*Applause.*] We do not hate them; we know better; we would freely give them a cup of water if they needed it. [*Applause.*] There is no room in our hearts for hate, except for the system, the social system in which it is possible for one man to amass a stupendous fortune doing nothing, while millions of others suffer and struggle and agonize and die for the bare necessities of existence. [*Applause.*]

President McKinley, as I have said, had been assassinated. I was first to speak at Portsmouth, having been booked there some time before the assassination. Promptly the Christian ministers of Portsmouth met in special session and passed a resolution declaring that "Debs, more than any other person, was responsible for the assassination of our beloved President." [*Laughter.*] It was due to the doctrine that Debs was preaching that this crime was committed, according to these patriotic parsons, and so this pious gentry, the followers of the meek and lowly Nazarene, concluded that I must not be permitted to enter the city. And they had the mayor issue an order to that effect. I went there soon after, however. I was to speak at Warren, where President McKinley's double-cousin was postmaster. I went there and registered. I was soon afterward invited to leave the hotel. I was exceedingly undesirable that day. I was served with notice that the hall would not be opened and that I would not be permitted to speak. I sent back word to the mayor by the only Socialist left in town — and he only remained because they did not know he was there — I sent word to the mayor that I would speak in Warren that night, according to schedule, or I would leave there in a box for the return trip. [*Applause.*]

The Grand Army of the Republic called a special meeting and then marched to the hall in full uniform and occupied the front seats in order to silence me if my speech did not suit them. I went to the hall, however, found it open, and made my speech. There was no interruption. I told the audience frankly who was responsible for the President's assassination. I said: "As long as there is misery caused by robbery at the bottom there will be assassination at the top." [*Applause.*] I showed them, evidently to their satisfaction, that it was their own capitalist system that was responsible; the system that had impoverished and brutalized the ancestors of the poor witless boy who had murdered the President. Yes, I made my speech that night and it was well received but when I left there I was still an "undesirable citizen."

Some years later I returned to Warren. It seemed that the whole population was out for the occasion. I was received with open arms. [*Applause.*] I was no longer a demagogue; no longer a fanatic or an undesirable citizen. I had become exceedingly respectable simply because the Socialists had increased in numbers and socialism had grown in influence and power. If ever I become entirely respectable I shall be quite sure that I have outlived myself. [*Laughter.*]

It is the minorities who have made the history of this world. It is the few who have had the courage to take their places at the front; who have been true enough to themselves to speak the truth that was in them; who have dared oppose the established order of things; who have espoused the cause of the suffering, struggling poor; who have upheld without regard to personal consequences the cause of freedom and righteousness. It is they, the heroic, self-sacrificing few who have made the history of the race and who have paved the way from barbarism to civilization. The many prefer to remain upon the popular side. They lack the courage and vision to join a despised minority that stands for a principle; they have not the moral fiber that withstands, endures and finally conquers. They are to be pitied and not treated with contempt for they cannot help their cowardice. But, thank God, in every age and in every nation there have been the brave and self-reliant few, and they have been sufficient to their historic task; and we, who are here today, are under infinite obligations to them because they suffered, they sacrificed, they went to jail, they had their bones broken upon the wheel, they were burned at the stake and their ashes scattered to the winds by the hands of hate and revenge in their struggle to leave the world better for us than they found it for themselves. We are under eternal obligations to them because of what they did and what they suffered for us and the only way we can discharge that obligation is by doing the best we can for those who are to come after us. [*Applause.*] And this is the high purpose of every Socialist on earth. Everywhere they are animated by the same lofty principles; everywhere they have the same noble ideals; everywhere they are clasping hands across national boundary lines; everywhere they are calling one another *Comrade,* the blessed word that springs from the heart of unity and bursts into blossom upon the lips. Each passing day they are getting into closer touch all along the battle line, waging the holy war of the working class of the world against the ruling and exploiting class of the world. They make many mistakes and they profit by them all. They encounter numerous defeats, and grow stronger through them all. They never take a backward step.

The heart of the international Socialist never beats a retreat. [*Applause.*]

They are pressing forward, here, there and everywhere, in all the zones that girdle the globe. Everywhere these awakening workers, these class-conscious proletarians, these hardy sons and daughters of honest toil are proclaiming the glad tidings of the coming emancipation; everywhere their hearts are attuned to the most sacred cause that ever challenged men and women to action in all the history of the world. Everywhere they are moving toward democracy and the dawn; marching toward the sunrise, their faces all aglow with the light of the coming day. These are the Socialists, the most zealous and enthusiastic crusaders the world has ever known. [*Applause.*] They are making history that will light up the horizon of coming generations, for their mission is the emancipation of the human race. They have been reviled; they have been ridiculed, persecuted, imprisoned and have suffered death, but they have been sufficient to themselves and their cause, and their final triumph is but a question of time.

Do you wish to hasten the day of victory? Join the Socialist Party! Don't wait for the morrow. Join now! [*Applause.*] Enroll your name without fear and take your place where you belong. You cannot do your duty by proxy. You have got to do it yourself and do it squarely and then as you look yourself in the face you will have no occasion to blush. You will know what it is to be a real *man* or *woman.* You will lose nothing; you will gain everything. [*Applause.*] Not only will you lose nothing but you will find something of infinite value, and that something will be yourself. And that is your supreme need — to find yourself — to really know yourself and your purpose in life. [*Applause.*]

You need at this time especially to know that you are fit for something better than slavery and cannon fodder. [*Applause.*] You need to know that you were not created to work and produce and impoverish yourself to enrich an idle exploiter. You need to know that you have a mind to improve, a soul to develop, and a manhood to sustain.

You need to know that it is your duty to rise above the animal plane of existence. You need to know that it is for you to know something about literature and science and art. You need to know that you are verging on the edge of a great new world. You need to get in touch with your comrades and fellow workers and to become conscious of your interests, your powers and your possibilities as a class. You need to know that you belong to the great majority of mankind. You need to know that as long as you are ignorant, as long as you are indifferent, as long as you are apathetic, unorganized and content, you will

remain exactly where you are. [*Applause.*] You will be
exploited; you will be degraded, and you will have to beg
for a job. You will get just enough for your slavish toil
to keep you in working order, and you will be looked
down upon with scorn and contempt by the very parasites that live and luxuriate out of your sweat and un-
paid labor.

If you would be respected you have got to begin by
respecting yourself. [*Applause.*] Stand up squarely and
look yourself in the face and see a man! Do not allow
yourself to fall into the predicament of the poor fellow
who, after he had heard a Socialist speech concluded that
he too ought to be a Socialist. The argument he had heard
was unanswerable. "Yes," he said to himself, "all the speaker said was true and I certainly ought to join the party."
But after a while he allowed his ardor to cool and he
soberly concluded that by joining the party he might
anger his boss and lose his job. He then concluded: "I
can't take the chance." That night he slept alone. There
was something on his conscience and it resulted in a
dreadful dream. Men always have such dreams when
they betray themselves. A Socialist is free to go to bed
with a clear conscience. He goes to sleep with his manhood and he awakens and walks forth in the morning
with his self-respect. He is unafraid and he can look the
whole world in the face [*applause and laughter*], without
a tremor and without a blush. But this poor weakling who
lacked the courage to do the bidding of his reason and
conscience was haunted by a startling dream and at midnight he awoke in terror, bounded from his bed and exclaimed: "My God, there is nobody in this room." [*Laughter.*] He was absolutely right. [*Laughter and applause.*]
There was nobody in that room.

How would you like to sleep in a room that had nobody in it? [*Laughter.*] It is an awful thing to be nobody.
That is certainly a state of mind to get out of, the sooner
the better.

There is a great deal of hope for Baker, Ruthenberg and Wagenknecht who are in jail for their convictions; but for the fellow that is nobody there is no pardoning power. He is "in" for life. Anybody can be nobody; but it takes a man to be somebody.

To turn your back on the corrupt Republican Party and the still more corrupt Democratic Party — the gold-dust lackeys of the ruling class [*laughter*] counts for still more after you have stepped out of those popular and corrupt capitalist parties to join a minority party that has an ideal, that stands for a principle, and fights for a cause. [*Applause.*] This will be the most important change you have ever made and the time will come when you will thank me for having made the suggestion. It was the day of days for me. I remember it well. It was like passing from midnight darkness to the noontide light of day. It came almost like a flash and found me ready. It must have been in such a flash that great, seething, throbbing Russia, prepared by centuries of slavery and tears and martyrdom, was transformed from a dark continent to a land of living light.

There is something splendid, something sustaining and inspiring in the prompting of the heart to be true to yourself and to the best you know, especially in a crucial hour of your life. You are in the crucible today, my Socialist comrades! You are going to be tried by fire, to what extent no one knows. If you are weak-fibered and fainthearted you will be lost to the Socialist movement. We will have to bid you goodbye. You are not the stuff of which revolutions are made. We are sorry for you [*applause*] unless you chance to be an "intellectual." The "intellectuals," many of them, are already gone. No loss on our side nor gain on the other.

I am always amused in the discussion of the "intellectual" phase of this question. It is the same old standard under which the rank and file are judged. What would become of the sheep if they had no shepherd to lead them out of the wilderness into the land of milk and honey?

Oh, yes, "I am your shepherd and ye are my mutton." [*Laughter.*]

They would have us believe that if we had no "intellectuals" we would have no movement. They would have our party, the rank and file, controlled by the "intellectual" bosses as the Republican and Democratic parties are controlled. These capitalist parties are managed by "intellectual" leaders and the rank and file are sheep that follow the bellwether to the shambles.

In the Republican and Democratic parties you of the common herd are not expected to think. That is not only unnecessary but might lead you astray. That is what the "intellectual" leaders are for. They do the thinking and you do the voting. They ride in carriages at the front where the band plays and you tramp in the mud, bringing up the rear with great enthusiasm.

The capitalist system affects to have great regard and reward for intellect, and the capitalists give themselves full credit for having superior brains. When we have ventured to say that the time would come when the working class would rule they have bluntly answered "Never! it requires brains to rule." The workers of course have none. And they certainly try hard to prove it by proudly supporting the political parties of their masters under whose administration they are kept in poverty and servitude.

The government is now operating its railroads for the more effective prosecution of the war. Private ownership has broken down utterly and the government has had to come to the rescue. We have always said that the people ought to own the railroads and operate them for the benefit of the people. We advocated that twenty years ago. But the capitalists and their henchmen emphatically objected. "You have got to have brains to run the railroads," they tauntingly retorted. Well, the other day McAdoo, the governor-general of the railroads under government operation, discharged all the high-salaried presidents and other supernumeraries. In other words, he fired the "brains" bodily and yet all the trains have been coming and going on schedule time. Have you noticed any change for the worse since the "brains" are gone? It is a brainless system now, being operated by "hands." [*Laughter.*] But a good deal more efficiently than it had been operated by so-called "brains" before. [*Laughter.*] And this determines infallibly the quality of their vaunted, high-priced capitalist "brains." It is the kind you can get at a reasonable figure at the market place. They have always given themselves credit for having superior brains and given this as the reason for the supremacy of their class. It is true that they have the brains that indicates the cunning of the fox, the wolf, but as for brains denoting real intelligence and the measure of intellectual capacity they are the most woefully ignorant people on earth. Give me a hundred capitalists just as you find them here in Ohio and let me ask them a dozen simple questions about the history of their own country and I will prove to you that they are as ignorant and unlettered as any you may find in the so-called lower class. [*Applause.*] They know little of history; they are strangers to science; they are ignorant of sociology and blind to art but they know how to exploit, how to gouge, how to rob, and do it with legal sanction. They always proceed legally for the reason that the class which has the power to rob upon a large scale has also the power to control the government and legalize their robbery. I regret that lack of time prevents me from discussing this phase of the question more at length.

They are continually talking about your patriotic duty. It is not *their* but *your* patriotic duty that they are concerned about. There is a decided difference. Their patriotic duty never takes them to the firing line or chucks them into the trenches.

And now among other things they are urging you to "cultivate" war gardens, while at the same time a government war report just issued shows that practically 52 percent of the arable, tillable soil is held out of use by the landlords, speculators and profiteers. They themselves do not cultivate the soil. They could not if they would. Nor do they allow others to cultivate it. They keep it idle to enrich themselves, to pocket the millions of dollars of unearned increment. Who is it that makes this land valuable while it is fenced in and kept out of use? It is the people. Who pockets this tremendous accumulation of value? The landlords. And these landlords who toil not and spin not are supreme among American "patriots."

In passing I suggest that we stop a moment to think about the term "landlord." "LANDLORD!" Lord of the Land! The lord of the land is indeed a superpatriot. This lord who practically owns the earth tells you that we are fighting this war to make the world safe for democracy — he, who shuts out all humanity from his private domain; he who profiteers at the expense of the people who have been slain and mutilated by multiplied thousands, under pretense of being the great American patriot. It is he, this identical patriot who is in fact the archenemy of the people; it is he that you need to wipe from power. It is he who is a far greater menace to your liberty and your well-being than the Prussian junkers on the other side of the Atlantic ocean. [*Applause.*]

Fifty-two percent of the land kept out of use, according to their own figures! They tell you that there is an alarming shortage of flour and that you need to produce more. They tell you further that you have got to save wheat so that more can be exported for the soldiers who are fighting on the other side, while half of your tillable soil is held out of use by the landlords and profiteers. What do you think of that?

Again, they tell you there is a coal famine now in the state of Ohio. The state of Indiana, where I live, is largely underlaid with coal. There is practically an inexhaustible supply. The coal is banked beneath our very feet. It is within touch all about us — all we can possibly use and more. And here are the miners, ready to enter the mines. Here is the machinery ready to be put into operation to increase the output to any desired capacity. And three weeks ago a national officer of the United Mine Workers issued and published a statement to the Labor Department of the United States government to the effect that the 600,000 coal miners in the United States at this time, when they talk about a coal famine, are not permitted to work more than half time. I have been around over Indiana for many years. I have often been in the coal fields; again and again I have seen the miners idle while at the same time there was a scarcity of coal.

They tell you that you ought to buy your coal right away; that you may freeze next winter if you do not. At the same time they charge you three prices for your coal. Oh, yes, this ought to suit you perfectly if you vote the Republican or Democratic ticket and believe in the private ownership of the coal mines and their operation for private profit. [*Applause.*]

The coal mines now being privately owned, the operators want a scarcity of coal so they can boost their prices and enrich themselves accordingly. If an abundance of coal were mined there would be lower prices and this would not suit the mine owners. Prices soar and profits increase when there is a scarcity of coal.

It is also apparent that there is collusion between the mine owners and the railroads. The mine owners declare there are no cars while the railroad men insist that there is no coal. And between them they delude, defraud and rob the people.

Let us illustrate a vital point. Here is the coal in great deposits all about us; here are the miners and the machinery of production. Why should there be a coal famine upon the one hand and an army of idle and hungry miners on the other hand? Is it not an incredibly stupid situation, an almost idiotic if not criminal state of affairs?

We Socialists say: "Take possession of the mines in the name of the people." [*Applause.*] Set the miners at work and give every miner the equivalent of all the coal he produces. Reduce the work day in proportion to the development of productive machinery. That would at once settle the matter of a coal famine and of idle miners. But that is too simple a proposition and the people will have none of it. The time will come, however, when the people will be driven to take such action for there is no other efficient and permanent solution of the problem.

In the present system the miner, a wage slave, gets down into a pit 300 or 400 feet deep. He works hard and produces a ton of coal. But he does not own an ounce of it. That coal belongs to some mine-owning plutocrat who may be in New York or sailing the high seas in his private yacht; or he may be hobnobbing with royalty in the capitals of Europe, and that is where most of them were before the war was declared. The industrial captain, so-called, who lives in Paris, London, Vienna or some other center of gaiety does not have to work to revel in luxury. He owns the mines and he might as well own the miners.

That is where you workers are and where you will remain as long as you give your support to the political parties of your masters and exploiters. You vote these miners out of a job and reduce them to corporation vassals and paupers.

We Socialists say: "Take possession of the mines; call the miner to work and return to him the equivalent of the value of his product." He can then build himself a comfortable home; live in it; enjoy it with his family. He can provide himself and his wife and children with clothes — good clothes — not shoddy; wholesome food in abundance, education for the children, and the chance to live the lives of civilized human beings, while at the same time the people will get coal at just what it costs to mine it.

Of course that would be socialism as far as it goes. But you are not in favor of that program. It is too visionary because it is so simple and practical. So you will have to continue to wait until winter is upon you before you get your coal and then pay three prices for it because you insist upon voting a capitalist ticket and giving your support to the present wage-slave system. The trouble with you is that you are still in a capitalist state of mind.

Lincoln said: "If you want that thing, that is the thing you want"; and you will get it to your heart's content. But some good day you will wake up and realize that a change is needed and wonder why you did not know it long before. Yes, a change is certainly needed, not merely a change of party but a change of system; a change from slavery to freedom and from despotism to democracy, wide as the world. [*Applause.*] When this change comes at last, we shall rise from brutehood to brotherhood, and to accomplish it we have to educate and organize the workers industrially and politically, but not along the zigzag craft lines laid down by Gompers, who through all of his career has favored the master class. You never hear the capitalist press speak of him nowadays except in praise and adulation. He has recently come into great prominence as a patriot. You never find him on the unpopular side of a great issue. He is always conservative, satisfied to leave the labor problem to be settled finally at the banqueting board with Elihu Root, Andrew Carnegie and the rest of the plutocratic civic federationists. When they drink wine and smoke scab cigars together the labor question is settled so far as they are concerned.

And while they are praising Gompers they are denouncing the I.W.W. There are few men who have the courage to say a word in favor of the I.W.W. [*Applause.*] I have. [*Applause.*] Let me say here that I have great respect for the I.W.W. Far greater than I have for their infamous detractors. [*Applause.*]

Listen! There has just been published a pamphlet called "The Truth About the I.W.W." It has been issued after long and thorough investigation by five men of unquestioned standing in the capitalist world. At the head of these investigators was Professor John Graham Brooks of Harvard University, and next to him John A. Fish of the Survey of the Religious Organizations of Pittsburgh, and Mr. Bruere, the government investigator. Five of these prominent men conducted an impartial examination of the I.W.W. To quote their own words they "followed its trail." They examined into its doings beginning at Bisbee where the "patriots," the cowardly business men, the arch-criminals, made up the mob that deported 1,200 workingmen under the most brutal conditions, charging them with being members of the I.W.W. when they knew it to be false.

It is only necessary to label a man "I. W. W." to have him lynched as they did Praeger, an absolutely innocent man. He was a Socialist and bore a German name, and that was his crime. A rumor was started that he was disloyal and he was promptly seized and lynched by the cowardly mob of so-called "patriots."

War makes possible all such crimes and outrages. And war comes in spite of the people. When Wall Street says war the press says war and the pulpit promptly follows with its *Amen*. In every age the pulpit has been on the side of the rulers and not on the side of the people. That is one reason why the preachers so fiercely denounce the I.W.W.

Take the time to read this pamphlet about the I.W.W. Don't take the word of Wall Street and its press as final. Read this report by five impartial and highly reputable men who made their investigation to know the truth, and that they might tell the truth to the American people. They declare that the I.W.W. in all its career never committed as much violence against the ruling class as the ruling class has committed against the I.W.W. [*Applause.*]

You are not now reading any reports in the daily press about the trial at Chicago, are you? They used to publish extensive reports when the trial first began, and to prate about what they proposed to prove against the I. W. W. as a gigantic conspiracy against the government. The trial has continued until they have exhausted all their testimony and they have not yet proven violence in a single instance. No, not one! They are utterly without incriminating testimony and yet 112 men are in the dock after lying in jail for months without the shadow of a crime upon them save that of belonging to the I.W.W. That is enough it would seem to convict any man of any crime and send his body to prison and his soul to hell. Just whisper the name of the I.W.W. and you are branded as a disloyalist. And the reason for this is wholly to the credit of the I.W.W., for whatever may be charged against it the I.W.W. has always fought for the bottom dog. [*Applause.*] And that is why Haywood is despised and prosecuted while Gompers is lauded and glorified by the same gang.

Now what you workers need is to organize, not along craft lines but along revolutionary industrial lines. [*Applause.*] All of you workers in a given industry, regardless of your trade or occupation, should belong to one and the same union.

Political action and industrial action must supplement and sustain each other. You will never vote the Socialist republic into existence. You will have to lay its foundations in industrial organization. The industrial union is the forerunner of industrial democracy. In the shop where the workers are associated is where industrial democracy has its beginning. Organize according to your industries! Get together in every department of industrial service! United and acting together for the common good your power is invincible.

When you have organized industrially you will soon learn that you can manage as well as operate industry. You will soon realize that you do not need the idle masters and exploiters. They are simply parasites. They do not employ you as you imagine but you employ them to take from you what you produce, and that is how they function in industry. You can certainly dispense with them in that capacity. You do not need them to depend upon for your jobs. You can never be free while you work and live by their sufferance. You must own your own tools and then you will control your own jobs, enjoy the products of your own labor and be free men instead of industrial slaves.

Organize industrially and make your organization complete. Then unite in the Socialist Party. Vote as you strike and strike as you vote.

Your union and your party embrace the working class. The Socialist Party expresses the interests, hopes and aspirations of the toilers of all the world.

Get your fellow workers into the industrial union and the political party to which they rightly belong, especially this year, this historic year in which the forces of labor will assert themselves as they never have before. This is the year that calls for men and women who have courage, the manhood and womanhood to do their duty.

Get into the Socialist Party and take your place in its ranks; help to inspire the weak and strengthen the faltering, and do your share to speed the coming of the brighter and better day for us all. [*Applause.*]

When we unite and act together on the industrial field and when we vote together on election day we shall develop the supreme power of the one class that can and will bring permanent peace to the world. We shall then have the intelligence, the courage and the power for our great task. In due time industry will be organized on a cooperative basis. We shall conquer the public power. We shall then transfer the title deeds of the railroads, the telegraph lines, the mines, mills and great industries to the people in their collective capacity; we shall take possession of all these social utilities in the name of the people. We shall then have industrial democracy. We shall be a free nation whose government is of and by and for the people.

And now for all of us to do our duty! The clarion

call is ringing in our ears and we cannot falter without being convicted of treason to ourselves and to our great cause.

Do not worry over the charge of treason to your masters, but be concerned about the treason that involves yourselves. [*Applause.*] Be true to yourself and you cannot be a traitor to any good cause on earth.

Yes, in good time we are going to sweep into power in this nation and throughout the world. We are going to destroy all enslaving and degrading capitalist institutions and re-create them as free and humanizing institutions. The world is daily changing before our eyes. The sun of capitalism is setting; the sun of socialism is rising. It is our duty to build the new nation and the free republic. We need industrial and social builders. We Socialists are the builders of the beautiful world that is to be. We are all pledged to do our part. We are inviting — aye challenging you this afternoon in the name of your own manhood and womanhood to join us and do your part.

In due time the hour will strike and this great cause triumphant — the greatest in history — will proclaim the emancipation of the working class and the brotherhood of all mankind. [*Thunderous and prolonged applause.*]

CANTON, OHIO, JUNE 16, 1918

28

ADDRESS TO THE JURY

On June 30, 1918, Debs was arrested in Cleveland, Ohio, charged with violating the Espionage Act. At the trial, which opened September 9, the prosecution cited the Canton speech as evidence that Debs had attempted to discourage enlistment and promote insubordination in the armed forces of the United States.

With the eyes of the world watching the trial of the man who had been a presidential candidate four times, he addressed the jury in his own defense. He admitted the correctness of the report of his speech, denied the charges in the indictment, and challenged the Espionage Act as a violation of the constitutional right of free speech.

Debs talked for almost two hours. This is an abridged selection of his speech to the jury.

May it please the court, and gentlemen of the jury:

For the first time in my life I appear before a jury in a court of law to answer to an indictment for crime. I am not a lawyer. I know little about court procedure, about the rules of evidence or legal practice. I know only that you gentlemen are to hear the evidence brought against me, that the court is to instruct you in the law, and that you are then to determine by your verdict whether I shall be branded with criminal guilt and be consigned, perhaps to the end of my life, in a felon's cell.

Gentlemen, I do not fear to face you in this hour of accusation, nor do I shrink from the consequences of my utterances or my acts. Standing before you, charged as I am with crime, I can yet look the court in the face, I can look you in the face, I can look the world in the face, for in my conscience, in my soul, there is festering no accusation of guilt.

Permit me to say in the first place that I am entirely satisfied with the court's rulings. I have no fault to find with the assistant district attorney or with the counsel for the prosecution.

I wish to admit the truth of all that has been testified to in this proceeding. I have no disposition to deny anything that is true. I would not, if I could, escape the results of an adverse verdict. I would not retract a word that I have uttered that I believe to be true to save myself from going to the penitentiary for the rest of my days.

Gentlemen, you have heard the report of my speech at Canton on June 16, and I submit that there is not a word in that speech to warrant the charges set out in the indictment. I admit having delivered the speech. I admit the accuracy of the speech in all of its main features as reported in this proceeding.

In what I had to say there my purpose was to have the people understand something about the social system in which we live and to prepare them to change this system by perfectly peaceable and orderly means into what I, as a Socialist, conceive to be a real democracy.

From what you heard in the address of the counsel for the prosecution, you might naturally infer that I am an advocate of force and violence. It is not true. I have never advocated violence in any form. I have always believed in education, in intelligence, in enlightenment;

and I have always made my appeal to the reason and to the conscience of the people.

I admit being opposed to the present social system. I am doing what little I can, and have been for many years, to bring about a change that shall do away with the rule of the great body of the people by a relatively small class and establish in this country an industrial and social democracy.

When great changes occur in history, when great principles are involved, as a rule the majority are wrong. The minority are usually right. In every age there have been a few heroic souls who have been in advance of their time, who have been misunderstood, maligned, persecuted, sometimes put to death. Long after their martyrdom monuments were erected to them and garlands woven for their graves.

This has been the tragic history of the race. In the ancient world Socrates sought to teach some new truths to the people, and they made him drink the fatal hemlock. This has been true all along the track of the ages. The men and women who have been in advance, who have had new ideas, new ideals, who have had the courage to attack the established order of things, have all had to pay the same penalty.

A century and a half ago when the American colonists were still foreign subjects; when there were a few men who had faith in the common people and their destiny, and believed that they could rule themselves without a king; in that day to question the divine right of the king to rule was treason. If you will read Bancroft or any other American historian, you will find that a great majority of the colonists were loyal to the king and actually believed that he had a divine right to rule over them. . . . But there were a few men in that day who said, "We don't need a king; we can govern ourselves." And they began an agitation that has immortalized them in history.

Washington, Jefferson, Franklin, Paine and their compeers were the rebels of their day. When they began to chafe under the rule of a foreign king and to sow the seed of resistance among the colonists they were opposed by the people and denounced by the press.... But they had the moral courage to be true to their convictions, to stand erect and defy all the forces of reaction and detraction; and that is why their names shine in history, and why the great respectable majority of their day sleep in forgotten graves.

At a later time there began another mighty agitation in this country. It was directed against an institution that was deemed eminently respectable in its time — the age-old, cruel and infamous institution of chattel slavery.... All the organized forces of society and all the powers of government upheld and defended chattel slavery in that day. And again the few advanced thinkers, crusaders and martyrs appeared. One of the first was Elijah Love-joy who was murdered in cold blood at Alton, Illinois, in 1837 because he was opposed to chattel slavery — just as I am opposed to wage slavery. Today as you go up or down the Mississippi River and look up at the green hills at Alton, you see a magnificent white shaft erected there in memory of the man who was true to himself and his convictions of right and duty even unto death.

It was my good fortune to personally know Wendell Phillips. I heard the story of his cruel and cowardly persecution from his own eloquent lips just a little while before they were silenced in death.

William Lloyd Garrison, Wendell Phillips, Elizabeth Cady Stanton, Susan B. Anthony, Gerrit Smith, Thaddeus Stevens and other leaders of the abolition movement who were regarded as public enemies and treated accordingly, were true to their faith and stood their ground. They are all in history. You are now teaching your children to revere their memories, while all of their detractors are in oblivion.

Chattel slavery has disappeared. But we are not yet

free. We are engaged today in another mighty agitation. It is as wide as the world. It means the rise of the toiling masses who are gradually becoming conscious of their interests, their power, and their mission as a class; who are organizing industrially and politically and who are slowly but surely developing the economic and political power that is to set them free. These awakening workers are still in a minority, but they have learned how to work together to achieve their freedom, and how to be patient and abide their time.

From the beginning of the war to this day I have never by word or act been guilty of the charges embraced in this indictment. If I have criticized, if I have condemned, it is because I believed it to be my duty, and that it was my right to do so under the laws of the land. I have had ample precedents for my attitude. This country has been engaged in a number of wars and every one of them has been condemned by some of the people, among them some of the most eminent men of their time. The war of the American Revolution was violently opposed. The Tory press representing the "upper classes" denounced its leaders as criminals and outlaws.

The war of 1812 was opposed and condemned by some of the most influential citizens; the Mexican war was vehemently opposed and bitterly denounced, even after the war had been declared and was in progress, by Abraham Lincoln, Charles Sumner, Daniel Webster, Henry Clay and many other well-known and influential citizens. These men denounced the President, they condemned his administration while the war was being waged, and they charged in substance that the war was a crime against humanity. They were not indicted; they were not charged with treason nor tried for crime. They are honored today by all of their countrymen.

The Civil War between the states met with violent resistance and passionate condemnation. In the year 1864 the Democratic Party met in national convention at Chicago and passed a resolution condemning the war as a failure. What would you say if the Socialist Party were to meet in convention today and condemn the present war as a failure? You charge us with being disloyalists and traitors. Were the Democrats of 1864 disloyalists and traitors because they condemned the war as a failure?

And if so, why were they not indicted and prosecuted accordingly? I believe in the Constitution. Isn't it strange that we Socialists stand almost alone today in upholding and defending the Constitution of the United States? The revolutionary fathers who had been oppressed under king rule understood that free speech, a free press and the right of free assemblage by the people were fundamental principles in democratic government. The very first amendment to the Constitution reads:

"Congress shall make no law respecting an establishment of religion, or prohibiting the free exercise thereof; or abridging the freedom of speech, or of the press; or the right of the people peaceably to assemble, and to petition the government for a redress of grievances."

That is perfectly plain English. It can be understood by a child. I believe the revolutionary fathers meant just what is here stated—that Congress shall make no law abridging the freedom of speech or of the press, or of the right of the people to peaceably assemble, and to petition the government for a redress of their grievances.

That is the right I exercised at Canton on the sixteenth day of last June; and for the exercise of that right, I now have to answer to this indictment. I believe in the right of free speech, in war as well as in peace. I would not, under any circumstances suppress free speech. It is far more dangerous to attempt to gag the people than to allow them to speak freely what is in their hearts.

I have told you that I am no lawyer, but it seems to me that I know enough to know that if Congress enacts any law that conflicts with this provision in the Constitution, that law is void. If the Espionage Law finally stands, then the Constitution of the United States is dead. If that law is not the negation of every fundamental principle established by the Constitution, then certainly I am unable to read or to understand the English language.

Now, in the course of this proceeding you gentlemen have perhaps drawn the inference that I am pro-German in the sense that I have sympathy with the imperial government of Germany. My father and mother were born in Alsace. They loved France with a passion that was holy. They understood the meaning of Prussianism, and they hated it with all their hearts. I did not need to be taught to hate Prussian militarism. I knew from them what a hateful, oppressive, and brutalizing thing it was and is. I cannot imagine how anyone can suspect for one moment that I could have the slightest sympathy with such a monstrous thing. I have been speaking and writing against it practically all my life. I know that the Kaiser incarnates all there is of brute force and murder.

With every drop of blood in my veins I despise Kaiserism, and all that Kaiserism expresses and implies. My sympathy is with the struggling, suffering people everywhere. It matters not under what flag they were born, or where they live, I sympathize with them all and I would, if I could, establish a social system that would embrace them all.

Now, gentlemen of the jury, I am not going to detain you too long.... I cannot take back a word I have said. I cannot repudiate a sentence I have uttered. I stand before you guilty of having made this speech.... I do not know, I cannot tell, what your verdict may be; nor does it matter much, so far as I am concerned.

Gentlemen, I am the smallest part of this trial. I have lived long enough to realize my own personal insignificance in relation to a great issue that involves the welfare of the whole people. What you may choose to do to me will be of small consequence after all. I am not on trial here. There is an infinitely greater issue that is being tried today in this court, though you may not be conscious of it. American institutions are on trial here before a court of American citizens. The future will render the final verdict.

And now, your honor, permit me to return my thanks for your patient consideration. And to you, gentlemen of the jury, for the kindness with which you have listened to me.

I am prepared for your verdict.

29

THE DAY OF THE PEOPLE

On September 14, 1918, Judge D. C. Westenhaver sentenced Eugene V. Debs, then nearing his sixty-third birthday, to ten years in prison.

Debs went home to Terre Haute pending the outcome of his appeal to the U. S. Supreme Court. But, undaunted by the prospect of spending the rest of his life in jail, he was not silent. The Russian Revolution of 1917, the German Spartacist uprising of 1918-1919, and the wave of strikes in the United States at the end of the war confirmed his revolutionary optimism and he voiced it in this article in the February 1919 issue of The Class Struggle, *then the organ of the left wing of the Socialist Party.*

Debs lost his legal appeal and went to prison in April 1919. As Prisoner No. 9653 he was the Socialist candidate for President in 1920 for the fifth and last time, and received 919,799 votes.

Debs' sentence was commuted by President Warren G. Harding December 25, 1921.

Upon his release he did not join those who left the Socialist Party and formed the Communist Party. He remained in the Socialist Party until his death in 1926. But he never recanted any of the ideas he had written or spoken on the need for uniting the working class in its own economic and political organizations for the social-

*ist revolution in the United States and throughout the
world.*

Upon his release from the Kaiser's bastille — the doors
of which were torn from their hinges by the proletarian
revolution — Karl Liebknecht, heroic leader of the rising
hosts, exclaimed: "The Day of the People has arrived!"
It was a magnificent challenge to the junkers and an inspiring battle cry to the aroused workers.

From that day to this Liebknecht, Rosa Luxemburg
and other true leaders of the German proletariat have
stood bravely at the front, appealing to the workers to
join the revolution and make it complete by destroying
what remained of the criminal and corrupt old regime
and ushering in the day of the people. Then arose the
cry that the people were not yet ready for their day, and
Ebert and Scheidemann and their crowd of white-livered
reactionaries, with the sanction and support of the fugi-
tive Kaiser, the infamous junkers and all the Allied powers, now in beautiful alliance, proceeded to prove that
the people were not yet ready to rule themselves by setting up a bourgeois government under which the working class should remain in substantially the same state
of slavish subjection they were in at the beginning of the
war.

And now upon that issue — as to whether the terrible
war has brought the people their day or whether its appalling sacrifices have all been in vain — the battle is
raging in Germany as in Russia, and the near future
will determine whether revolution has for once been really triumphant or whether sudden reaction has again
won the day.

In the struggle in Russia the revolution has thus far
triumphed for the reason that it has not compromised.
The career of Kerensky was cut short when he attempted
to turn the revolutionary tide into reactionary bourgeois
channels.

Lenin and Trotsky were the men of the hour and under their fearless, incorruptible and uncompromising leadership the Russian proletariat has held the fort against the combined assaults of all the ruling class powers of earth. It is a magnificent spectacle. It stirs the blood and warms the heart of every revolutionist, and it challenges the admiration of all the world.

So far as the Russian proletariat is concerned, the day of the people has arrived, and they are fighting and dying as only heroes and martyrs can fight and die to usher in the day of the people not only in Russia but in all the nations on the globe.

In every revolution of the past the false and cowardly plea that the people were "not yet ready" has prevailed. Some intermediate class invariably supplanted the class that was overthrown and "the people" remained at the bottom where they have been since the beginning of history. They have never been "ready" to rid themselves of their despots, robbers and parasites. All they have ever been ready for has been to exchange one brood of vampires for another to drain their veins and fatten in their misery.

That was Kerensky's doctrine in Russia and it is Scheidemann's doctrine in Germany. They are both false prophets of the people and traitors to the working class, and woe be to their deluded followers if their vicious reaction triumphs, for then indeed will the yokes be fastened afresh upon their scarred and bleeding necks for another generation.

When Kerensky attempted to sidetrack the revolution in Russia by joining forces with the bourgeoisie he was lauded by the capitalist press of the whole world. When Scheidemann patriotically rushed to the support of the Kaiser and the junkers at the beginning of the war, the same press denounced him as the betrayer of socialism and the enemy of the people. And now this very press lauds him to the heavens as the savior of the German nation! Think of it! Scheidemann the traitor has become

Scheidemann the hero of the bourgeoisie. Could it be for any other reason on earth than that Scheidemann is doing the dirty work of the capitalist class?

And all this time the prostitute press of the robber regime of the whole world is shrieking hideously against Bolshevism. "It is worse than Kaiserism" is the burden of their cry. Certainly it is. They would a thousand times rather have the Kaiser restored to his throne than to see the working class rise to power. In the latter event they cease to rule, their graft is gone and their class disappears, and well do they know it. That is what we said from the beginning and for which we have been sentenced as disloyalists and traitors.

Scheidemann and his breed do not believe that the day of the people has arrived. According to them the war and the revolution have brought the day of the bourgeoisie. Mr. Bourgeois is now to take the place of Mr. Junker — to evolute into another junker himself by and by — while Mr. Wage Slave remains where he was before, under the heels of his master, and all he gets out of the carnage in which his blood dyed the whole earth is a new set of heels to grind into his exploited bones and a fresh and lusty vampire to drain his life-blood.

Away with all such perfidious doctrines; forever away with such a vicious subterfuge and treacherous betrayal!

The people *are* ready for their day. *THE PEOPLE*, I say. Yes, *the people!*

Who are the people? The people are the working class, the lower class, the robbed, the oppressed, the impoverished, the great majority of the earth. They and those who sympathize with them are the people, and they who exploit the working class, and the mercenaries and menials who aid and abet the exploiters, are the enemies of the people.

That is the attitude of Lenin and Trotsky in Russia and was of Liebknecht and Rosa Luxemburg in Germany, and this accounts for the flood of falsehood and calumny which poured upon the heads of the brave leaders and their revolutionary movement from the filthy mouthpieces of the robber regime of criminal capitalism throughout the world.

The rise of the working class is the red specter in the bourgeois horizon. The red cock shall never crow. Anything but that! The Kaiser himself will be pitied and forgiven if he will but roll his eyes heavenward, proclaim the menace of Bolshevism, and appeal to humanity to rise in its wrath and stamp out this curse to civilization.

And still the "curse" continues to spread — like a raging conflagration it leaps from shore to shore. The reign of capitalism and militarism has made of all peoples inflammable material. They are ripe and ready for the change, the great change which means the rise and triumph of the workers, the end of exploitation, of war and plunder, and the emancipation of the race. Let it come! Let us all help its coming and pave the way for it by organizing the workers industrially and politically to conquer capitalism and usher in the day of the people.

In Russia and Germany our valiant comrades are leading the proletarian revolution, which knows no race, no color, no sex, and no boundary lines. They are setting the heroic example for world-wide emulation. Let us, like them, scorn and repudiate the cowardly compromisers within our own ranks, challenge and defy the robber-class power, and fight it out on that line to victory or death!

From the crown of my head to the soles of my feet I am Bolshevik, and proud of it.

"The Day of the People has arrived!"

30

WALLS AND BARS

*In 1927, after his death, the only full-length book writ-
ten by Debs was published by the Socialist Party. Twelve
chapters of the book had originally been written for the
Bell Syndicate upon his release from the federal penitentiary in Atlanta as a series on his prison experiences.
Only nine of them were published and in some cases
even those were edited to delete sections considered "propaganda" or "too radical" by the capitalist press.*

*In the introduction to his book, dated July 1, 1926,
Debs wrote:*

*"To the twelve original articles there have been added
three chapters for the purpose not only of amplifying
the treatment of the subject, but that the writer might
discuss more critically and fundamentally the vital
phases of the prison question, including especially the
cause of and responsibility for this crying evil, than was
possible in the newspaper articles. . . .*

*"In the latter chapters I have undertaken to show that
the prison in our modern life is essentially a capitalistic
institution, an inherent and inseparable part of the social
and economic system under which the mass of mankind
are ruthlessly exploited and kept in an impoverished
state, as a result of which the struggle for existence, cruel and relentless at best, drives thousands of its victims
into commission of offenses which they are forced to ex-*

piate in the dungeons provided for them by their masters.

"The prison as a rule, to which there are few exceptions, is for the poor. . . .

"The prison at present is at best a monumental evil
and a burning shame to society. It ought not merely to
be reformed but abolished as an institution for the punishment and degradation of unfortunate human beings."

We reproduce here the first chapter, which introduced
the newspaper series, and the three chapters Debs added
later to discuss the prison question more fundamentally.

The current concern of all capitalist politicians with
the "increase in crime and lawlessness" and the "need for
more and better prisons," and the latter-day prison reform movements add timeliness to Debs' socialist view of
the prison question.

The Relation of Society to the Convict

A prison is a cross section of society in which every human strain is clearly revealed. An average prison, and
its inmates, in point of character, intelligence and habits, will compare favorably with any similar number of
persons outside of prison walls.

I believe that my enemies, as well as my friends, will
concede to me the right to arrive at some conclusions
with respect to prisons and prisoners by virtue of my
personal experience, for I have been an inmate of three
county jails, one state prison and one federal penitentiary. A total of almost four years of my life has been
spent behind the bars as a common prisoner; but an
experience of such a nature cannot be measured in point
of years. It is measured by the capacity to see, to feel
and to comprehend the social significance and the human
import of the prison in its relation to society.

In the very beginning I desire to stress the point that
I have no personal grievance to air as a result of my
imprisonment. I was never personally mistreated, and

no man was ever brutal to me. On the other hand, during my prison years I was treated uniformly with a peculiar personal kindliness by my fellow prisoners, and not infrequently by officials. 1 do not mean to imply that any special favors were ever accorded me. I never requested nor would I accept anything that could not be obtained on the same basis by the humblest prisoner. I realized that I was a convict, and as such I chose to share the lot of those around me on the same rigorous terms that were imposed upon all.

It is true that I have taken an active part in public affairs for the past forty years. In a consecutive period of that length a man is bound to acquire a reputation of one kind or another. My adversaries and I are alike perfectly satisfied with the sort of reputation they have given me. A man should take to himself no discomfort from an opinion expressed or implied by his adversary, but it is difficult, and often times humiliating to attempt to justify the kindness of one's friends. When my enemies do not indulge in calumny I find it exceedingly difficult to answer their charges against me. In fact, I am guilty of believing in a broader humanity and a nobler civilization. I am guilty also of being opposed to force and violence. I am guilty of believing that the human race can be humanized and enriched in every spiritual inference through the saner and more beneficent processes of peaceful persuasion applied to material problems rather than through wars, riots and bloodshed. I went to prison because I was guilty of believing these things. I have dedicated my life to these beliefs and shall continue to embrace them to the end.

My first prison experience occurred in 1894 when, as president of the American Railway Union, I was locked up in the Cook County Jail, Chicago, because of my activities in the great railroad strike that was in full force at that time. I was given a cell occupied by five other men. It was infested with vermin, and sewer rats scurried back and forth over the floors of that human cesspool in such numbers that it was almost impossible for me to place my feet on the stone floor. Those rats were nearly as big as cats, and vicious. I recall a deputy jailer passing one day with a fox terrier. I asked him to please leave his dog in my cell for a little while so that the rat population might thereby be reduced. He agreed, and the dog was locked up with us, but not for long, for when two or three sewer rats appeared the terrier let out such an appealing howl that the jailer came and saved him from being devoured.

I recall seeing my fellow inmates of Cook County Jail stripping themselves to their waists to scratch the bites inflicted by all manner of nameless vermin, and when they were through the blood would trickle down their bare bodies in tiny red rivulets. Such was the torture suffered by these men who as yet had been convicted of no crime, but who were awaiting trial. I was given a cell that a guard took the pains to tell me had been occupied by Prendergast, who assassinated Mayor Carter H. Harrison. He showed me the bloody rope with which Prendergast had been hanged and intimated with apparent glee sparkling in his eyes that the same fate awaited me. His intimation was perhaps predicated upon what he read in the newspapers of that period, for my associates and I were accused of every conceivable crime in connection with that historic strike. I was shown the cells that had been occupied by the Chicago anarchists who were hanged, and was told that the gallows awaited the man in this country who strove to better the living conditions of his fellowmen.

Such was my introduction to prison life. I can never forget the sobbing and screaming that I heard, while in Cook County Jail, from the fifty or more women prisoners who were there. From that moment I felt my kinship with every human being in prison, and I made a solemn resolution with myself that if ever the time came and I could be of any assistance to those unfortunate souls, I would embrace the opportunity with every ounce of my strength. I felt myself on the same human level with those Chicago prisoners. I was not one whit better than they. I felt that they had done the best they could with their physical and mental equipment to improve their sad lot in life, just as I had employed my physical and mental equipment in the service of those about me, to whom I was responsible, whose lot I shared and the energy expended had landed us both in jail. There we were on a level with each other.

With my associate officers of the American Railway Union I was transferred to the McHenry County Jail, Woodstock, Illinois, where I served a six months' sentence in 1895 for contempt of court in connection with the federal proceedings that grew out of the Pullman strike in 1894. My associates served three months, but my time was doubled because the federal judges considered me a dangerous man and a menace to society. In the years that intervened some national attention was paid to me because I happened to have been named a presidential candidate in several successive campaigns.

But there was no real rejoicing from the influential and powerful side of our national life until June, 1918, when I was arrested by Department of Justice agents in Cleveland for a speech that I had delivered in Canton, Ohio. I was taken to the Cuyahoga County Jail, and when the inmates heard that I was in prison with them there was a mild to-do about it, and they congratulated me through their cells. A deputy observed the fraternity that had sprung up, and I was removed to a more remote corner. Just after I retired that Sunday midnight I heard a voice calling my name through a small aperture and inquiring if I were asleep. I replied no.

"Well, you've been nominated for Congress from the Fifth District in Indiana. Good luck to you!" he said.

When a jury in the federal court in Cleveland found me guilty of violating the Espionage Law, through a speech delivered in Canton on June 16, 1918, Judge Westenhaver sentenced me to serve ten years in the West

Virginia State Penitentiary, Moundsville. This prison had entered into an agreement with the government to receive and hold federal prisoners for the sum of forty cents per day per prisoner. On June 2, 1919, the State Board of Control wrote a letter to the Federal Superintendent of Prisons complaining that my presence had cost the state $500 a month for extra guards and requested that the government send more federal prisoners to Moundsville to meet this expense. The government could not see its way clear to do this, since it was claimed there was plenty of room at Atlanta, and if, as the State Board of Control averred, I was a liability rather than an asset to the state, the government would transfer me to its own federal prison at Atlanta, which it did on June 13, 1919, exactly two months after the date on which I began to serve my ten years' imprisonment — a sentence which was commuted by President Warren G. Harding on Christmas day, 1921.

I was aware of a marvelous change that came over me during and immediately after my first incarceration. Before that time I had looked upon prisons and prisoners as a rather sad affair, but a condition that somehow could not be remedied. It was not until I was a prisoner myself that I realized, and fully comprehended, the prison problem and the responsibility that, in the last analysis, falls directly upon society itself.

The prison problem is directly co-related with poverty, and poverty as we see it today is essentially a social disease. It is a cancerous growth in a vulnerable spot of the social system. There should be no poverty among hard-working people. Those who produce should have, but we know that those who produce the most — that is, those who work hardest, and at the most difficult and most menial tasks, have the least. But of this I shall have more to say. After all, the purpose of these chapters is to set forth the prison problem as one of the most vital concerns of present-day society. A prison is an institution to which any of us may go at any time. Some of us go to prison for breaking the law, and some of us for upholding and abiding by the Constitution to which the law is supposed to adhere. Some go to prison for killing their fellowmen, and others for believing that murder is a violation of one of the Commandments. Some go to prison for stealing, and others for believing that a better system can be provided and maintained than one that makes it necessary for a man to steal in order to live.

The prison has always been a part of human society. It has always been deemed an essential factor in organized society. The prison has its place and its purpose in every civilized nation. It is only in uncivilized places that you will not find the prison. Man is the only animal th'at constructs a cage for his neighbor and puts him in it. To punish by imprisonment, involving torture in every conceivable form, is a most tragic phase in the annals of mankind. The ancient idea was that the more cruel the punishment the more certain the reformation. This idea, fortunately, has to a great extent receded into the limbo of savagery whence it sprang. We now know that brutality begets brutality, and we know that through the centuries there has been a steady modification of discipline and method in the treatment of prisoners. I will concede that the prison today is not nearly as barbarous as it was in the past, but there is yet room for vast improvement, and it is for the purpose of causing to be corrected some of the crying evils that obtain in present-day prisons and making possible such changes in our penal system as will mitigate the unnecessary suffering of the helpless and unfortunate inmates that I set myself the task of writing these articles before I turn my attention to anything else.

It has been demonstrated beyond cavil that the more favorable prison conditions are to the inmates, the better is the result for society. We should bear in mind that few men go to prison for life, and the force that swept them into prison sweeps them out again, and they must

go back into the social stream and fight for a living.
I have heard people refer to the "criminal countenance."
I never saw one. Any man or woman looks like a criminal behind bars. Criminality is often a state of mind
created by circumstances or conditions which a person
has no power to control or direct; he may be swamped
by overwhelming influences that promise but one ave-
nue to peace of mind; in sheer desperation the distressed
victim may choose the one way, only to find he has broken the law — and at the end of the tape loom the tur-
rets of the prison. Once a convict always a convict. That
is one brand that is never outworn by time.

How many people in your community would be out
of prison if they would frankly confess their sins against
society and the law were enforced against them?

How many lash and accuse themselves of nameless
and unnumbered crimes for which there is no punishment save the torment visited upon the individual conscience? Yet, they who so accuse themselves, assuming
there exist reasons to warrant accusation, would never
admit to themselves the possession of a criminal countenance. In Atlanta Prison I made it a point to seek out
those men that were called "bad." I found the men, but
I did not find them bad. They responded to kindness
with the simplicity of a child. In no other institution on
the face of the earth are men so sensitive as those who
are caged in prison. They are ofttimes terror-stricken;
they do not see the years ahead which may be full of
promise, they see only the walls and the steel bars that
separate them from their loved ones. I never saw those
bars nor the walls in the nearly three years that I spent
in Atlanta. I was never conscious of being a prisoner.
If I had had that consciousness it would have been tan-
tamount to an admission of guilt, which I never attached
to myself.

It was because I was oblivious of the prison as a
thing that held my body under restraint that I was able
to let my spirit soar and commune with the friends of

freedom everywhere. The intrinsic me was never in prison. No matter what might have happened to me I would
still have been at large in the spirit. Many years ago,
when I made my choice of what life had to offer, I realized, saw plainly, that the route I had chosen would
be shadowed somewhere by the steel bars of a prison
gate. I accepted it, and understood it perfectly. I consider that the years I spent in prison were necessary to
complete my particular education for the part that I am
permitted to play in human affairs. I would certainly not
exchange that experience, if I could, to be President of
the United States, although some people indulge the erroneous belief that I have coveted that office in several
political campaigns.

The time will come when the prison as we now know
it will disappear, and the hospital and asylum and farm
will take its place. In that day we shall have succeeded
in taking the jail out of man as well as taking man out
of jail.

Think of sending a man out from prison and into the
world with a shoddy suit of clothes that is recognized by
every detective as a prison garment, a pair of paper
shoes, a hat that will shrink to half its size when it rains,
a railroad ticket, a five-dollar bill and seven cents car-
fare! Bear in mind that the railroad ticket does not necessarily take a man back into the bosom of his family,
but to the place where he was convicted of crime. In other words a prisoner, after he has served his sentence,
goes back to the scene of his crime. Society's responsibility ends there—so it thinks. But does it? I say not.
With the prison system what it is, with my knowledge
of what it does to men after they get into prison, and
with the contempt with which society regards them after
they come out, the wonder is not that we have period-
ical crime waves in times of economic and industrial depression, but the wonder is that the social system is not
constantly in convulsions as a result of the desperate
deeds of the thousands of men and women who pour

in and pour out of our jails and prisons in never-ending streams of human misery and suffering.

But society has managed to protect itself against the revenge of the prisoner by dehumanizing him while he is in prison. The process is slow, by degrees, like polluted water trickling from the slimy mouth of a corroded and encrusted spout—but it is a sure process. When a man has remained in prison over a certain length of time his spirit is doomed. He is stripped of his manhood. He is fearful and afraid. He has not been redeemed. He has been crucified. He has not reformed. He has become a roving animal casting about for prey, and too weak to seize it. He is often too weak to live even by the law of the fang and the claw. He is not acceptable even in the jungle of human life, for the denizens of the wilderness demand strength and bravery as the price and tax of admission.

Withal, a prison is a most optimistic institution. Every man somehow believes that he can "beat" his sentence. He relies always upon the "technical point" which he thinks has been overlooked by his lawyers. He sometimes imagines that fond friends are busily working in his behalf on the outside. But in a little while the bubble breaks, disillusion appears, the letters from home become fewer and fewer, and the prisoner in tears of desperation resigns himself to his lot. Society has won in him an abiding enemy. If, perchance, he is not wholly broken by the wrecking process by the time his sentence is served, he may seek to strike back. In either case society has lost.

I do not know how many prisoners came to me with their letters soaked in tears. They sought my advice. They believed I could help them over the rough edges. I could do nothing but listen and offer them my kindness and counsel. They would stop me in the corridors, and on my way to the mess room and say: "Mr. Debs, I want to get a minute with you to tell you about my case." Or, "Mr. Debs, will you read this letter from my wife; she says she can't stand the gaff any longer." Or, "Mr. Debs, my daughter has gone on the town; what in God's name can you do about it?" What could I do about it? I could only pray with all my heart for strength to contribute toward the rearrangement of human affairs so that this needless suffering might be abolished. Two or three concrete cases will suffice as examples of the suffering that I saw.

Jenkins, but that is not his name, was a railroad man. Aged, 35. Married and six children; the oldest a daughter, aged 16 years. His wages were too small to support his family in decency. He broke into a freight car in interstate commerce. Sentenced to five years in Atlanta. He received a letter a little while before his term expired telling him that his daughter had been seduced and was in the "red light" district. This man came to me with his tears and swore he would spend the rest of his life tracking down the man who ruined his daughter, and, upon finding him, he would kill him. For days I sought that man out and talked with him, and persuaded him against his rash program. His wife stopped writing to him. She had found an easier, but a sadder, way of solving her economic problems. His home was completely broken up by the time he got out of prison.

Another prisoner who had been a small tradesman, married and the father of eight children, also broke into a freight car. It was his first offense. He got five years. He showed me a letter from his wife saying there was no food in the house and no shoes for the children. The landlord had threatened them with eviction. That man was thirsting for revenge. Society had robbed his family of the breadwinner. The mother had too many children to leave them and work herself. If society deprives a family of their provider should it not provide for the family? It would have been more humane to have sent the whole family to prison.

Another young man, aged 25, showed me a letter from his wife. He was married a little while before he was convicted. His wife was pregnant and was living with the prisoner's invalid mother. She had written to him saying that unless she got relief from somewhere both herself and his mother had made up their minds to commit suicide. They were destitute. They had been refused further credit. They could endure the misery no longer.

Many men attempt suicide in prison. One of the most damaging influences in prison life is the long sentence. It produces a reaction in the heart and mind of the man who receives it that defeats its intended purpose.

Every prison of which I have any knowledge is a breeding place for evil, an incubator for crime. This is especially true about the influence of the prison upon the prison upon the youth and young man.

Capitalism and Crime

Crime in all of its varied forms and manifestations is of such a common nature under the capitalist system that capitalism and crime have become almost synonymous terms.

Private appropriation of the earth's surface, the natural resources, and the means of life is nothing less than a crime against humanity, but the comparative few who are the beneficiaries of this iniquitous social arrangement, far from being viewed as criminals meriting punishment, are the exalted rulers of society and the people they exploit gladly render them homage and obeisance.

The few who own and control the means of existence are literally the masters of mankind. The great mass of dispossessed people are their slaves.

The ancient master owned his slaves under the law and could dispose of them at will. He could even kill his slaves the same as he could any domestic animal that belonged to him. The feudal lord of the Middle Ages did not own his serfs bodily, but he did own the land without which they could not live. The serfs were not allowed to own land and could work only by the consent of the feudal master who appropriated to himself the fruit of their labor, leaving for them but a bare subsistence.

The capitalist of our day, who is the social, economic and political successor of the feudal lord of the Middle Ages, and the patrician master of the ancient world, holds the great mass of the people in bondage, not by owning them under the law, nor by having sole proprietorship of the land, but by virtue of his ownership of industry, the tools and machinery with which work is done and wealth produced. In a word, the capitalist owns the tools and the jobs of the workers, and therefore they are his economic dependents. In that relation the capitalist has the power to appropriate to himself the products of the workers and to become rich in idleness while the workers, who produce all the wealth that he enjoys, remain in poverty.

To buttress and safeguard this exploiting system, private property of the capitalist has been made a fetish, a sacred thing, and thousands of laws have been enacted and more thousands supplemented by court decisions to punish so-called crimes against the holy institution of private property.

A vast majority of the crimes that are punished under the law and for which men are sent to prison, are committed directly or indirectly against property. Under the capitalist system there is far more concern about property and infinitely greater care in its conservation than in human life.

Multiplied thousands of men, women and children are killed and maimed in American industry by absolutely preventable accidents every year, yet no one ever dreams of indicting the capitalist masters who are guilty of the crime. The capitalist owners of fire traps and of fetid sweating dens, where the lives of the workers are ruthlessly sacrificed and their health wantonly undermined, are not indicted and sent to prison for the reason that they own and control the indicting machinery just as they own and control the industrial machinery in their system.

The economic-owning class is always the political ruling class.

Laws in the aggregate are largely to keep the people in subjection to their masters.

Under the capitalist system, based upon private property in the means of life, the exploitation that follows impoverishes the masses, and their precarious economic condition, their bitter struggle for existence, drives increasing numbers of them to despair and desperation, to crime and destruction.

The inmates of an average county jail consist mainly of such victims. They also constitute the great majority in the state prisons and federal penitentiaries. The inmates of prisons are proverbially the poorer people recruited from what we know as the "lower class." The rich are not to be found in prison save in such rare instances as to prove the rule that penitentiaries are built for the poor.

Capitalism needs and must have the prison to protect itself from the criminals it has created. It not only impoverishes the masses when they are at work, but it still further reduces them by not allowing millions to work at all. The capitalist's profit has supreme consideration; the life of the workers is of little consequence.

If a hundred men are blown up in a mine a hundred others rush there eagerly to take the places of the dead even before the remnants of their bodies have been laid away. Protracted periods of enforced idleness under capitalism have resulted in thousands of industrious workingmen becoming tramps and vagabonds, and in thousands of tramps and vagabonds becoming outcasts and criminals.

It is in this process that crime is generated and proceeds in its logical stages from petty larceny to highway robbery and homicide. Getting a living under capitalism — the system in which the few who toil not are millionaires and billionaires, while the mass of the people who toil and sweat and produce all the wealth are victims of poverty and pauperism — getting a living under this inexpressibly cruel and inhuman system is so precarious, so uncertain, fraught with such pain and struggle that the wonder is not that so many people become vicious and criminal, but that so many remain in docile submission to such a tyrannous and debasing condition.

It is a beautiful commentary on human nature that so little of it is defiled and that so much of it resists corruption under a social system which would seem to have for its deliberate purpose the conversion of men into derelicts and criminals, and the earth into a vast poorhouse and prison.

The prison of capitalism is a finished institution compared to the cruder bastilles of earlier periods in human history. The evolution of the prison has kept pace with the evolution of society and the exploitation upon which society is based.

Just as the exploitation of the many by the few has reached its highest cultivation and refinement under present-day capitalism, and is now carried on more scientifically and successfully, and is yielding infinitely richer returns than ever before, so has the prison under this system been cultivated and refined in the infliction of its cruelty, and in its enlarged sphere and increased capacity.

Externally, at least, the prison under capitalism presents a beautiful and inviting appearance, but behind its grim and turreted walls the victims still crouch in terror under the bludgeons of their brutal keepers, and the progress of the centuries, the march of Christian civilization, mean little to them, save that the prisons of capitalism are far more numerous and capacious, and more readily accessible than ever before in history. They signalize the civilization of our age by being composed of steel and concrete and presenting a veritable triumph in architectural art.

Capitalism is proud of its prisons which fitly symbolize the character of its institutions and constitute one of the chief elements in its philanthropy.

I have seen men working for paltry wages and other men in enforced idleness without any income at all sink by degrees into vagabondage and crime, and I have not only found no fault with them, but I have sympathized with them entirely, charging the responsibility for their ruin on the capitalist system, and resolving to fight that system relentlessly with all the strength of mind and body that I possess until that system is destroyed root and branch and wiped from the earth.

During my prison years I met many men who were incarcerated as the victims of capitalism. Let me tell of one in particular. This will typify many other cases with variations, according to the circumstances.

This man has spent nearly forty-eight years in reformatories and prisons. His father died when he was a child and his mother was poor and could ill provide for her offspring. At the tender age of seven years he found himself in a so-called House of Correction. There he was starved and beaten and learned to steal.

Escaping from that institution, he was captured and returned. From that time on he was marked and his life was a continuous battle. He was dogged and suspected and the little time that he was out of jail was spent in dodging the detectives who were ever on his track like keen-scented hounds in pursuit of their prey. They were determined that he should be inside of prison walls. In this cruel manner his fate was sealed as a mere child. The House of Correction for poor boys and girls comes nearer being a House of Destruction.

I spent many hours talking with this victim of the sordid social system under which we live. Despite the cruelties he had suffered at its hands, he was as gentle as a child and responded to the touch of kindness as quickly as anyone I ever knew. Society, which first denied him the opportunity to acquire a decent means of living and subsequently punished him for the crime which it had committed against him and of which he was the victim, could have won an upright and useful member in this man.

As I have already stated in a foregoing chapter, I declined to attend the prison chapel exercises. There were many other convicts who lent their presence to the mockery of religious worship over which guards presided with clubs because they were compelled so to do. The particular prisoner to whom I have referred addressed a letter to the warden protesting that he did not wish to attend devotional exercises and stated the reason for his attitude. He wrote and gave to me a copy of the letter and I introduce it here as indicating that this victim of the brutality of the capitalist system, in spite of the fact that he had spent nearly half a century behind prison bars, still possessed sufficient manhood and courage to assert himself in face of his cruel captors.

The letter follows as he wrote it:

"Sir:

"I desire to be excused from attendance on all religious services here which no longer appeal to my curiosity or sense of obligation. I need practical assistance not spiritual consolation.

"My imagination has already been overworked to the impairment of my other mental faculties.

"I do not believe in the Christian religion. I have formulated a creed agreeable to my mind.

"I have always been fearful of those to whom government grants the special privilege to furnish a particular brand of theology.

"I deny the right of government to compel me to attend any kind of religious service. I claim and proclaim my religious freedom under the U. S. Constitution.

Note:

"In reformatory and penal institutions I have attended

religious service every Sunday for forty-odd years — *to what purpose?*"

The entire career of this unfortunate prisoner was determined by his imprisonment in his childhood, and as well might he have been sentenced for life in his cradle. The system in which he was worn in poverty condemned him to a life of crime and penal servitude in which he typifies the lot of countless thousands of others doomed to a living death behind prison walls.

Poverty and the Prison

There is an intimate relation between the poorhouse and the prison. Both are made necessary in a society which is based upon exploitation. The aged and infirm who remain docile and submissive through the struggle for existence, to whatever straits it may reduce them, are permitted to spend their declining days in the county house and to rest at last in the potters' field.

But they who protest against their pitiless fate rather than yield to its stern decrees, they who refuse to beg, preferring to take the chances of helping themselves by whatever means seem most available, are almost inevitably booked for the jail and the prison.

Poverty has in all ages, in every nation, and under every government recorded in history, been the common lot of the great mass of mankind. The many have had to toil and produce in poverty that the few might enjoy in luxury and extravagance. But however necessary this may have been in the past, it need no longer be true in our day.

Through invention and discovery and the application of machinery to industry, the productive forces of labor have been so vastly augmented that if society were properly organized the great body of the people, who constitute the workers and producers, instead of being poor and miserable and dependent as they now are, would be happy and free and thrill with the joy of life.

There can be no question about the simple and self-evident facts as here set forth:

First, here in the United States we live in as rich a land as there is on earth.

Second, we have all the natural resources, all the raw materials from which wealth is produced in practically unlimited abundance.

Third, we have the most highly efficient productive machinery in the world.

Fourth, we have millions of workers skilled and unskilled not only ready, but eager, to apply their labor to the industrial machinery and produce a sufficiency of all that is required to satisfy the needs and wants of every man, woman and child under a civilized standard of living.

Then why should millions be idle and suffering, millions of others toiling for a pittance, and all the victims of poverty, and of a bleak and barren existence?

The answer is, that capitalism under which we now live has outlived its usefulness and is no longer adapted to the social and economic conditions that today confront the world. Profit has precedence over life, and when profit cannot be made, industry is paralyzed and the people starve.

Here let it be said again, and it cannot be repeated too often nor made too emphatic, that poverty and ignorance, with which poverty goes hand in hand, constitute the prolific source from which flow in a steady and increasing stream most of the evils which afflict mankind.

It is poverty from which the slums, the red light districts, the asylums, the jails and the prisons are mainly recruited.

It was in the so-called panic of 1873, which lasted five years and during which millions were in a state of enforced idleness due to "overproduction," that the "tramp" made his appearance in American life. The industrious workingman, turned by his employer into the street because he had produced more goods than could be sold, became a tramp; the tramp in some instances became a beggar and in others a thief and criminal. From that time to this the tramp has been a fixed institution in American life, and epidemics of crime are reported with regularity in the daily press.

Poverty breeds misery and misery breeds crime. It is thus the prison is populated and made to prosper as a permanent and indispensable adjunct to our Christian civilization. The most casual examination of the inmates of jails and prisons shows the great majority of them at a glance to be of the poorer classes.

When, perchance, some rich man goes to prison the instance is so remarkable that it excites great curiosity and amazement. A rich man does not fit in prison. The prison was not made for him. He does not belong there and he does not stay there. The rich man goes to prison only as the exception to prove the rule.

The social system that condemns men, women and children to poverty at the same time pronounces upon many of them the sentence of the law that makes them convicts. And this social system in the United States rests on the foundation of private ownership of the social means of common life.

Two percent of the American people own and control the principal industries and the great bulk of the wealth of the nation. This interesting and amazing fact lies at the bottom of the industrial paralysis and the widespread protest and discontent which prevail as these lines are written. The daily papers are almost solid chronicles of vice and immorality, of corruption and crime.

In the city of Chicago the authorities frankly admit being no longer able to cope with crime and, happily, Judge W. M. Gammill, of that city, comes to the rescue by recommending the re-establishment of the whipping post as a deterrent for the crimes and misdemeanors committed by the victims of a vicious social system which Judge Gammill upholds. The distinguished judge's Christain spirit as well as his judicial mind are vindicated in his happy and thoughtful suggestion which is finding ready echo among ruling class parasites and mercenaries who, no doubt, would experience great delight in seeing the poor wretches that are now only jailed for the crimes that the injustice of society forces them to commit, tied to a post and their flesh lacerated into shreds by a whip in the hands of a brute.

Commenting upon Judge Gammill's advocacy of the whipping post the *Tribune* of Terre Haute, the city in which I live, has the following illuminating editorial in its columns dated April 12, 1922:

"Revival of the whipping post, Judge W. M. Gammill, of Chicago, yesterday told the committee on law enforcement of the American Bar Association, would have a great effect on the reduction of crime. He cited examples where flogging tended to reduce crime and presented figures showing the number of murders in the large cities. In 1921 his figures showed that St. Louis had 26 murders; Philadelphia, 346; New York, 261; Chicago, 206; Boston, 102; and Washington, 69.

"There is a good deal to this. Mushy sentiment regarding 'honor system,' and the soft theories that criminals are not criminals but sick men, and other things of this sort, have reduced the fear of the law to a minimum and desperate characters no longer hesitate at desperate crimes.

"Half-baked minds will register horror at the idea of restoring the whipping post. These will cry that the world is 'returning to barbarism.' The fact is that the world can return to 'barbarism' with the forces of law and order directing the 'return,' or it can return to the barbarism of the criminal, where life and property are held at naught, and rule is by the pistol, blackjack and terrorism. The present crime wave indicates that the world is well on its way to return to the latter form of 'barbarism' and the law-abiding people of the world are getting very much the worst of it. The general re-establishment of the whipping post would stop the present well-advanced return to barbarism. The whipping post should hold terror for but one class, and the sooner this class is banished from our society the better. No law-abiding citizens should have any apprehension over Judge Gammill's suggestion."

This editorial, reflecting as it does the enlightened opinion of the ruling class of which it is a recognized organ in the community, is its own sufficient commentary.

In the chapter which follows I shall show how poverty as it now exists may be abolished, and how in consequence of such an organic social change the prison as such would no longer be necessary.

For the present I feel impelled to emphasize the fact that poverty is mainly responsible for the prison and that, after all, it is poverty that is penalized and imprisoned under the present social order.

It is true that people may be poor and not go to prison, but it is likewise true that most of those who serve prison sentences do so as the result of their poverty.

From the hour of my first imprisonment in a filthy county jail I recognized the fact that the prison was essentially an institution for the punishment of the poor, and this is one of many reasons why I abhor the prison, and why I recognize it to be my duty to do all in my power to humanize it as far as possible while it exists, and at the same time to put forth all my efforts to abolish the social system which makes the prison necessary by creating the victims who rot behind its ghastly walls.

Socialism and the Prison

Socialism and prison are antagonistic terms.

Socialism means freedom and when the people are free they will not be under the necessity of committing crime and going to prison. Such exceptional cases as there may be requiring restraint for the protection of society will be cared for in institutions and under conditions betokening a civilization worthy of the name.

Socialism will abolish the prisons by removing its cause and putting an end to the vicious conditions which make such a hideous thing as the prison a necessity in the community life.

I am aware in advance that what is said here in regard to abolishing the prison will be met with incredulity, if not derision, and that the theory and proposal I advance will be pronounced visionary, impractical and impossible. Nevertheless, my confidence remains unshaken that the time will come when society will be so far advanced that it will be too civilized and too humane to maintain a prison for the punishment of an erring member, and that man will think too well of himself to cage his brother as a brute, place an armed brute over him, feed him as a brute, treat him as a brute, and reduce him to the level of a brute.

Socialism proposes that the people — all the people — shall socially own the sources of wealth and social means with which wealth is produced; that the people, in other words, shall be the joint proprietors upon equal terms of the industries of the nation, that these shall be cooperatively operated and democratically managed; it proposes that the people shall appropriate to themselves the whole of the wealth they create to freely satisfy their normal wants instead of turning the bulk of that wealth over, as they now do, to idlers, parasites and nonproducers while they suffer in poverty and want.

When the community life is organized upon a cooperative basis according to the socialistic program, every man and woman will have the inalienable right to work with the most improved modern machinery and under the most favorable possible conditions with the assurance that they will receive in return the equivalent of their product, and that they may enjoy in freedom and peace the fruit of their labor.

In such a society there will be a mutuality of interest

and a fraternity of spirit that will preclude the class antagonism and the hatred resulting therefrom which now prevail, and men and women will work together with joy, not as wage slaves for a pittance, but in economic freedom and in an atmosphere of mutual goodwill and peace. The machine will be the only slave, the workday will be reduced in proportion as the productive capacity is increased by improved machinery and methods, so that each life may be assured sufficient leisure for its higher and nobler development.

What incentive would there be for a man to steal when he could acquire a happy living so much more easily and reputably by doing his share of the community work? He would have to be a perverted product of capitalism indeed who would rather steal than serve in such a community. Men do not shrink from work, but from slavery. The man who works primarily for the benefit of another does so only under compulsion, and work so done is the very essence of slavery.

Under socialism no man will depend upon another for a job, or upon the self-interest or good will of another for a chance to earn bread for his wife and child. No man will work to make profit for another, to enrich an idler, for the idler will no longer own the means of life. No man will be an economic dependent and no man need feel the pinch of poverty that robs life of all joy and ends finally in the county house, the prison and potters' field.

The healthy members of the community will all be workers, and they will be rulers as well as workers, for they will be their own masters and freely determine the conditions under which they shall work and live. There will be no arrogant capitalists on the one hand demanding their profits, nor upon the other cowering wage slaves dependent upon paltry and insufficient wages.

Industrial self-government, social democracy, will completely revolutionize the community life. For the first time in history the people will be truly free and rule themselves, and when this comes to pass poverty will vanish like mist before the sunrise. When poverty goes out of the world the prison will remain only as a monument to the ages before light dawned upon darkness and civilization came to mankind.

It is to inaugurate this world-wide organic social change that the workers in all lands and all climes are marshaling their forces, recognizing their kinship, and proclaiming their international solidarity.

The world's workers are to become the world's rulers. The great transformation is impending and all the underlying laws of the social fabric and all the irresistible forces of industrial and social evolution are committed to its triumphant consummation.

Capitalism has had its day and must go. The capitalist cannot function as such in free society. He will own no job except his own as a worker and to hold that he must work for what he gets the same as any other worker. No man has, or ever did have, the right to live on the labor of another; to make a profit out of another, to rob another of the fruit of his toil, his liberty and his life.

Capitalism is inherently a criminal system for it is based upon the robbery of the working class and cornerstoned in its slavery. The title deed held by the capitalist class to the tools used by the working class is also the title deed to their liberty and their lives.

Economic slavery is at the foundation of every other slavery of body, mind and soul. But the capitalists rob not only the workers, but also themselves in appropriating what is produced in the sweat and misery of their toil. They lapse into a state of parasitism that robs them of their higher development, the intellectual and spiritual estate to which all human beings are heirs who live in accordance with the higher laws of their being.

Often at night in my narrow prison quarters when all about me was quiet I beheld as in a vision the majestic march of events in the transformation of the world.

I saw the working class in which I was born and reared, and to whom I owe my all, engaged in the last great conflict to break the fetters that have bound them for ages, and to stand forth at last, emancipated from every form of servitude, the sovereign rulers of the world.

It was this vision that sustained me in every hour of my imprisonment, for I felt deep within me, in a way that made it prophecy fulfilled, that the long night was far spent and that the dawn of the glad new day was near at hand.

In my prison life I saw in a way I never had before the blighting, disfiguring, destroying effects of capitalism. I saw here accentuated and made more hideous and revolting than is manifest in the outer world the effects of the oppression and cruelty inflicted upon the victims of this iniquitous system.

On the outside of the prison walls the wage slave begs his master for a job; on the inside he cowers before the club of his keeper. The entire process is a degenerating one and robs the human being, either as a wage slave walking the street or as a convict crouching in a cell, of every attribute of sovereignty and every quality that dignifies his nature.

Socialism is the antithesis of capitalism. It means nothing that capitalism means, and everything that capitalism does not.

Capitalism means private ownership, competition, slavery and starvation.

Socialism means social ownership, cooperation, freedom and abundance for all.

Socialism is the spontaneous expression of human nature in concrete social forms to meet the demands and regulate the terms of the common life.

The human being is a social being, and socialism would organize his life in the social spirit, under social conditions and along social lines of advancement.

What more natural than that things of a social nature in a community should be socially owned and socially administered for the individual and social well-being of all!

What more unnatural, what more antagonistic to every

social instinct, than the private ownership of the social means of life!

Socialism is evolving every hour of the day and night and all attempts to arrest its progress but increase its power, accelerate its momentum, and insure its triumph for the liberation of humanity throughout the world.

INDEX

Also from Pathfinder

Episodes of the Cuban Revolutionary War, 1956–58

Ernesto Che Guevara

Guevara's firsthand account of the military campaigns and political events that culminated in the January 1959 popular insurrection that overthrew the U.S.-backed dictatorship in Cuba. With clarity and humor, Guevara describes his own political education. He explains how the struggle transformed the men and women of the Rebel Army and July 26 Movement led by Fidel Castro. And how these combatants forged a political leadership capable of guiding millions of workers and peasants to open the socialist revolution in the Americas. Complete for the first time in English. $23.95

The Changing Face of U.S. Politics

Working-Class Politics and the Trade Unions

Jack Barnes

A handbook for workers coming into the factories, mines, and mills, as they react to the uncertain life, ceaseless turmoil, and brutality of capitalism in the closing years of the twentieth century. It shows how millions of workers, as political resistance grows, will revolutionize themselves, their unions, and all of society. $19.95

Defending Cuba, Defending Cuba's Socialist Revolution

Mary-Alice Waters

In face of the greatest economic difficulties in the history of the revolution. Cuba's workers and farmers are defending their political power, their independence and sovereignty, and the historic course they set out on more than 35 years ago. In *New International* no. 10. $14.00

Lenin's Final Fight

Speeches and Writings, 1922–23

V. I. Lenin

The record of Lenin's last effort to win the leadership of the Communist Party of the USSR in the early 1920s to maintain the political course that had enabled the workers and peasants of the old tsarist empire to carry out the first successful socialist revolution and begin building a world communist movement. The issues posed in that political battle remain at the heart of world politics today. $19.95

To Speak the Truth

Why Washington's 'Cold War' against Cuba Doesn't End

Fidel Castro and Che Guevara

In historic speeches before the United Nations and its bodies, Guevara and Castro address the workers of the world, explaining why the U.S. government is determined to destroy the example set by the socialist revolution in Cuba and why its effort will fail. $16.95

Opening Guns of World War III

Washington's Assault on Iraq

Jack Barnes

The U.S. government's murderous assault on Iraq heralded increasingly sharp conflicts among imperialist powers, the rise of rightist and fascist forces, growing instability of international capitalism, and more wars. In *New International* no. 7. Also includes "Communist Policy in Wartime as well as in Peacetime" by Mary-Alice Waters. $12.00

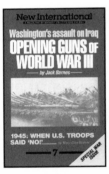

Cosmetics, Fashions, and the Exploitation of Women

Joseph Hansen, Evelyn Reed, and Mary-Alice Waters

How big business promotes cosmetics to generate profits and perpetuate the oppression of women. In her introduction, Mary-Alice Waters explains how the entry of millions of women into the workforce during and after World War II irreversibly changed U.S. society and laid the basis for a renewed rise of struggles for women's equality. $12.95

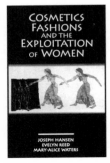

The Communist Manifesto

Karl Marx, Frederick Engels

Founding document of the modern working-class movement, published in 1848. Explains why communists act on the basis not of preconceived principles but of *facts* springing from the actual class struggle, and why communism, to the degree it is a theory, is the generalization of the historical line of march of the working class and the political conditions for its liberation. Also available in Spanish. Booklet. $3.95

The History of the Russian Revolution

Leon Trotsky

The social, economic, and political dynamics of the first socialist revolution. The story is told by one of the revolution's principal leaders writing from exile in the early 1930s, with these historic events still fresh in his mind. Also available in Russian. Unabridged edition, 3 vols. in one. 1,358 pp. $35.95

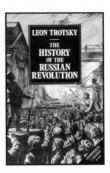

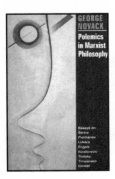

Polemics in Marxist Philosophy

George Novack

Novack defends scientific socialism—the generalization of the historic line of march of the working class, first advanced by Karl Marx and Frederick Engels. He answers those in the twentieth century who, parading as the true interpreters of Marx, have provided a "philosophical" veneer for the anti-working-class political course of Stalinist and social democratic misleaderships around the world. $19.95

Malcolm X Talks to Young People

"I for one will join in with anyone, I don't care what color you are, as long as you want to change this miserable condition that exists on this earth"—Malcolm X, Britain, December 1964. Also includes his 1965 interview with the *Young Socialist* magazine. $10.95

Imperialism: The Highest Stage of Capitalism

V.I. Lenin

"I trust that this pamphlet will help the reader to understand the fundamental economic question, that of the economic essence of imperialism," Lenin wrote in 1917. "For unless this is studied, it will be impossible to understand and appraise modern war and modern politics." Booklet $3.95

Capital

Karl Marx

Marx explains the workings of the capitalist system and how it produces the insoluble contradictions that breed class struggle. He demonstrates the inevitability of the revolutionary transformation of society into one ruled for the first time by the producing majority, the working class. Vol. 1, $14.95; vol. 2, $13.95; vol. 3, $14.95

Revolutionary Continuity

Marxist Leadership in the United States

Farrell Dobbs

How successive generations of fighters took part in the struggles of the U.S. labor movement, seeking to build a leadership that could advance the class interests of workers and small farmers and link up with fellow toilers around the world. 2 vols. $16.95 each

WRITE FOR A FREE CATALOG.
SEE FRONT OF BOOK FOR ADDRESSES.